Transforming Higher Education

Higher Education Policy Series
Edited by Maurice Kogan

This series offers information and analysis of new developments and provides reflective accounts of the impacts of higher education policy. The International Study of Higher Education Reforms forms a set of books within the series.

Maurice Kogan is professor of Government and Social Administration at Brunel University and Joint Director of the Centre for the Evaluation of Public Policy and Practice.

The International Study of Higher Education Reforms
Set ISBN 1 85302 958 0

Transforming Higher Education
A Comparative Study
Maurice Kogan, Marianne Bauer, Ivar Bleiklie and Mary Henkel
ISBN 1 85302 882 7
Higher Education Series 57

Academic Identities and Policy Change in Higher Education
Mary Henkel
ISBN 1 85302 662 X
Higher Education Series 46

Reforming Higher Education
Maurice Kogan and Stephen Hanney
ISBN 1 86302 715 4 pb
Higher Education Policy 50

Transforming Universities
Changing Patterns of Governance, Structure
and Learning in Swedish Higher Education
Marianne Bauer, Susan Marton, Berit Askling and Ference Marton
ISBN 1 85302 674 3 hb
ISBN 1 85302 675 1 pb
Higher Education Policy 48

International Study of Higher Education: Norway
Ivar Bleiklie, Roar Høstaker and Agnete Vabø
ISBN 1 85302 705 7 hb
Higher Education Policy Series 49

HIGHER EDUCATION POLICY SERIES 57

Transforming Higher Education

A Comparative Study

Maurice Kogan, Marianne Bauer,
Ivar Bleiklie and Mary Henkel

Jessica Kingsley Publishers
London and Philadelphia

The right of the contributors to be identified as authors of this work has been asserted by them in accordance with the Copyright, Designs and Patents Act 1988.

First published in the United Kingdom in 2000 by
Jessica Kingsley Publishers Ltd,
116 Pentonville Road, London
N1 9JB, England
and
325 Chestnut Street,
Philadelphia PA 19106, USA.

www.jkp.com

© Copyright 2000 Maurice Kogan, Marianne Bauer,
Ivar Bleiklie and Mary Henkel

Library of Congress Cataloging in Publication Data
A CIP catalog record for this book is available from the Library of Congress

British Library Cataloguing in Publication Data
A CIP catalogue record for this book is available from the British Library

ISBN 1 85302 882 7

Printed and Bound in Great Britain by
Athenaeum Press, Gateshead, Tyne and Wear

Contents

Introduction

This work is based on an international study, comprising three national projects, of the higher education reforms that were put into place primarily in the1980s and 1990s in England, Norway and Sweden. The studies were conducted by teams from the Department of Government, Brunel University, England, the Department of Education and Education Research and the Department of Political Science, Gothenburg University, Sweden and the Norwegian Research Centre in Organisation and Management, University of Bergen, Norway.

They originated from informal discussions with senior members of the Swedish academic world. Our Swedish discussants, the directors of the Swedish Council for Studies in Higher Education, the Bank of Sweden Tercentenary Foundation, the Karolinska Institute and Uppsala University, expressed support for a bi-national project which was formulated by the English and Swedish teams. By good fortune, colleagues at the University of Bergen were working on similar themes in Norway and it was decided to make it a tri-country study.

It was agreed that each country would produce its own national account, now published (Bauer *et al.* 1999; Bleiklie, Hostaker and Vabø 2000; Henkel 2000; Kogan and Hanney 1999), but then combine our results in a comparative study. To this end the three groups ensured that the research frames were compatible and capable of being read across. We noted how major changes were occurring in all three welfare states and in the concept of the state. It seemed obvious that different kinds of change in the different countries must affect the way in which higher education policy was being formulated and the ways in which policy changes would have an impact on academic working and values. The studies were intended to reflect on the particular and idiosyncratic case of higher education policy and on the relationships between the worlds of policy and academe – important and fascinating in its own right – but also to illuminate policy generation and its impacts as a generalisable set of phenomena.

The authors are indebted to a large number of individuals and funding bodies for the achievement of this work and the four other published works on which it feeds. The initial encouragement came from Johnny Andersson, Dan Brändström, Lars Ekholm and Thorsten Nybom who at congenial meetings in Reykajvik and Stockholm encouraged us to formulate and seek funds for the project. The principal source of funding for the English and Swedish projects was the Swedish Council for Studies in Higher Education. We are indebted to Professor Sigbrit Franke and her colleagues for the confidence and support which they lent to our efforts. In particular we owe a massive debt to the Council's Director, Professor Thorsten Nybom, whose expert knowledge and support accompanied and sustained us throughout the years in which the project was carried out. The Norwegian study was initially financed by the Norwegian Research Council; support from the Meltzer Fund of the University of Bergen made completion of the study possible.

We also owe debts of gratitude to the Swedish government's Committee on Follow-up of the 1993 Higher Education Reform, the Spencer Foundation of Chicago, the Leverhulme Trust (for an emeritus fellowship awarded to Maurice Kogan which enabled a particular part of the English study to be completed) and to the Bank of Sweden Tercentenary Foundation which provided funds assisting us with the last stage of the project and its dissemination.

The list of names of the editorial team on the cover of this book in no sense exhausts the account of its authorship or of those responsible for the contributory country studies. Our equal partners in the whole exercise have been Stephen Hanney (England), Berit Askling and Susan Gerard Marton (Sweden), and Roar Høstaker and Agnete Vabø (Norway). The names of individual authors are to be found at the beginning of each chapter. Throughout the five years of our project we have enjoyed an intellectual camaraderie which enabled the experience of different cultures and systems to flow into our research.

We are also indebted to Tom Kogan for expert copy-editing of the final version.

An editorial note

This book contains material based on empirical work undertaken in English institutions. But many of the policies and issues described in it apply to UK policies more generally. We have therefore referred to either England or the UK as seemed appropriate. Not all of the points covered were directly researched in our national projects and we have referred freely to the work of other scholars to complement our own analyses.

Bergen, Gothenburg, London, Stockholm
February 2000

PART I

Themes, Concepts and Methods

Chapter 1

Comparison and Theories

Ivar Bleiklie and Maurice Kogan

Introduction

Between the years of 1965 and the late 1990s higher education in a number of West European countries, including England, Norway and Sweden, went through a period of unprecedented growth, both in terms of its scope and its comprehensiveness. The purpose of this book is to render a social science analysis of this period. Our aim is to develop an understanding of the changes that the higher education system has undergone in the last 30 years, what these changes mean in terms of the relationship between knowledge and political power, and the perspectives the observed developments raise for the future 'education society'. In our analysis we shall do this by trying to identify and explain commonalities and variation of the change processes in the three countries. This will prevent us from committing the obvious fallacy of implicitly assuming that policy changes are generated exclusively within the confines of nation states and help us identify the interaction between national processes and international developmental trends. Empirically, the main emphasis is put on the role of the universities within higher education, and the present book gives a political science analysis of higher education politics, administration and organisation of educational institutions. It gives a sociological analysis of educational institutions, research disciplines, processes of social differentiation and the formation of academic status hierarchies and identities. It gives a comprehensive depiction of the reform policies and changes that have affected the higher education system in the three countries in recent years. Finally, it analyses the impact of changes in policy formation, policies on academic values and working, and changes in conceptions of knowledge.

The task of providing a social science analysis of changes within higher education policies and educational institutions is an exciting one. Working with this book and the collaboration between the three research teams have provided the authors with an opportunity to develop insights into a social institution that will have a central position in discussions about the development of our societies at the beginning of the twenty-first century. The university represents forceful traditions through the 800-year history of the institution. Yet it also represents the future to the extent that higher education and research will be a central driving force in the ongoing formation of society. This being said, it is important to bear in mind that most universities in the world are young institutions which have been established since World War II. However, the idea of being part of a century-old tradition is also frequently cultivated by these younger institutions.

The fact that this analysis is exciting prevents it neither from being difficult nor from raising a number of specific methodological problems. One such problem is represented by the fact that the researchers are studying a policy field and a type of institution in which they themselves are active participants. The present study is also characterised by the fact that we venture into an area of higher education reform that has been dominated by polemics and easily predictable views, whereas thoughtful analyses have been harder to come by. The risks notwithstanding, it is therefore our ambition to develop an empirically-based conceptual understanding of higher education as a social, political, organisational and educational phenomenon.

The topic

From the perspective of educational policy the topic of our analysis is historically delimited by two important reform periods in higher education – one in the late 1960s and early 1970s and a second during the late 1980s and 1990s. In between we find a third period. Although it may not have been characterised by high-profile national reform efforts to the same extent, it nevertheless brought with it important changes within higher education.

Seen from the perspective of organisational sociology and organisation theory, our topic turns on how the higher education system, primarily university education, has changed during the course of a long period of expansion. The expansion has been characterised by two periods of rapid growth during the years before and after 1970 and shortly before and after 1990, alternating with a relative standstill in the intermediate period in the case of the universities. The reform periods have coincided with the growth periods but, as will be demonstrated below, they have been related in different ways. The two growth periods represent simultaneously two important stages of the transition process in which the role of higher education in society is about to change from 'elite education' via 'mass education' and possibly to 'universal education' (Trow 1970, 1974).

There is an important ideological similarity between the reforms of the 1960s and 1970s and those of the 1980s and 1990s. They were both based on the recognition that higher education was of great socio-economic importance and ought to be exploited as a means in order to reach major political goals. However, whereas higher education in the 1960s and 1970s was considered a welfare benefit and emphasised issues related to its distribution, the reforms of the 1980s and 1990s regarded higher education as a necessary tool and a resource in international economic competition. Accordingly, production efficiency (student flow and publication frequency) and product quality (students' achievements, academically good and socially useful research) were the focus of attention.

Although similar trends seem to have affected all three countries, there are important differences between them and their reforms that need to be further explored. In the chapters that follow we shall address a number of questions about change over time and across national boundaries related to the purpose, national policy and system characteristics of higher education, the management and organisation of academic institutions, and the characteristics of academic identity and work. Before we embark on this analysis, however, we need to clarify our comparative methodology and our conceptual approach. These two issues will be addressed in the following two sections.

Perspective on comparative policy studies

Within the relatively small world of academic studies of higher education there are contending assumptions about methods which spill over into perspectives on comparative studies. The comparative study of public policy and administration to which the analysis of higher education policies belongs is, as Heady (1990) argues, struggling to accommodate two seemingly inconsistent tendencies. One tendency is to try to 'generalise by making comparisons that are as inclusive as possible and by searching for administrative knowledge that transcends national regional boundaries' (p.3). The other tendency is towards case-specific or idiosyncratic analyses 'with only scant attention, or none at all, to foreign experience' (ibid.).

Page (1995) divides comparative studies under four headings: single country studies; juxtapositions; thematic comparisons; and causal explanations. The comparative studies of all kinds account for nearly three-quarters of empirically-based articles published in leading English language public administration journals. They can be

classed as comparative inasmuch as they add to knowledge in specifying what it is that marks off one set of administrative arrangements
from another. Those offering a particular study need not undertake
the comparison. The fact that one-offs are available in the literature,
however, makes it possible for comparisons to be made somewhere
within the universe of scholars. The many edited collections of essays
on a range of countries that are published are obvious examples of
these. Moreover, the analysis can be based on comparisons between
different periods of change, rather than comparisons between countries.

Juxtapositions bring together single country studies and, at minimum, allow a relatively rapid impression of the range of experiences
to be secured.

It is with thematic comparisons that we have our best hope of
finding a systematic presentation of evidence that allows common
questions about different political systems to be asked. At the most
ambitious level, facts can be used reiteratively as explanatory factors
when the institutions are examined one by one (Finer 1956).
Thematic comparisons might include specified objectives of the comparison and gather common data in order to generalise on the basis of
those data. They attempt to establish regularities in different patterns
of administration and deviation from these patterns. Finer hoped that
the process might lead to causes, although such a quest often leads to
banality rather than illumination. But even if one might be able to
determine causal relationships, data collection does not of itself
produce fruitful theorising. Some daring assumptions of a prioris
based on the wider literature of other cases seem a necessary prerequi-
site.

The notion of thematic comparisons may be made more precise if
specified in terms of what Alexander George (1979) calls the method
of 'structured, focused comparison' of cases. This approach relies on
a common set of questions to examine a small number of cases for
comparability and similarity. In their award-winning book on deterrence theory, George and Smoke (1974, p.98) justify the strategy of
constructing a set of common questions when neither the empirical
nor the theoretical literature provides the investigator with hypotheses or questions 'which are precise, operationally significant, and
adequate'. They continue by arguing that in the absence of a clear set
of testable hypotheses, the investigator's research design becomes:

> at least informally and for practical purposes, an iterative one.
> Tentative questions and ideas are tried out against two or three
> case studies in a preliminary way, and are then refined and
> expanded upon on the basis of the tentative results. A new trial is

made, and the process of question-asking and -answering iterates back and forth, until a satisfactorily full menu of hypotheses or questions can be arrived at for more formal application to all one's case study material. (George and Smoke 1974, p.98)

However, this approach implies that the researcher takes a stand on two closely related issues, that of causality and that of generalisability. In order to identify our position we shall borrow Theda Skocpol's (1980) distinction between research strategies in historical sociology where she defines three major strategies (pp.356–391). Our ambition is similar to what she calls analysing causal regularities. It positions itself between the ambitious quest for grand theories to find general causal models, based on concepts of common properties of phenomena that are supposed to be valid irrespective of time and place, and comparisons where concepts are used to arrive at meaningful interpretations of each distinctive case. We share the ambition to look for explanations, but believe that such explanations need to be socially and historically grounded, i.e. that they have to be specified in time and space. In practice we realise that our ability to arrive at an analysis of causal regularities is limited and that realistically we should start out with a set of concepts in terms of which we may arrive at meaningful interpretations by identifying similarities and differences between our cases. The next step in the analysis is then to try to identify factors that can explain patterns or regularities in the reform processes.

Our position is different from the more ambitious attempts at arriving at more general causal explanations taken by Leo Goedegebuure and Frans van Vught (Goedegebuure *et al.* 1994; Goedegebuure and van Vught 1994). They offer a helpful framework of themes within an international perspective. They are, however, somewhat critical of what they regard as 'individual hobbyhorses' which they think will be 'curbed' by providing an overarching framework to 'maximise comparability of outcomes of the constituent parts'. They offer thematic blocks against which they organise national characteristics. In their position we thus find both the ambition of developing general explanations and a top-down perspective on higher education policy.

Limitations of top-down macro analysis

Goedegebuure and van Vught follow Ragin (1987) in his claim that comparative method in the social sciences is distinguished by its use of attributes of macro-social units in explanatory statements. An example from van Vught and Goedegebuure is the hypothesis that the extent to which steering mechanisms are facilitatory or controlling affects the propensity of curriculum reforms to go through. Our criticism would be that the macro analysis is not too meaningful without linked fine-grained analyses of curriculum and institutional changes, some of them unique.

There is a tendency to regard the internal logic of governmental systems as sufficient to explain policy. Without the detailed knowledge of social processes that requires micro analysis, however, untidy and difficult to generalise though it is, generalisation at the macro level will not be true for one country, let alone in comparison across countries. As Teichler (1993) rightly points out: 'Higher education research does not seem to move to any balance regarding theories, disciplines and themes, but rather research-linked management and policy issues seem to take over the scene.' In our view, policy and management issues not only take over the scene but their pursuit fails to have much force if they do not take account of the true criteria variables, namely changes in research, scholarship, teaching and learning in which particularity rather than commonality is likely to be the rule.

Limitations of general hypothesising

Page, quoting Sartori (1970), notes that the whole of political science is a trade-off between configurative or detailed discussion of one case or a few cases and broader and more abstract theoretically-based generalisations which 'are best seen as a continuum rather than as categories of comparison'.

Archer (1979) has noted that it has proved virtually impossible to make an adequate match between micro analysis, in which the verities of close-grained empirical studies can be demonstrated, and macro analysis, in which more generally applicable propositions can be announced and interrogated.[1] The world of knowledge has increasingly accepted that more than one incommensurate or apparently inconsistent proposition can be advanced simultaneously. In the social domain, in particular, reality does not pile up in well-connected hierarchies of paradigm and theorems.

If stating hypotheses from previous accumulated knowledge and testing, verifying and adding to them were to be our dominant intellectual and research procedure, we would be subscribing to a major hypothesis which is dubious in its own right. The presumption would be that there are sufficient regularities in social experience for them to be capable of being incorporated into overarching frameworks and hypotheses. Such an intellectual procedure is based on the presumption that the phenomenon under study is both objectively and unequivocally given and subject to some form of rigid regularity. However, phenomena such as public 'higher education policy', 'the higher education system', 'academic disciplines', 'the academic profession', 'teaching', 'learning' and 'research' are social constructions. Their contents vary according to time and place. It would be odd to presume that phenomena, the actual content of which may vary under different circumstances, can be conceptualised as objective variables arranged in clear causal chains of cause and effect. Thus the data may emerge in topological rather than progressive arrangements and one of the necessary tasks in a comparative study like ours is to identify the precise content of the phenomenon we study. While we can certainly look for juxtapositions and thematic comparisons, and attempt to find causal explanations, we will be tying ourselves into an unnecessary bed of nails if we try to direct our research on the basis of pre-structured hypotheses. Where there are usable hypotheses we prefer to use them as assumptions that we may explore for the purpose of thematic comparisons.

Comparative approach

Our own approach, as elaborated by Susan Marton (1994), follows that of Castles (1989) who, by using methods of comparison, attempts 'to comprehend the purposes for which and the strategies by which policy is elaborated' (p.8). One method he suggests is the use of comparative case studies of two or more countries, the distinctiveness or similarity of whose policy outcomes is highlighted by the similarities or differences in other respects. The substantive method employed is that of thematic comparisons. The issues which we pursue thematically over the three countries are:

1. Changes in the ideologies of the state.

2. Changes in the mechanisms of government and the salience of central government.

3. Policy formation and the place of government agencies, educational institutions, elites, interest groups and actor networks of various kinds.

4. The nature of the reforms created by government.

5. The impacts of the reforms in terms of the academic profession, epistemic identities and working practices of academics in a range of disciplines, and in a range of institutions in the three countries.

6. The generation, application and impacts of quality assurance policies in the three countries.

Comparisons can be made across the three countries by working strongly from inductive methodologies which are essentially bottom-up and starting from the analysed experiences and not the other way round. But this does not mean that we start with atheoretical perceptions. This will become clear in our discussion of the actor–context model later in this chapter and in the conceptual analyses of the data presented in the chapters that follow. In these analyses we shall draw on a wide range of theories such as the theory of elites, interest groups and pressure groups in order to see how differences in their presence, position and operation reflect differences in the national political culture or expectations of the higher education systems. Furthermore we want to clarify to what extent these differences affect policies in the three countries. Finally, we shall use theories about the nature of knowledge generation and transmission, the academic profession and academic identity which can be played against the three country examples.

Why the three systems?

Our choice of three systems for comparisons was initially opportunistic: that is, we took advantage of opportunities presented to us for funding and access and for work with colleagues known and respected by each other. Given the intention to work intensively in the qualitative mode, we accepted in any case that we could not hope to work with a full representative sample of national systems. But familiarity with each system reassured us that there were significant differences that would make the comparisons worthwhile.

In all three countries throughout the 1970s the traditional assumptions about the welfare state – of which higher education formed one element – remained firm, if somewhat battered by economic hazards and growing lack of confidence in the capacity of public systems to deliver services with sufficient responsiveness and economy. But the first casualty within assumptions about the welfare state was less its distributive policies than its assumptions about the state's duty to support public professions largely on their own recognisance.

The differences between countries were, however, significant. The Scandinavian countries had been centralist in their public policies while the British were highly devolutionary. At the same time there were substantial differences between the Norwegian and Swedish approaches to centralised planning – Sweden was the *locus classicus* of social engineering (Åasen 1993) while Norway offered a mixture of rule-governed administration and fierce localism (Eide 1993). The advent of that ambiguous confection known as New Public Management (Pollitt 1993) had quite different implications for the three countries because they started from quite different assumptions about the modes through which policy could be generated and implemented. The structures of influence and the nature and working of elites, too, were different, as were the nature of state–university relations and the assumptions about the inner government of institutions. Finally, the nature of teaching and learning displayed significant differences.

Our methods

We give a full account of the methods adopted in our projects in the four books which report them, and have also summarised them in the appendix to this chapter. For the most part, our methods were qualitative and based on documentary and interview material.

Conceptual framework

The object of our study is straightforward and may be outlined in terms of a simple explanatory model. We aim at explaining the dependent variable, change in higher education, over a specified time period from about 1960 till 1995. Change within higher education systems is a complicated affair, as indicated above. In public higher education systems it is often regarded as an outcome of public policy and is usually conceptualised as follows. New policies are initially formulated in a top-down process by national policy-making bodies. They are subsequently translated into laws and resources and are implemented within educational institutions. Finally they affect the behaviour of individual faculties and the way in which they conduct their research, teaching and administrative tasks. This process is usually understood as a hierarchical process that spans what is usually considered different 'levels' of analysis: the macro level of national politics, the meso level of institutional behaviour and the micro level of individual behaviour. The process normally runs like this: decisions made at a higher level become structural conditions that affect behaviour at lower levels. Alternatively, the process may be 'reversed', so that influence moves the other way, from the bottom up. In the study of public policy and particularly in the field of policy implementation, there is an extensive literature on such processes (Berman 1978; Bleiklie 1997; Elmore 1979; Lester and Goggin 1999; Sabatier 1986; Sabatier and Jenkins-Smith 1993; Schneider and Ingram 1997).

When the problem is conceptualised like this, the question of how the levels are related to one another presents itself. Examples of general sociological discussions on the topic are found in, for example, Alexander *et al.* (1987). Because the discussion is framed in terms of a hierarchical model, the range of possible answers is given. The levels are related through chains of events as reflected in the discussion about top-down versus bottom-up perspectives on public policy making. In addition to the methodological problems pointed out above, there are additional reasons why this conceptual separation of levels often does not facilitate analysis of real world change processes. Quite to the contrary, the analyst is presented with a world that is conceptually divided into segments to which he or she must relate. In practice it is our experience that decisions in the different contexts of higher education are highly interwoven in a number of different ways that make a separate levels model unsuitable. Indeed it may even obscure rather than illuminate analysis. We shall therefore prefer the concept of 'fields of social action', where a field is an institutionalised area of activity in which actors struggle about something that is of importance to them.

We thus combine two definitions. The first part about social activity is derived from Powell and DiMaggio's (1991) definition of 'organisational field' as a 'recognised area of institutional life' (p.64f), and the second part from Bourdieu's (1988) concept of 'social field'. However, we shall still use the concept of 'levels' where it is appropriate for heuristic reasons. The point is not, therefore, to conceal the obvious fact that so many policy initiatives come from the political centre and are implemented in bodies and institutions at formally lower levels in a governmental hierarchy. The theoretical point we make here is that while admitting the obvious existence of a formal hierarchy, we seek to retain an analytical openness that is particularly important in a field of social life where multiple forces so clearly work together in forming the system. The significance of the autonomy of academic institutions, the role of academic disciplines and academic professional interests, testify to this. One of the advantages of this definition is that it is easier to incorporate in the theoretical framework the fact that certain influential individuals may affect simultaneously processes in many different contexts, their department, university and national policies. Reform ideas may furthermore move around and take effect in very complicated patterns, as the following example from Norway may illustrate. Reform ideas on graduate education were originally imported from the USA by Norwegian scientists in the 1950s. They managed to get their universities to introduce new graduate education degrees during the 1960s. In the 1980s the same reform ideas came back as national graduate education reforms in the humanities and social sciences. These reforms were not the product of top-down or bottom-up processes within a formal hierarchy, but of multiple interlocking processes within international academic disciplines, academic institutions and central authorities that finally resulted in national reform.

Although there are important characteristics particular to each nation, we can say that higher education in practice is regulated by more than one system: the governmental and the academic. Governmental regulation takes place through the central policy-making bodies and bureaucracies, the allocative bodies and the quality assurance bodies. These provide the frame for the policies for the universities, which then seek to find their particular identities and niches within them. At the same time, a different set of policies is formed through the invisible colleges of academics. They decide the award of the more prestigious academic posts and honours, reputational statuses and, interlocking with the allocative systems, the awards and differential allocation of funds. There are thus two policy- and decision-making systems, that have no formal connection, but which affect and generate energy between each other. Their action can be likened to that of tectonic plates [2] which shifting under the surface of the earth generate energy between them.

This tension and energy is created through the allocative functions that academics exercise on behalf of government within institutions or on decision-making bodies like research councils. In these functions the academic not only has to balance the needs of the government against those of academia, but also operates within a field of social action that requires him or her to reconcile social systems which are subject to different modi operandi and driven by forces of bureaucracy and politics opposed to the development of knowledge within academic disciplines and institutions. These points indicate the exceptionalism of policy making within higher education.

The reach of decisions made by groups or individuals defines the different fields within higher education politics. This reach may vary from decisions that concern national policy choices, via those affecting individual higher education institutions, academic disciplines or individual departments to those that concern only the individual academics themselves. Our dependent variable, accordingly, is change within three different fields of social action: national policy, educational institutions and academic work within different disciplinary settings.

We shall explain the changes in terms of a simple explanatory model where we assume that change is affected by two sets of independent variables. On the one hand we assume that the actors are bounded rational actors. We assume accordingly that they seek some kind of satisfying outcome defined in terms of specific goals, rather than trying to maximise some exogenously given utility function. Since preferences are not exogenously given they must be identified empirically.

In order to understand the nature of the choices actors make we need to see how their attempts to reach specific goals interact with the second set of independent variables which is the institutional context in which they act. Among approaches to 'the New Institutionalism' we find considerable variation both as to what extent human agency plays a role and how it interacts with the institutional context (Peters 1999, pp. 142ff). Regarding the latter aspect we can identify two kinds of ideas that we may consider opposites. There is institutional rational choice, as formulated by authors such as Ostrom (1990) and Scharpf (1997). Here institutions, defined as a set of rules, act as constraints on goal-seeking behaviour. There is also normative institutionalism as presented by March and Olsen (1984, 1989). In their rendition institutions do not constrain behaviour. They shape it. Institutions are defined as a collection of values, rules and routines that are developed in order to implement and enforce those values (Peters 1999, p.29). It follows from their concept of a logic of appropriateness that institutions and human agency are inseparable, because the latter is a product of the former.

If we return to the question of the extent to which actors play an important independent part in these models, neither the rational nor the normative version of institutionalism per se offers unambiguous and clear-cut answers. In the case of institutional rational choice the answer turns on how severely actors are constrained in the pursuit of their goals by institutional rules. This is partly an empirical question and partly a question of analytical focus. We may thus focus on how choices and choice opportunities are limited by the rules, or we may focus on how the actors try to use, bend or circumvent rules in order to achieve their goals. However, the rational choice approach is, in the words of Fritz Sharpf (1997), 'an actor-centred' institutionalism, and the analytical focus is on the actors and their choices, whereas rules are secondary limitations or constraints. Correspondingly, in the case of normative institutionalism we may choose between a focus on how institutions shape preferences in order to be effective or on how actors themselves are carriers of normative expectations. By expressing and communicating these expectations they develop, reinforce or shape institutions (cf. Peters 1999, p.57f, 107f). However, the main focus is on individuals, not as atomistic utility maximisers, but as actors embedded within a normative order. The analytical emphasis is on routines rather than rules. As rules are internalised rather than external, actors embody and represent institutions by normally doing the appropriate thing. Thus in trying to explain the resistance of academics to merging university departments (Chapter 7), the rational institutionalist is likely to assume that the reform threatened academic privileges and interests. The normative institutionalist would be more likely to assume that the reforms clashed with the established norm that a proper academic discipline has its own department. The academic would furthermore defend this view regardless of how it might affect his or her immediate interests.

In order to understand change in higher education we believe that it is fruitful to combine these perspectives. Historical institutionalism may be helpful in this connection because it seeks to find a middle ground between the extreme positions outlined above (Thelen and Steinmo 1995). Researchers within this tradition find the opposition between interest driven and normative behaviour that is posited explicitly by rational choice and normative institutionalism to be artificial. In practice human agency is guided by and drawn between these two driving forces. The interesting question is therefore usually not whether we ought to focus on one or the other, but how the tension between the two principles plays out in specific settings. We agree with their view and will accommodate this position by introducing more explicitly the temporal dimension in the analysis.

Although both institutions and human agency are constantly shaping and affecting the outcome of political processes, their role and significance vary according to characteristics of the situation at hand as well as to the theoretical perspective applied. We emphasise, therefore, the tension between what Becher and Kogan (1992, p.176) call organic growth and radical change. The implication for how we regard policy change is that the notion of consciously designed reforms and radical change needs to be supplemented. We propose therefore to add the idea of gradual change where new structures and values imposed by reforms are grafted onto established arrangements in a process of meandering and sedimentation that gives policies and institutions their character of complexity and ambiguity (Bleiklie and Marton 1998). These two explanatory foci may also supplement one another, ceteris paribus, in the following sense. The more macroscopic the scope and the longer the time frame of the analysis, the more relevant are the relatively stable structural arrangements for explaining patterns of behaviour. The more microscopic the scope and the shorter the time frame, the more relevant will choices and strategies made by individual actors be for explaining the outcome of a given policy process.

We expect that the implications of these perspectives as to how higher education may be shaped by processes of change are pretty straightforward. The reform period of about thirty years on which we focus is fairly short in a historic perspective. This means that we should be able to close in on the actors and that their environment is relatively stable. The analysis should therefore focus on the actors, and the problem of to what extent they manage to realise their goals within given constraints. However, given our premise that we cannot assume what the goals and choices of the actors really are, we need to identify them by focusing on the setting in which they find themselves.

The main model is therefore applied like this (Figure 1.1). First we shall describe the situation at T^1, which is the starting point for the reform period in question, with a particular view to the structural, normative and material setting, i.e. the constellation of actors, their objectives, resources and values. However, we shall also venture into occasional historical analyses over longer time spans in order to understand the original context better. Second, we want to analyse the reform process itself, focusing on actor behaviour, the choices they make and how successful they are. Finally we shall describe the situation at T^2 and compare with the situation at T^1, in order to spell out the changes that have taken place and explain the outcome in terms of the two sets of independent variables: human agency and institutional characteristics. [3]

The question of change in higher education is not, however, a simple one of either/or. Whereas some aspects of higher education such as ideologies or formal organisational structures may change drastically in a relatively short time period, other aspects such as faculty or student behaviour and identities may change more slowly and gradually. The same may be true of certain basic technologies such as academic lectures or study techniques. This indicates that in an analysis of developments over shorter periods of time we should also be open to the tension between organic growth and radical change. Finally, we may find that actors' ability to induce change and the degree of structural constraints they face may vary over time and from place to place. We expect this to be clear from the cross-national comparison of our three countries. We shall demonstrate that the capacity of the British government to induce drastic change in the

T^1 ➔ Process shaped by actors and institutions ➔ T^2

Figure 1.1. The actor–context model of higher education change

higher education system seems to be greater than that of the Swedish government and much more so than the Norwegian central government. In the latter case the impression of continuity and gradual change is comparatively strong.

Research issues

When we try to define and explain these policy changes we shall focus on a number of aspects of change such as the values that characterise the policies and processes of change, the actors that formulate the policies, the policy content and the outcome and implications of the policies that are adopted and how they interact with other ongoing processes of change. We aim at binding together analyses of political reforms and of processes of social change as they manifest themselves at different levels of analysis: the national, the institutional, the disciplinary and the individual. We shall focus on the tension between the practical tasks that actors seek to solve through goal-oriented action and the cognitive maps and social norms that direct them (Becher and Kogan 1992; March and Olsen 1995). These ideas form a general conceptual framework around the work, although in the different chapters we will make use of specific conceptual approaches in the analyses of national policy formation, the implementation of reforms, the policy impacts and processes of change at educational institutions and within disciplinary groups. The 'synoptic model' of higher education may illustrate the complexity of the higher education system and the way in which it is affected by policy initiatives. This model emphasises how the multilevel character of the system, in combination with normative and instrumental or operational modes which are generated both within and outside the system, creates a multifaceted system that is formed by a multiplicity of social forces (Becher and Kogan 1992, pp.7–21).

These forces play themselves out within different contexts. We shall follow Burton Clark's argument (Clark 1983) that higher education institutions find themselves within a triangular field of co-ordinating forces constituted by state authority, academic oligarchy and the market (see also Chapter 4). By co-ordinating forces is meant those forces that represent sufficient power and authority to pull higher education systems together in the face of a complex and disparate array of tasks, beliefs and forms of authority that pull in different directions (Clark 1983, pp.137–145) (see Chapter 4). Becher and Kogan (1992), adapting Premfors, (1983) added a welfare state force. The co-ordinating forces, furthermore, manifest themselves in different ways at the level of national policies, educational institutions and individual academics within their disciplinary departments.

Within the field of national politics three sets of considerations apply in this connection. One consideration concerns the understanding of political change. Here we are concerned with the tension and interplay between the strategic and institutional aspect, i.e. between the conscious attempts at creating change in order to achieve instrumental goals and the habitual and rule-bound processes where change takes place gradually and less noticeably. On this basis two interpretations of reform processes are at hand. We may regard them as conscious clearly distinguishable attempts at achieving specific goals, or we may see them as embedded processes that form parts of more comprehensive social and political processes of change. In this latter perspective reforms may be regarded as expressions of how public authorities react to such phenomena as rising student numbers, changed conceptions of the significance of higher education, research and the different disciplines or changes in philosophies about higher education governance. These questions are addressed in particular in Chapter 2.

The second consideration concerns the understanding of the field of higher education as a public policy domain. In this connection we have developed an analysis of policy regimes along two dimensions. One is the influence dimension where we apply a typology of influence according to the actors or constellations of actors who dominate policy formation: central authorities, higher education institutions, higher education elites or interest organisation. The other dimension concerns the relationship between the actors that may range from relatively tightly knit, stable and cohesive policy communities to transient and loosely coupled issue networks. A dynamic regime approach has been developed in order to analyse the political processes within higher education policy regimes. This analysis is found in Chapter 3.

The third consideration relates to the way in which we seek to understand policy content. We emphasise three aspects of higher education policy:

1. The ideological aspect appears through the values that are promoted, the actors' understanding of reality and the justifications they provide for the policies.

2. The organisational aspect manifest itself through the way in which procedures by which influence and authority are sought and distributed.

3. The educational and research policy aspects appear through the way in which education and research activities are designed and through the resources that are invested. (These two aspects are analysed in Chapters 4 and 5.)

In the analysis of the fields of institutional and individual practices we shall focus on the interplay between institution, discipline and the individual academic. Two questions will be at the centre of our attention.

The first question turns on the position of the academic profession which we shall address in Chapter 6. In this connection we shall consider important questions relating to university policy and how it interacts with dominant conceptions of knowledge and the position of various academic disciplines.

The second question turns on how reforms had an impact on academic identity and how characteristics of academic disciplines and academic identity contribute to the formation of university policy and local practices. This is the topic of Chapter 7.

In analysis of the institutional field in these two chapters we shall mainly make use of two kinds of theoretical approaches. First, the underlying theme is the struggle for social recognition within hierarchical social institutions (Bourdieu 1988). In this analysis we focus on status hierarchies within disciplines, hierarchies of disciplines and hierarchies of disciplines and other social groups at the universities as well as their position within wider social structures. The second approach is based on Tony Becher's (1989) concepts of research modes and disciplinary cultures. In this connection we shall emphasise how different disciplines form the basis of different types of communities based on specific modes of work, organisational patterns and common values.

In the analyses we shall focus on the dynamics of the various social forces which these perspectives are aiming to capture. Central among them are the dynamics between the struggles for social status, disciplinary and professional values, organisational patterns and forms of practice, political reform efforts and other external events of significance to the actors involved. In the final analysis we are concerned with how the processes that are brought together within academic institutions affect the basic conceptual understanding and the epistemic structures on which the activity of each individual academic is based.

Taking the different aspects of change we mentioned at the beginning of this section as a point of departure, we shall argue in this book that: *Changes in formal structures (such as higher education reform) and size (increased student enrolment) do not necessarily change behaviour or all aspects of social relationships as, for example, power and autonomy.* The thrust of this argument is that social behaviour and social relationships are far too complex and ambiguous to be fruitfully analysed in terms of a mechanistic model that assumes simple causation as the engine of social change. We support the view that social causes and effects, in order to be meaningfully identified, must be located in time and space. One implication of this view is that social causation cannot be assumed, but must be discovered. The assumptions of grand theories or generalised models of society must therefore be tested. One cannot presume that changes in social relationships and behaviour within higher education follow from reforms that change social structures. Neither can the causes of actual behavioural changes be read back into structural causes. These ideas about the nature of change in higher education systems will be developed further in Chapters 2 and 3 on the higher education policy process. An important subset of these assumptions is that academics have a dual accountability to their invisible colleges of fellow academics and to their institution. On this hypothesis it is indeed possible to compare systems and, at any one time, to denote the extent to which one force, e.g. managerial as against collegial or civil society as opposed to market criteria, is driving the system.

The nature and pace of change in higher education systems are affected by national socio-political peculiarities. Most major theoretical perspectives on higher education development and change, such as idealism, functionalism and rationalism, assume that the co-ordinating forces within higher education have changed fundamentally. They tend to assume, furthermore, that the autonomy of academic institutions and individual academics has been reduced, and that the influence of the market and/or public authorities has increased. This is usually considered to be a consequence of the development of higher education from elite via mass to universal higher education. We argue that there is a considerable variation depending on national political and educational and research traditions. However, in trying to identify commonalities across national boundaries, we may develop alternative assumptions from the functionalist theory of organisations based on the concept of socio-technology. Joan Woodward (1965) developed the theme that social relationships develop in response to the underlying technology which an institution performs. Thus the traditional view of collegial academic governance followed the assumption that the process was based on diverse and individualistic work. The main production unit was the free academic who required freedom to generate good research and teaching. It followed from this that the structures of higher education would be collegial rather than managerial. By contrast, if the civil society functions of higher education predominate, academic freedom is tempered by social concern, which requires a somewhat more hierarchical channel of authority to secure it.

Events outside the realm of national politics such as changes in student preferences may affect the higher education system at least as much as national policies. Much of the rhetoric about higher education policy is based on the notion that higher education systems are shaped by political decisions and preferences. We seek to demonstrate how a number of events and processes, such as educational choices made by young people, the dynamics of academic labour markets and academic prestige hierarchies, have exerted equally important influences on higher education.

Social practices at the organisational and individual levels have changed less than formal structural changes may indicate. The argument rests on a number of premises. Reform policies are often based on the assumption that target groups can be counted on to act as if they are subject to no other influences than the policy itself. However, policy reforms and organisational changes represent but two of several factors that affect the behaviour of individuals and organisations. In this connection it is important to bear in mind the set of three co-ordinating forces pointed out by Clark (1983). In addition to the public authorities or bureaucracy in Clark's model, there are the forces of the market and the academic oligarchy that potentially at least may shape higher education, and possibly compete with or prevent the efforts of public authorities to reach their goals through higher education policies. The way in which reform policies affect behaviour thus depends on at least the following factors: the extent to which a policy is clearly identifiable in terms of operational goals and tangible policy instruments; the extent to which a policy is welcome in terms of compatibility with the values and interests of target groups; the extent to which a policy is relevant in terms of how likely it is to affect core activities of target groups. One assumption we shall explore is that this process is likely to be affected by the relationships between the types of knowledge being generated and disseminated and the higher education organisation required to sustain them. This point taken from work by Basil Bernstein (1963) relates to the extent to which forms of knowledge, hard and soft, the collected and integrated curriculum, affect and are affected by its social or organisational forms. It follows that higher education organisation, such as decentralisation, binary systems, more power to rectors, are/should be determined in part by the extent to which they are applicable to the component knowledge structures in teaching and research. We may assume furthermore with Geertz (1964) and Archer (1981) that forms of knowledge, feeling or value become shaped and structurated into procedures, processes and structures. Both these assumptions thus refer to a basic generative process in higher education development where policy movements from above interact with disciplinary processes from below.

Processes of change at the level of national policy, within academic institutions and disciplinary groups, are only partially co-ordinated. The implication of this argument is that changes within these fields of social action are, like tectonic plates, driven by different forces. It is thus an open question how and to what extent academic institutions and practices are affected by major policy changes. This depends on the extent to which the changes are welcomed by, relevant to, and moulded and absorbed by academic institutions and practices. Conversely, academic disciplines and their development may, for instance, be formed by processes such as academic drift that may go unheeded by national political actors.

Contents of the book

In the following chapters we shall flesh out the actor–context model and its institutionalist argument. In doing so we shall deal with changes within the three tightly interwoven fields of national policy and politics (Chapters 2–4), educational institutions (Chapter 5), academic identity and work (Chapters 6–7).

In Chapter 2 Maurice Kogan and Marianne Bauer provide an outline of the recent higher education policy history of the three countries. Chapter 3 by Ivar Bleiklie analyses the relationship between policies and the actors and patterns of influence in the policy process. Chapter 4 by Maurice Kogan and Susan Gerard Marton deals with the relationship between the state and higher education and theories of the state and of academic autonomy relevant to that relationship. Chapter 5 by Berit Askling and Mary Henkel analyses the relationship between academic institutions, national political authorities and the framing of academic authority. Chapter 6 by Roar Høstaker focuses on the academic profession and how its has been affected by policy changes. Chapter 7, by Mary Henkel and Agnete Vabø, deals with the impact of higher education reforms on academic identity. Chapter 8 sums up and draws conclusions from the analyses in the preceding chapters.

Appendix
Procedures and data

More detailed accounts of methods are given in the four national studies published separately. The common procedures for the whole project were, however, as follows:

1. Joint identification by the three teams of the substantive content and methods of the national studies and hence of the comparative study. This process was conducted through workshops and the exchange of drafts.

2. Study of policy documentation to tabulate changes in the governing structures of higher education. Intensive documentary study was undertaken in all three projects, but most intensively in Norway and Sweden where more detailed current policy documentation was more readily available, which to some extent balanced the amount of data available to the three projects.

   In Norway, secondary material included statistics and reports from the following sources: (a) Norwegian Institute for Studies in Research and Higher Education; (b) Central Bureau of Statistics; (c) the online Ministry Database on Higher Education (DBH) provided by the Norwegian Social Science Data Services.

   Swedish material and data were derived from documents, including parliamentary and government reform documents and material from central agencies. Reports and descriptions of organisation and the distribution of authority and responsibility, as well as accounts of their systems for quality assurance and development, were collected from the institutions in the study. When relevant, documented information from other Swedish higher education institutions was employed. The statistics were obtained from Statistics Sweden, the National Higher Education Agency and individual institutions and departments.

3. Selected interviews with policy formers and other past and present key informants on changes in the policies and structures of central government in relation to higher education. The total number of those interviewed specifically for the English study of policy formation was 90 ministers and former ministers, senior civil servants, and other key informants, e.g. journalists. The project also benefited from

interviews with both policy makers or observers and academics conducted for our contemporaneous evaluation of the Foresight Initiative, funded by the Nuffield Foundation.

The Norwegian study included interviews with 12 national level actors including a minister, three senior civil servants, the Secretary-General of the Council of Norwegian Universities and the Director of the Norway Network Council. Eight interviews were undertaken with institutional leaders.

In Sweden, at the macro level, the purpose of conducting the interviews was to shed light on and confirm the information obtained from official government documents. This was quite different from the micro and meso levels where the interviews comprised a large part of the primary empirical material. A total of 12 interviews were conducted (approximately two and a half hours in length) during the time period of February 1996 to March 1998 with the majority taking place during 1996.

4. Interviews with academics of different levels in a range of institutions and subject areas. All of the studies concentrate on the more academic fields of knowledge and excluded, for example, the more professionally oriented faculties of law, medicine and engineering. This limitation was applied in all three countries on the assumption that change or non-change in values and attitudes among academic staff would be better observed within more traditional disciplinary fields. These would be the *a fortiori* examples, because change would be least expected in them.

    Within the English project, studies were made through documentation and over 300 semi-structured interviews within the following subject areas: biochemistry, chemistry, economics, English, history, physics and sociology. This part of the project also comprised two case studies of quality assurance. Work on the enterprise in higher education initiative also incorporated interviews with those involved at national level in the two specific policy areas, as well as with members of senior academic management teams and administrators in seven universities and academics in seven disciplines. The more general study was based largely on interviews with individual academics from six disciplines in four more universities.

The Norwegian case focused on change and reform within the three different fields of action: national policy, educational institutions and the individual academic. The analysis tried to overcome the uniqueness of the single case by describing it in terms of general theoretical variables and located the case as a particular value on each variable for the more detailed investigation in the various empirical chapters. They selected the two largest of Norway's four universities, the universities in Bergen and Oslo. Within the two universities the humanities and social sciences faculties were selected, which together employ 70 per cent of all Norwegian academics within these types of university faculty. Thus the selection of disciplines at the institutional level was somewhat different from the two other country studies. Forty-six semi-structured interviews were made with actors or respondents operating at different levels. At the disciplinary level 32 academics at the two faculties of the humanities and social sciences in Bergen and Oslo were interviewed.

In addition, there were two surveys of the whole faculty at the faculty of the humanities and faculty of social sciences, the University of Bergen (N = 334, 85 per cent response rate) and the faculty of the humanities and faculty of social sciences, the University of Oslo (N = 425, 81 per cent response rate).

In Sweden, four universities were selected as study objects – two large and two smaller ones of varying age. However, in order to cover the institutional variance of the Swedish comprehensive higher education system, one large and one smaller college were included.

Six disciplines were selected to cover the range from the humanistic and social sciences to the natural sciences: history, modern languages, sociology, economics, physics and biochemistry. In both the English and Swedish studies, the interviewees were guaranteed anonymity and are therefore not identified. Such an undertaking was not considered realistic in the smaller and more specific Norwegian project.

Interviews were held with the rectors, other institutional leaders, deans and top administrators (two to five persons at each institution). At the micro level, seven to fourteen academics (including the head of department) from each of the six disciplines were interviewed, that is 108 interviews in all. The rectors of the six institutions all gave very positive responses to our request to let their institutions take part in the study. Everyone approached for interview immediately agreed (only one person found it impossible to find a suitable time for the interview). Several people expressed appreciation at the opportunity to talk about these matters. Interviews with the 108 academic teachers/researchers were structured in three groups of themes.

5.   Most of our empirical work was placed on databases which enabled us to read across interview, documentary and secondary material under discrete thematic headings. The analysis of material was assisted by the creation of detailed coding frames against which our data could be recorded. The recording was an onerous task. If we have any counsel to offer, it is to be relatively parsimonious in the coding heads selected and to avoid over-allocation of empirical sections when creating the codes.

Notes

1   For a thorough discussion of the limitations of macro-oriented survey research see Castles (1989).

2   This metaphor of tectonic plates has also appealed to Professor Ronald Barnett who used it in his inaugural lecture at the London Institute of Education. This appears to have been spontaneous adoption of the metaphor on both sides.

3   It is important to note that we use the word 'institution' in two different meanings: used as a theoretical concept 'institution' refers to formal or informal structures that regulate behaviour; used as concrete denomination 'institution' refers to a specific organization, such as a university or a college.

PART II

History, Policy
and Structure

Chapter 2

Higher Education Policies
Historical Overview

Maurice Kogan and Marianne Bauer

Introduction

Before entering on the analysis of change processes in higher education between 1965 and 1995 we shall describe common features and
contrasts in higher education policies and systems in the three countries as they existed at the starting point (T^1) of our study. We shall
also note the periodisation of each country's reform as these have
been documented in our three national reports. In spite of the complexities and variations that such periodisation may involve, we will
analyse similarities and differences in the changes in national policies
and systems within the time span of our study and interpret them in
terms of sources of change. We shall in particular focus on the extent
to which political actors have been able to formulate preferences and
impose change or, alternatively, the extent to which policy changes
are the product of evolutionary processes of change in social structures.

The situation before the 1960s (T^1)

In the period, post the 1939–45 war the political frame of higher education in the three countries was similar in some respects. They all
more or less adhered to welfare state ideologies and practices. All had
had left or centrist administrations for much of the post-war period
and even when more conservative governments came into office they
were reluctant to alter the substantive thrust of redistributive policies.
From the 1950s, as in the rest of Europe, they experienced a steep
increase in student demand for higher education and the beginning of
questioning of the university elite system. This demand was met by
the establishment of new institutions and the expansion of existing
ones. Abundant resources were assigned to higher education and
research.

However, there were as well deep-seated differences between the three countries, primarily in their relationships between the state and the higher education institution. These originated from different basic models and developed within different traditions: the Norwegian and Swedish systems in the traditions of continental Europe with two strong centres of power, the government and the faculties, while in the British system power had been concentrated in the basic units of the universities under relaxed central control (Clark and Youn 1976).

In the two Nordic countries there were close relationships between the universities and the state, which has also funded them. In Sweden, from the fifteenth century, universities were responsible for the training of higher civil servants in accordance with a fairly strict degree system, which reflected the demands of the national state, its schools, church and judicial system (Askling 1999). Until the 1990s the Swedish universities were subordinate to the state in recruiting professors and teachers. In Norway, from the founding of the first university in 1811 in Oslo, the main purpose of the university was to fulfil the need of the emerging Norwegian nation state for educated manpower (Bleiklie 1999). As in Sweden, Norwegian university teachers were and are civil servants, and parliament until recently formally made decisions on detailed matters such as the establishment of new professorships.

In the UK the universities were almost wholly free of state control. Their funding came in quinquennial tranches determined in advance on assumptions that entailed maximum autonomy. Universities were assumed to be private institutions but sanctioned by charter and entitled to receive all necessary funding that they could not earn or otherwise find themselves ('deficiency funding'). In like fashion, all full-time undergraduate students were entitled to free tuition and subsistence allowances, subject to parental income. Higher education was thus a fully subsidised emanation of the welfare state. By contrast, the Norwegian and Swedish systems allowed generous allocations for institutional funding and free tuition, but only repayable loans for students.

The differences between British and continental European higher education government have been remarked by Neave (1986, p.109) in the following terms: 'in the Continental European countries the revolutions of the late eighteenth and nineteenth centuries ensured that the university was incorporated in the national bureaucracy'. By contrast in the UK, 'the status of academia as a property owning corporation of scholars, the purest expression of which was in the two ancient British universities, was preserved ... Until the First World

War ... there existed a broadly held view which regarded education ... as ill-served by state intervention'.

Other factors that generated different conditions for policy development and impact between the three countries were the size and age of the higher education systems. In Norway, the top civil servants and university professors all belonged to the small national civil service elite, and the question of autonomy could for a long period be settled within the homogeneous community of this elite. The long tradition in Sweden of close relations between the universities and the state meant that while the institutions were state governed, within this fairly small system, rules and regulations were often laid down after long and respectful negotiations between the government and the professors (Askling 1999). Within such a tradition Swedish universities never had the legally autonomous status of the Anglo-Saxon universities (Lane 1992).

A further national characteristic of these higher education systems due to policies was their degrees of differentiation. While within the British system there developed ranking orders between the autonomous universities with a clear elite summit, in both the Scandinavian countries differentiation of their higher education institutions was counteracted. In Norway a national hierarchy was avoided by way of regionalisation, and in Sweden through a deep-seated ambition of equivalence of all higher education. The propensity to differentiate occurred more easily in the UK system, which even before the ending of the binary system included 45 universities, while the much smaller Norwegian (four universities) and Swedish (six universities) systems could assume greater degrees of homogeneity.

Sweden stands out as the country that traditionally has had the strongest state control (a position which was modified by an increasing influence of corporate structures by the reforms of the 1970s). England was located at the other extreme with little state interference and a high degree of institutional autonomy combined with a strong co-operation of academic elites with central government. Although Norway, like Sweden, had an almost completely state-owned higher education system, it was characterised by a fairly high degree of autonomy combined with a strong role of academic institutions operating as regional actors in a political system characterised by strong regionalist influences.

From T^1 to T^2 – the whole of our period – strong forces making for continuity interacted with attempts at reform. These included the inheritance of buildings and equipment, tenured staff and other resources, reputations and academic culture and values.

Periodisation of reform

Our three national studies reflect changes taking place over a period roughly from the 1960s to the present time with particular concentration on the latter period. In comparing the different periods and content of change which we note here, we can discuss later whether causes and processes of change were different between the countries. In Norway there were three periods of higher education policy:

- *1960s to early 1970s*: the policy of expansion developed in the Kleppe (1961) and Ottosen (1965) Commissions.

- *1970s to 1980s*: the policy of selectivity; district colleges, an outcome of the Ottosen Commission.

- *Late 1980s to 1990s*: the policy of quality and integration inaugurated by the Hernes Commission (1988).

There was rapid growth in student numbers during the 1960s, reaching its peak in 1972 and again between 1985 and 1995 with a relative standstill in between. Reforms coincided with growth but were related to it in different ways. The first wave was an attempt to meet greater student numbers, but academic resistance to key reforms of the structure of degree patterns led the government to create and put its additional resources into regional colleges. During the 1970s, in a wave of strong vocationalism and criticism of the universities as 'ivory towers', a large number of district colleges were established in non-university towns and villages all over Norway. The universities were left in benign neglect and both their budgets and student numbers were allowed to diminish. This was the time of the democratisation of universities (Bleiklie, Høstaker and Vabø 2000).

Two political tendencies contributed to this development. First, regional policy became an important instrument for increased investment for higher education purposes, and contributed to a political climate that was unfavourable to the universities. Second, budgetary growth became detached from the school systems' need for teachers. Instead growth became linked with changes in student numbers as the universities' main tasks were transformed from the production of a necessary minimum of qualified candidates to the civil service and the professions to the distribution of education as a welfare benefit.

In the second period of change (1970s to 1980s), the emphasis shifted back to the development of universities, their quality and efficiency, and concern for the building up of graduate studies. In the third period, the Hernes Commission argued for an integrated system as epitomised in 'the Norway Network' and for the creation of research academies, that is graduate schools. It thus looked towards essentially US patterns of structure.

In governmental terms the Norwegians joined the universal surge of interest in explicit quality measures and towards public service 'activity planning' and away from rules-led government. Higher education was no longer conceived primarily as a welfare benefit and was instead envisaged by government primarily as a tool of economic development. Our study reflects on the extent to which this view was shared by the academics.

The Swedish reforms can be characterised by the following time stages:

- *1960 to 1977*: expansion of higher education paving the way for structural reform in 1977.

- *1978 to 1993*: tinkering with decentralisation leading to a major reform in 1993.

- *1994 onwards*: further expansion and partial return to a more centralist policy.

In the 1960s the student numbers more than tripled. Most of the students chose the faculties of humanities and social sciences and courses that did not fit the structure of the labour market. Continuous efforts were made by the government to manage this expansion, e.g. by introducing a lecturer position for teaching only, establishing institutions and fixed study plans. Finally, the U68 Commission was set up with the task not only of coping with the expansion but also with the idea of the higher education system as a tool for reforming society.

Nearly ten years later, after a thorough preparation phase, parliament decided to set the extensive reform into action in 1977. All post-secondary education was integrated in 'Högskolan' and subordinated to a Higher Education Law and Ordinance. Under this unitary attire, however, a binary system was concealed, in that only the universities received basic funding for research. Access to higher education was centrally regulated to a fixed number of study places in universities and colleges and funding for undergraduate education was earmarked to the study lines and courses of the new system.

After strong criticism of the inflexibility of the new higher education system in the 1980s, the Social Democratic Party gradually retracted from its centralist policy and took several steps towards deregulation and decentralisation in order to improve flexibility and efficiency of the system. Student numbers were kept practically constant during this decade in spite of a considerable increase in applications for study places. The confidence in the public sector decreased and at the end of the 1980s a new steering system for the entire sector was introduced, based on goal-oriented regulation and extensive autonomy combined with accountability. Concern about the quality of undergraduate education was raised by student criticism and a commission was called upon to scrutinise the state of teaching and suggest improvements.

With a change to a Conservative/Liberal government in 1991 higher education was seen as a tool, not for reforming society, but for supporting national interests in an international competitive marketplace. A series of propositions and bills were delivered announcing a more profound devolution of power and responsibilities. In 1993 the 'Freedom for Quality' reform was launched which brought more responsibility to the vice chancellors and boards and power on matters such as internal organisation, allocation of resources and establishing of professorships. Important changes were also a performance-based resource allocation system for undergraduate education and the obligation to establish internal quality assurance systems in all institutions.

The number of student places had continuously increased during the 1990s, but access was still centrally regulated. With the return of a Social Democratic government in 1994 there was a restrengthening of central influence, e.g. by appointing external representatives as chairs of the institutional boards and establishing a new central agency for higher education.

In the UK, from the 1960s it is possible to analyse the reforms in higher education in the following time segments:

- *1945 to 1963*: a period of growth in demand and provision but essentially continuing a pattern in which research-led universities were divided from non-university and teacher training institutions, all within a highly selective system. The non-university sector itself, other than teacher training, was somewhat undifferentiated and included technical and further education colleges offering courses of advanced study at the same time as they offered craft and technician training.

- *1963 to 1975*: a period of moderate growth and consolidation stretching from the legitimation of expansion, under broadly continuing conditions, by the Robbins Report (1963). During this time, the non-university sector grew in parallel to the universities and gained strength with the creation of 30 polytechnics. Numbers continued to rise but the participation rate levelled off and there was increasing financial stringency.

- *1975 to 1981*: the ending of the quinquennial system in 1973–4 was a decisive turning point, with 1975 marking the start of the post-quinquennium period. From the 1980s distinctive ideologies were pursued alongside drastic reductions in the units of resource.

- *1981 to 1997*: a period of change in which the finance, government evaluation and substantive content of higher education were subjected to radical changes, but in which also from the mid-1980s there was a return to rapid expansion.

Common features and contrasts in changes to three national systems

The sequence of policy change was much the same in all three countries. Social expectation and economic demand stimulated student recruitment and led to the transformation from elite towards mass higher education systems. This in its turn evoked governments' insistence on quality assurance, cost effectiveness and interplay with the market. But the countries also differed in important respects

At the end of the 1970s an important common feature was that all three welfare states came under challenge. Almost all countries felt the economic stress engendered by the oil crises of the first few years of the 1970s. This led to the first questioning of the assumption that higher education must be allowed to grow, under constant cost per unit, in response to qualified demand. However, between 1985–6 and 1996–7 expenditure in the UK went up more in higher education than in all education, or on the armed services, the police or even health and social security. The contradiction between the general backlash against the welfare state and the growth of higher education has been even more marked in the UK than other European countries (Scott 1995). But if student numbers increased, the cost per student was forced down. In Sweden too higher education was long prioritised and sheltered from cuts compared with most other public sectors. Between 1988 and 1993 this was also the case in Norway.

While the three countries started from different points they were all deeply affected by the obligations placed on universities by the expansion of student demand. Underlying those demands were similar social and economic expectations of higher education. The combination of economic stress and growing student demand raised questions as to whether the basic qualities and values of higher education were under threat and whether available resources were used efficiently. This led to pressures, common to all countries, on the higher education institutions for accountability and explicit quality assurance. This, in turn, demanded shifts in assumptions about the traditional university–state relationships.

Norway and Sweden attempted to strengthen the government of higher education, but through the exercise of stronger leadership at the institutional level and a corresponding relaxation of government through rules. Especially in Sweden, with its long tradition of detailed central control, deregulation, finally codified by a comprehensive reform, was of significant scope. In Norway, with the stability that has characterised its state–university relations, the change has taken place piecemeal and gradually, and the intensity with which central government authorities have tried to interfere with university affairs has never fundamentally changed the relationship between state and university. In the UK, while the institutions were expected to assert their authority and thus reduce academic power, the central authorities increasingly strengthened their position through the requirements of institutional plans, quality assurance, research assessment and the legalisation of the system. The changes in state–university relations were more acute in the UK, partly because of the strong ideological position taken by radical Conservative governments in the 1980s and partly because they started from a position in which universities had had autonomy. A further difference was that while the changes in Norway and Sweden can be described as forms of de-bureaucratisation, the UK, in strengthening the authority of central institutions, did not become bureaucratic in the sense of imposing detailed rules.

There were thus substantial differences in reform of government and administration because the three countries started from different positions, and also due to varied traditions in the use of reform instruments, where Sweden stands out in its use of large comprehensive reforms.

Common goals, different means

The universal conditions of economic stress, increased demands for and the importance of higher education in the developing 'knowledge society' thus led to similar goals in the three countries: both quantity and quality of higher education should increase, and closer relationships with society and industry should be established in order for higher education both to contribute better to their development and to gain a larger proportion of its funding from the 'market'. However, the means and instruments to cope with these problems varied between the countries, depending on their ideological traditions and state–institutions relationship. (For the different outcomes of attempted reforms see Chapters 6–8.) We shall use two examples for our analysis: changes in the institutional systems and in the policies and systems of quality assurance.

CHANGES IN THE INSTITUTIONAL SYSTEMS

The quantity/quality problem was first tackled (in the 1960s and 1970s) by means of institutional development including differentiation and strengthening of the institutional role.

In both Norway and the UK the solution was binary systems, where polytechnics and district colleges respectively were established in order to accommodate the need for a vocationally oriented higher education alternative to the traditional universities, and in Norway for shorter courses. The universities although larger, operated as previously and the tasks of university teachers did not change significantly. In the UK the non-university sector grew in parallel to the universities and gained strength with the creation of 30 polytechnics but with lower teacher–student ratios, which reflected the assumption that research, while not restricted, was not centrally funded. Similarly, in Norway, as the universities resisted reforms to become more socially 'relevant' and useful, the government set up the district colleges to make more student places available all over the country. This new kind of educational institution comprised shorter vocational studies, university-like disciplinary subjects and multi- or cross-disciplinary subjects, but were not funded for research. Contrary to this, in Sweden with its more centralist policy the model became a unitary, integrated higher education system containing, however, a binary divide concerning teaching and research. The Swedish solution was a more radical transformation of the existing university education in a more vocationally oriented direction. This also meant that the teacher role within the universities became more differentiated, with a corps of staff restricted to teaching operating alongside the traditional university professors who combine teaching and research functions (Askling 1999; Bauer *et al.* 1999).

In the 1990s, with more emphasis on quality, the three types of systems changed in different ways. In the UK, the end of the binary system in 1992 constitutes a major case study in the post-1970s politics of higher education. Central government responded to those interests whose objectives coincided with theirs. Suspicion of local government and ministers' perceptions of the shortcomings of universities must have persuaded them that their interests need not be accommodated and that the polytechnics' interests should be advanced instead. The issue was decided by the interaction of quite closed interests and politics. It was also decided by ministers who lacked the deference to academe of a previous political generation.

The moves against local authority control of polytechnics and their promotion to university status were connected with changing assumptions about public institutions. Originally there had been the parallel theories of the free universities, best able to use their freedom to produce excellent research and scholarship, while the polytechnics would be more aligned with public purposes through their connections with local government. Now there was a theory of institutions free to compete with each other but working within far tighter funding and demands for accountability as largely expressed through quality assurance.

The result of these changes at the system level has yet to be evaluated although some of the impacts on individual academics and on institutional governance have been assessed (e.g. Henkel 2000; Kogan and Hanney 1999; see also Chapters 5 and 7). The 'old' universities lost the protection accorded to those whose standards were accepted without challenge. Some reshuffling of the order of esteem, particularly at the point of previous overlap, could be expected. The most esteemed institutions would remain secure or indeed better secured because comparisons difficult to make before could be made through national assessments of the quality of teaching and research. Alongside legal homogeneity went a creed of diversity, which continued to accommodate both elite and mass strata of academic existences.

In Norway, at the end of the 1980s the universities were accused of mediocrity and failing ambitions. In the Hernes Commission Report (1988) emphasis was put on quality of both teaching and research and the aim was an integrated, flexible and efficient higher education system. Integration was seen as an important means for raising quality. Institutional fragmentation was considered a problem both at universities with small departments and in the college sector with its many small units. The suggested solution was a co-operative network of institutions in the higher education sector – 'the Norway Network' – implying mergers of small colleges as well as closer co-operation between universities and district colleges. The district colleges retained their status as a particular kind of college until 1995 when they were integrated into the state college sector under the new higher education legislation. Thus, in spite of a clear integration policy, the binary system with its relatively clear distinction between the university and college sectors was sustained – a positive feature from the perspectives of university teachers. However, the early ambition of the district colleges to be different from the universities faded as their teachers simultaneously fought for the right to do research and for university-like autonomy, an 'academic drift' that might undermine the Norwegian binary system.

In Sweden the integrated higher education system inaugurated by the 1977 reform survived the reform of 1993, but with a new common Higher Education Ordinance signifying a shift from uniformity to pluralism and to widened autonomy for the institutions. The 'hidden binarity' within this integrated system was based on discrimination between institutions with and without basic funding of research and the rights to award doctoral degrees. The reason for this differentiation was fear of scattering limited research resources to small research milieus, which might reduce both quality and efficiency. However, in Swedish higher education 'academic drift' has also been apparent and partly successful. Thus, after being scrutinised for meeting university criteria, the three largest colleges have received university status and others are about to qualify for it. Furthermore, all colleges have received funding for research and are stimulated to develop their research competence within chosen areas. This means that in Sweden the integration trend is also gaining force, with the aim of strengthening the quality criterion of research-based education and increasing the number of graduate students and doctors' degrees.

POLICIES AND SYSTEMS FOR QUALITY ASSURANCE

Another policy trend directed at managing the risks of diminishing quality as student numbers rose while funding decreased was the development of 'the evaluative state', i.e. arrangements which guaranteed that higher education kept its standards and further developed its quality. Again, even though the goals were similar, the quality assurance policies and undertakings in the three countries were different; in the cases of the UK and Sweden they were practically opposite.

In Sweden, where quality had been secured (or was believed to be) by central regulation of study lines and courses, there was a significant change in policy that put the primary responsibility on the higher education institutions themselves. The resource allocation system for undergraduate education had been based entirely on student numbers. It was changed to a 60 per cent performance-based system – a shift that could imply a threat to the quality level in order to let enough students pass the examination. Therefore, all institutions were obliged to set up and demonstrate their own quality assurance systems, while the Higher Education Agency kept a low profile in carrying out audits of the local systems and a few national programme assessments. Evaluation of research has mainly been a task of the research councils. Neither kind of national evaluation has been connected with resource allocation.

In contrast, the UK quality assurance policy for the formerly autonomous and self-regulating universities put the responsibility for evaluations of both research and education on the government's funding bodies. Evaluation of teaching was eventually placed with a central Quality Assurance Agency, the evaluative orientations of which were not to the universities' liking. However, unlike the Research Assessment Exercise (RAE), it was not linked to funding. Since 1985 the RAE, established by the University Grants Committee, has been an important means of rationalising the stratification of universities and concentration of research resources (Henkel 2000).

In Norway, following the traditional state–institution relationship, questions concerning assurance and development of quality were handled in a much more hesitant manner, while observing what was going on in other European countries and cautiously copying some of their experiments, such as performance indicators and programme evaluation. There was a stronger belief in raising the quality of the whole system by merging institutions and departments and their integration through the 'Norway Network'.

'Organic' evolution or imposed change?

To what extent were the changes the results of the 'organic' evolution of systems of higher education, and to what extent were they more the results of imposed change, perhaps encouraged by imitation of other examples internationally? There were powerful elements of systems that acted as sources of continuity. They included the power of the academic elites whose position within academe was reinforced by the part they played in the state's allocation of resources, processes which could not operate without academic judgements. Academics still possessed professional and expert status within society and the generation of knowledge relied upon the capacity to use and regenerate knowledge passed on by previous generations of academics. The 'invisible colleges' (Clark 1983), that is the networks of disciplines and subject areas, engaged in inter-institutional judgement forming and decision making. The institutions possessed an accumulation of assets in buildings, laboratories and tenured faculties and, in the case of some UK universities, considerable wealth which made them to some extent independent of current policy preferences.

But in all three countries the universities had to come to terms with the dynamics of the system as it responded, sometimes unwillingly and almost unknowingly, to external pressures. Intentionality, individual consciousness and free will are always present, but free individuals get used to what they regard as inevitable.

Thus, the propensity of higher education to expand was influenced by both the economic dynamic of demand for greater knowledge and skills and personal desires for access to better jobs and greater social mobility – all consequences of rising standards of living and expectations for the better. We have seen how expansion often did not result from consistent planning, although at times politicians were at least in part responsible. Yet it is so universal a phenomenon that it all but acquires the status of a natural and inevitable force.

Expansion was further driven by an opportunistic use of student demand and from the political weakness of institutions in the face of demands that they take more students on greatly reduced resources. In each case expansion was blessed and legitimised once it was underway and became a source of strength for previously less well-recognised institutions.

By the end of our period, the UK government was resisting demands for an even higher level of recruitment; it had been surprised by the rapid success of the market approach to funding which encouraged institutions to recruit. In Sweden government was still planning for continuous growth of higher education. In these respects, therefore, higher education showed less an internal dynamic than a propensity to respond, when it had to, to external pressures. Left to themselves in the late 1950s, the universities would probably have been content to remain relatively inactive. In the UK the polytechnics responded with full vigour in the 1980s, partly when stimulated by the universities' reluctance to take in their previous levels of students on reduced funding, but much more as the decade went on as they sought the opportunity to build maturing institutions. It has been argued that they have always believed in keeping the door open to those seeking opportunity.

The systems all responded to the power of contextual factors: demography, the changing economic frames, the secular demands for better education and the ideologies of economic growth and equality of opportunity – all with origins outside higher education but fed by and feeding higher education. But then certain of the major trends seem likely to have resulted from virtually universal propensities to systemic development. Granted expansion, restratification in the UK was part product of policy determination and part of organic development. There is a natural propensity for systems both to create their own new subject specialisations (Clark 1983) and to create or reformulate their own strata as the range of student recruitment and research and teaching balances widens. In Sweden the institutions were challenged to enhance their 'profiles' by developing their best fields and areas. This process was powerfully reinforced in the UK by policies. The implosion of the binary system seemed to follow a trend manifest in other systems which allows institutions to mature to a point where, for both academic and political or social reasons, they were admitted to independent status; in Sweden one by one after scrutiny. This must also have been associated with changing assumptions about what constituted the boundaries of university-provided research and teaching.

The contextual factors interacted with shifting ideologies concerning the nature of the state to promote change, if in no systematic fashion. Massification led directly to changes in the functions and operational modes of higher education. The development of evaluation and accountability was a key factor in reducing the autonomy of UK academics and universities, but in Sweden it was, on the contrary, seen as part of their widened self-regulation. The changes in the nature of the state, including New Public Management and rise of the evaluative state, and the formulation contained in Clark's triangle of co-ordination, are perhaps the most appropriate framework to use for considering these changes.

It is important, however, not to exaggerate the effects of radical changes – they varied in each country. Changes introduced by the reforms in many cases turned out to reflect, or even reinforce, salient characteristics of each country. In England, academic excellence still remained the leading and most prized criterion, against all the claims of competing ideology, as represented by the allocation of funds and the award of quality assurance grading through the Research Assessment Exercise and the quality assurance systems. In Norway and Sweden, expansion and the regionalisation of the universities was accompanied by an equalisation in their statuses. The existing UK hierarchies of esteem, already steep, were reinforced rather than reduced by these changes, although expansion and the implosion of the binary system allowed for some readjustment, particularly in the middle of the pecking order, of statuses between institutions. So, far from enforcing single ideologies upon higher education government, perhaps through avoidance of fundamental reappraisal, seemed content to allow several ideologies, policies and practices to run in parallel with each other.

Some changes, or at least the rhetoric surrounding them, may have come about from imitation. Thus the fashion of planning seems to have emerged strongly in the 1960s, perhaps under the advocacy of the OECD and its country reviews. The current emphases on quality review and market style arrangements almost certainly spread from country to country. But the deeper changes – massification, changing state university relations, stratification between systems, the new emphasis on curriculum and its delivery – might all be described as the natural evolution of systems once certain contextual factors were in place.

In this chapter we have attempted to provide a descriptive basis upon which the more analytic treatments which follow can build. In Chapter 4 we follow a particular strand of the historical sequence in terms of changing theories of the state and how they affected concepts of higher education government. But first we pursue in detail the nature of policy regimes and policy making.

Chapter 3

Policy Regimes and Policy Making

Ivar Bleiklie

Introduction

The analysis of higher education policy change in this chapter seeks to combine two perspectives. A number of theoretical approaches to the study of public policy share a common and popular assumption: policy change is the outcome of changing preferences among political actors. According to such *an actor's perspective*, policy change is the outcome of changing preferences in actors or changing power constellations between actors with different preferences (Ostrom 1990). Sabatier and Jenkins-Smith (1993) advocate another version of an actor's perspective and emphasise that policy change is normally caused by external system events such as changes in economic and political conditions that affect actors' belief systems. An alternative to an actor's perspective is *a structural perspective* that emphasises how underlying norms and values shape policy change. This perspective explains policy change as an outcome of shifting values or constellations of values (March and Olsen 1989; Skocpol 1992). Such shifts may in turn be caused either by the internal dynamics of and problems within political institutions or by external events that cause internal disruptions.

Based on the actor–context model it is a likely assumption that both social action and structural sources of change may be located within the policy field in question or outside it. Actors may change behaviour because of changing preferences resulting from experiential learning or changing positions within the field, or because their belief systems change as a result of shifting external conditions of action. Similarly, structural change may have endogenous or exogenous sources. It may be caused by internal structural tensions or result from reactions to tensions caused by changing environmental conditions such as reduced autonomy and legitimacy that may threaten the resource base of the system. In higher education systems where institutional autonomy is a central concern, much attention tends to be given to the question of the extent to which change is generated by actors and events within the system or the extent to which changes are introduced and driven through by outside forces.

The analysis in this chapter is based on *a dynamic regime* approach (Bleiklie and Marton 1998).[1] We shall argue that variations in policy can be explained in terms of *policy regimes* defined as the network of actors and patterns of influence that are particular to a policy area or an entire polity.[2] This does not mean that the content of policies *per se* can be deduced from particular regime characteristics, but it does mean that the processes which bring about change in policy can. We define policy content in terms of *policy design* where design is regarded as a set of characteristics that are observable by the policy instruments which are deployed (Ingram and Schneider 1990).[3]

The next section outlines and analyses the policy design of the recent reforms by focusing on the choice of policy instruments. Then in the third section we turn to the regime characteristics of higher education policy and develop the concepts that will be used for the analysis of regime changes. We discuss both the roles of the main actors, including central government agencies, local institutions, elites and interest groups, and the relationship between the actors. The fourth section discusses the processes of change within dynamic policy regimes and the main empirical analyses of regime changes and emerging policies under the current policy regime. The analysis is based on data from two main sets of sources, written documents and personal interviews with politicians, ministry officials and university leaders.

Policy design

Policy changes in higher education since 1945 may be described empirically in terms of the measures that have been introduced. The first two periods of policy change took place roughly between 1960 and 1980 and were first characterised by growth, then by democratisation and to some extent by bureaucratisation (Daalder and Shils 1982). Our main focus here is on the third period of transition, characterised by unprecedented expansion and systemic integration that began during the latter half of the 1980s.

However, in order to define the dependent variable more precisely we shall use the concept of *policy design*. Policy design may be defined in different ways and two major perspectives are found in the literature. It may be understood in terms of a rationalistic concept where policy makers regard themselves as some sort of architect or engineer, and public policy is seen as the mechanical application of means in order to realise given ends (Brobrow and Dryzek 1987). Alternatively, policy design can simply be understood as a set of characteristics that distinguish a given policy in one field from policies in other fields, countries or periods, including policy attributes that affect the orientation and behaviour of target populations. Design in this latter version is not the outcome of any master plan, but reflects the decisions of many different people and organisational units, often acting in different contexts and places. They are not necessarily logical or even coherent (Ingram and Schneider 1993, p.71f; Rein 1983, pp.xi–xii). The two above definitions are also different in the sense that whereas the first refers to an activity, the second refers to a set of characteristics.

We prefer this latter definition and shall regard policy design as a set of characteristics. The reason for this choice is that where the former definition presumes a rational actor model, the latter does not presuppose one specific explanation. As we assume that we need a theoretically integrated perspective in order to understand higher education policy change, the choice does not mean that we want to exclude the possibility that rational action may in fact explain policy design.

We shall take Ingram and Schneider's (1990) behavioural characteristics of policy instruments as a point of departure because their taxonomy corresponds particularly well with the policy dimensions that we find interesting for the study of higher education policy development. The underlying assumption of their taxonomy is 'that public policy almost always attempts to get people to do things they might not otherwise do; or it enables people to do things they might not have done otherwise' (p.513). They identify five different reasons why people are not taking actions needed to ameliorate social, economic or political problems:

> They may believe the law does not direct them or authorise them to take action; they may lack incentives or capacity to take the actions needed; they may disagree with the values implicit in the means or ends; or the situation may involve such high levels of uncertainty that the nature of the problem is not known, and it is unclear what people should do or how they might be motivated. (Ingram and Schneider 1990, p.514)

Then they distinguish between five broad categories of corresponding instruments according to the behavioural assumptions on which they are based. Below we shall first discuss how higher education reform policy can be described in terms of policy instruments. When we refer to specific measures under one kind of policy tool, this does not mean that they belong to this specific category *per se*. This depends in the final analysis upon what assumptions a measure is based; nor does it mean that policy tools are mutually exclusive.

Changes in policy design

Over time, significant changes have taken place regarding the policy instruments that are employed, both with respect to what kinds of instruments are used and the way in which particular types of instruments are applied. The most striking development is the increasing array of instruments that are deployed. Whereas policies used to be concentrated on authority and capacity measures, they now encompass all the above categories of instruments. Second, existing types of instruments are used in different ways. In particular, the changing management philosophies have altered the way in which authority instruments are used (decentralisation/deprofessionalisation). Finally, in certain cases discussion may arise as to what category a particular instrument belongs because the behavioural assumptions behind its use are unclear or contested.

Comparing the three countries we shall highlight similarities and differences between them rather than presenting the reform policies in detail. For a detailed presentation of reforms we refer to the national accounts.

AUTHORITY TOOLS

Authority tools are simply statements backed by the legitimate authority of government that grant permission, prohibit or require action under designated circumstances. These tools assume agents and targets are responsive to the organisational structure of leader–follower relationships (Ingram and Schneider 1990, p.514). Authority tools have always been important in the state management of higher education and university affairs. However, such measures have traditionally been much more salient in the almost entirely state-owned higher education systems of Norway and Sweden than in England, where state authorities hardly tried to wield any authority at all. In the former countries, however, university legislation and other legislative measures determined such important issues as the degree structure, examinations and the obligations of the academic faculty. Both in Norway and even more so in Sweden, parliament made decisions on detailed matters such as the appointment of individual professors. However, from the perspective of the universities this formal control did not present a problem so long as they felt that their autonomy and qualified judgement in academic matters were respected. In England until 1981 'there was very little government policy for higher education' (Kogan and Hanney 1999). Whether measured in terms of the legal status of the institutions, academic authority, mission, governance, finances, employment and academic decentralisation, English universities scored high in terms of autonomy. Although in England the relationship between the state and universities used to be close, it was characterised by a benevolent regime under which the universities enjoyed extensive autonomy and little authority was exercised by the state.

The reforms of the 1980s and 1990s signalled new directions in higher education policies in all three countries, but with different emphases. In England there was a clear centralisation trend, although denied by central politicians and officials, whereas in Norway and Sweden the reforms came with the message that in the name of quality a new freedom was to be bestowed upon higher education by means of a move from regulation to performance control. The policy design was supposed to be radically altered by less emphasis on the traditional rule-oriented use of authority tools than previously and more emphasis on goal formulation and performance. This was portrayed as a process whereby state authority was rolled back and autonomy and decentralised decision making were put in its place. One characteristic that applied to all three countries was that higher education had become more politically salient over the years. Accordingly central government authorities, whatever their leaning, were more concerned about the cost of higher education and more interested in affecting the product of higher education institutions in terms of candidates and both basic and applied research than previously. This meant that although some governments might steer in a more decentralised manner than previously, they were interested in steering a wider array of affairs and in this sense power was centralised rather than decentralised.

In England the replacement of the University Grants Committee (UGC) by the University Funding Council (UFC) and later the Higher Education Funding Council for England (HEFCE) meant that the benevolent 'private government of public money' style of the former was replaced.[4] Within the new regime the government started to formulate goals for the universities and apply legislative and financial means in order to reach those goals with relatively little consultation with the academic community. The message from Norwegian university leaders was also almost unanimous that a shift in the direction of less state control did not take place. Although new forms of *ex post* control had been introduced (e.g. activity planning and performance indicators), the new instruments did not replace but came in addition to the traditional detailed legislation that regulated an increasing array of university affairs. New legislation had also been introduced over the years in areas such as civil service regulations and work environment regulation in addition to the new national higher education legislation. Finally, parliament showed an increasing willingness to interfere in rather detailed policy questions. Swedish reforms were more consistent with the officially stated goals of decentralisation and autonomy. In particular the 1993 reform meant to some extent a retreat from the previous relatively tight central government control that had characterised the 1977 reform. As we shall see in Chapters 4 and 5, academic institutional autonomy was strengthened by the replacement of a dual leadership of a rector that combined academic and administrative institutional leadership functions. The universities furthermore gained the right to appoint their own professors. The centrally determined 'study line system' was abandoned and academics regained influence on curricular matters. Yet government-appointed external representatives took up a strengthened position on the university boards. Thus the use of authority tools was reduced in the Swedish case. However, both economic difficulties with rising unemployment and the Social Democratic return to power in 1994 resulted in a gradual return to more centralist policies with more use of authority tools.

INCENTIVE TOOLS

Incentive tools include those that rely on tangible payoffs, positive or negative, to induce compliance or encourage utilisation. Incentives have traditionally been important tools in the life of academic institutions, whether the use of student grading, competition for fellowships, research money and tenured or untenured academic positions. However, they have not been considered policy tools, but rather tools that were integral to the academic community and used to cater to its internal concern with maintaining academic quality. Incentives were thought of as tools used by and within the 'republic of scholars' to motivate individuals. Conscious political use of incentive tools first commenced in the late 1980s.

In England a shift in the direction of extensive and active use of incentive tools began with the introduction from 1985–86 of the Research Assessment Exercises (RAE) that were repeated in modified versions in 1989, 1992 and 1996. The idea of the RAE was to rank qualified basic units in hierarchical categories according to their research performance. Most of the research funds were dedicated to the top categories and no research funding to the bottom category. The characteristic that distinguished the English use of incentive tools was the systems perspective on which it was based. The incentives were ostensibly directed at selective research funding on a meritocratic basis, but the system also resulted in positioning departments in a hierarchy of esteem in which non-performing institutions were excluded from research funding.

In Norway the most important incentive tool, both financially and from a principle point of view, was the funds that were tied to the production of new graduates. The grants based on production of undergraduate candidates went to the institutions, but for students at master and doctoral level the money was intended for the individual professors who served as their advisers. In addition there was the incentive money for publications. Thus the funds for graduate candidates and publications were supposed to be distributed as research funds to the individual teacher. A performance pay system was also introduced, but played an insignificant and largely symbolic role. Norwegian incentive tools were thus supposed to increase production of undergraduate candidates by motivating institutions to produce more graduate candidates. Furthermore the idea was to produce more quality research by motivating individual teachers to be more efficient advisers and produce more research for publication in international journals and books.

The Swedish reforms represented yet another version of design and use of incentive tools by being exclusively directed at institutions in order to enhance competition between them. A performance-based funding system was established. The money partly followed enrolment and performance of undergraduate students and was partly dependent on the number of PhDs produced. In order not to encourage universities to focus too much on the competition for students and student processing without regard for quality, 5 per cent of their funding should be based on an evaluation of the institutions' quality development work. However, the latter measure was revoked by the incoming Social Democratic Education Minister in 1994 and never really took effect.

CAPACITY TOOLS

Capacity tools provide information, training, education and resources to enable individuals, groups, or agencies to make decisions or carry out activities. Capacity tools in connection with university policy are primarily about money.[5] Changes in the use of capacity tools over the last decades may be studied from a number of angles. One may focus on anything from the overall level of funding via the distribution of funds between individual institutions, classes of institutions, disciplines or activities (like research or teaching) to the way in which the funds are used in terms of external control and long-term commitment (e.g. quinquennial, triennial or annual budgets). Three characteristics were common across the three countries: the formidable growth of the higher education system, the reduced per unit cost and the assumption behind government policies that higher education institutions needed to be more responsible and accountable for the resources they received. In addition it was generally believed that they ought to generate more of their own resources from other sources through competition for students and research funding. However, if we define the capacity of the higher education system in terms of qualified teachers and research funding it is clear that both the direction and use of capacity tools varied considerably.

During the early 1980s English universities faced severe cutbacks and the definite end of the quinquennial budgets. From the late 1980s and during the first half of the 1990s the system expanded sharply in student as well as budgetary terms until the age participation rate reached 30 per cent. By the mid-1990s the growth was halted and the government introduced measures to prevent student numbers rising much above current levels.

The Norwegian reforms aimed both at expanding the system considerably and improving the level of funding from 1988 on, but student demand far exceeded the plans and the anticipated real budget growth barely helped to keep up the level of funding. From 1993 the policy of growth was replaced by austerity and budget cuts. Politically salient shifts have also taken place in the distribution of funds between different kinds of institutions. With the exception of the late 1980s and early 1990s, the state colleges (or previously district colleges) have tended to be relatively favoured at the expense of universities and scientific institutions.

The Swedish government sought to expand the higher education system in the early 1990s as part of a government strategy to fight unemployment and strengthen the economic competitiveness of the nation. However in the face of increasing budget deficits the government had to cut expenditure and limit growth. Although the Swedish system grew much less in the first five years of the last decade (from 1988) compared with both England and Norway, it had an even growth curve and a stronger growth than Norway from 1993.

SYMBOLIC AND HORTATORY TOOLS

Symbolic and hortatory tools assume that people are motivated from within and decide whether or not to take policy-related actions on the basis of their beliefs and values. Symbolic and hortatory tools are important in university and higher education politics, among other things, because universities are institutions imbued with value, have a long history and embrace a fairly well codified although not necessarily consistent set of values and widespread norms. The most recent reforms represented a value shift and changing fundamental notions of what the university was all about; with it a new set of symbolic tools has emerged (Bleiklie 1996, 1998). As is evident from the policy documents, other written statements and our respondents, the idea of the university as a community of scholars, student or disciplines and as a public agency to some extent yielded to the idea of the university as a corporate enterprise. In Burton Clark's (1998) recently coined concept, the idea of 'the entrepreneurial university' was on the rise. The changing symbols had at one level apparently far-ranging and deep consequences because they redefined the mission of the institution as well as the content of what it was doing, the roles of the main actors and the power relationships between them. Academic institutions and individual researchers were requested to cultivate competition and entrepreneurship. The symbolic tools that come with the corporate enterprise notion of the university are closely related to other policy tools such as the authority and incentive tools discussed above.

It is hard to discern clear differences between the three countries with regard to the symbolic and hortatory tools that were introduced. They may all be adequately described and analysed in terms of the corporate enterprise idea of the university and co-exist in a more or less tension-ridden relationship with more traditional academic values. However, the implications of apparent ideological innovations are often exaggerated and do not necessarily threaten traditional values. As this study intends to bear out, their impact depends very much on how the new values are interpreted and what practical arrangements they sustain. The interesting comparative material lies in the fact that these apparently identical symbolic tools are used to justify different policies, as should be fairly evident from our discussion of other policy tools.

LEARNING TOOLS

Learning tools are used when the basis upon which target populations might be moved to take problem-solving action is unknown or uncertain. Learning tools are also fairly tightly related to the corporate enterprise notion of the university and New Public Management ideology with which that notion is related. The idea that target groups can learn from experience is integral to this ideology (Olsen and Peters 1996). In all three countries this led to the introduction of new policy tools, such as evaluation and changes in existing methods such as planning, reporting and accounting procedures. The underlying idea was that the organisation formulates goals in mission statements, activity plans and budgets and receives feedback by means of evaluation exercises, annual reporting and accounting. From this information the organisation was supposed be able to enter into a learning process by which it might gradually improve its performance. By and large these were the policy tools that the actors involved seemed to have the greatest doubts about. Whereas proponents dreamed of a more efficient and goal-oriented administration, opponents portrayed them as threats to academic freedom, open dialogue and reflection. With hindsight, the tools were questioned on the grounds of their ritualistic character, their feeble if any effects and their symbolic rather than substantial impact. Another unintended consequence of their introduction was the sensation that the administration of the tools and the information that had to be gathered, processed and analysed led to bureaucratic expansion rather than improved performance.

Policy regimes

Having observed these changes in higher education policy, it is time to consider explanations of how the changes came about. The following approach is based on the idea that a policy field such as higher education is governed by policy regimes and is based on three considerations:

1. Policy regimes are networks of actors. The focus on the relationship between policy regimes, defined as dynamic actor networks, and policy design is influenced by the policy network literature. The concept of a policy regime may therefore at first glance seem quite similar to the policy network concept, but it differs in several important respects. Most policy network approaches present the networks as rather static, structural arrangements for interest representation, characterised by goal-oriented behavior (Atkinson and Coleman 1992; John and Cole 1997; Knoke *et al.* 1996; Raab 1994; Rhodes and Marsh 1992; Richardson 1997). Policy regimes are dynamic in the sense that the actors and the relationship between them change over time.

2. The network of actors within the policy regime is not exclusively engaged in interest politics, but may comprise any type of action that potentially bears on public policy.

3. The policy process within the dynamic regimes is not only driven by goal-oriented rational action, but may also be

driven by rule-oriented institutionalised behaviour and communicative action.

Compared with the policy networks literature, the dynamic regime perspective makes fewer assumptions about the actors by allowing for greater dynamism, functional diversity and variation in actors' motives. The idea is that particular types of policy regimes can be identified in terms of their actor network characteristics. By using the dynamic network concept as a heuristic device, we emphasise that the constellation of actors involved in policy making may vary over time as well as cross-nationally and involve a wide array of different actors who are motivated by a diversity of factors.

Dimensions of policy regimes

Theories of how policy regime characteristics affect the content of public policy abound. In order to simplify somewhat, we shall initially distinguish between two dimensions that have been important to theory formation in the area and can be helpful to the formulation of ideas about relevant regime characteristics of policy networks. The first dimension turns on the distribution of *influence* between actors within a field of policy making. The second dimension, *cohesion*, refers to how tightly or loosely the actors are related to one another. Regarding the first, we shall distinguish between two classes of theories relevant to the policy field under scrutiny. The first class of theories comprises those assuming that higher education policies are made by one dominant institution or set of institutions: in our case either the central government or individual, autonomous, local institutions. In addition, we find theories assuming that higher education policies are made through some form of mediation either via elites or organised interests.

INFLUENCE

State domination means that state agencies formulate policies which individual subordinate agencies are supposed to implement. To the extent that they are conceived as parts of the civil service, they find themselves within a hierarchical bureaucratic order and in principle put their services at the disposal of superior political administrative units. In this capacity *loyalty* is the central expectation directed towards individual higher education institutions, the primary task of which is to implement state policies.

To what extent the state seeks to manage the institutions by tight-knit control, usually manifests itself through legislation and budgetary policy. Based on current knowledge in the areas of comparative public policy and administration, there are ample reasons to expect considerable variation in the tightness of central control across nations, policy sectors and over time (Heidenheimer, Heclo and Adams 1983; Lægreid and Pedersen 1999). Sources of such variations may be found in traditions of political steering, the relationship between civil service and higher educational institutions and finally in views of the role of education and research in relation to the realisation of national political goals (Becher and Kogan 1992; Clark 1993; Salter and Tapper 1994).

Institutional autonomy at its most extreme means that individual institutions, or institutions under government control, are free to make decisions independently and manage their own affairs as they see fit. The concept of autonomy is complicated and can be analysed along a number of dimensions. Here we start out with the above fairly simple actor-oriented definition that we shall elaborate further in Chapter 4. The organisational arrangements for sustaining autonomy vary (as we shall point out in Chapter 4) in the comparison of English charter institutions and the civil service status of Norwegian and Swedish universities. In either case autonomy may but does not have to imply that central government policies in a policy area amount to little more than the sum of the institutions' actions. Institutions within a certain policy sector may enjoy such freedom, much as public research universities traditionally have in many West European countries (Ben-David and Zloczower 1991; Rothblatt and Wittrock 1993). Similarly, some national policy-making 'styles', such as the Norwegian, tend to favour decentralised patterns of decision making that leave relatively substantial decision-making authority with local agencies or institutions (Olsen 1983).

Institutional autonomy can thus be based on (at least) two different principles. There is the idea that authority should be based on knowledge which is the basis for the autonomy of universities and various degrees of independence granted to research institutions and specialised technical branches of government such as health administration, agricultural administration, military defence (see Chapter 4); or there is the idea that authority should be based on proximity to those who are affected by the decisions, whether it manifests itself within the context of local democracy or the context of business life and the value of consumerism. In a European context there has been increased political support for two versions of institutional autonomy at local level in recent years. The first is the principle of subsidiarity promoted by the EU, which means that decisions should be made as close as possible to the level where functions are performed and services are actually delivered (Blichner and Sangolt 1994). The second version is the idea of decentralisation, a central element in the New Public Management ideology which has characterised administrative reforms in a number of European Countries (Christensen and Egeberg 1997; Pollitt 1993, 1995).

The idea that *elites* of various kinds are important in order to understand public policy making in modern democracies has been increasingly popular during recent years after a period of bleak existence in the periphery of political science theory (Etzioni-Halevy 1993). Elite theories assume that smaller groups of power holders can be distinguished from the powerless majority. In their classic versions they distinguish elites according to their group consciousness, coherence and conspiracy. In terms of power, organisation or other resources, they are able to exploit their positions to preserve the elite's domination (Marton, Hanney and Kogan 1995). For analytical purposes, the typical strategy of elite analysis is to study top positions to find out by whom they are controlled and where key decisions are made (Hunter 1953).

The pluralist view, often called democratic elite theory, emphasises the concept of multiple and autonomous elites. The autonomy of the elites, both from the government as well as from the other elite groups, is an important factor in preventing the abuse of power by one ruling class. In this regard, the idea of co-optation, 'the process of absorbing new elements into the leadership of policy-determining structures of an organisation, as a means of averting threats to its stability or existence' (Kogan 1984), puts in question the idea of autonomous elites. Similar concerns appear in Saward's (1992) attempt to build a model of policy making in terms of co-optation.

In order to study how elites operate in higher education policy we may adopt the approach suggested by Becher and Kogan (1992) and Kogan (1992) for the analysis of academic elites in higher education policy making. They suggest three different directions along which co-opted academic elites may operate:

- as part of government decision making through membership in government appointed bodies
- by internalising, interpreting and helping implementation of government policies
- by creating hierarchies of resource and esteem.

One may then formulate assumptions about how the role of elites has been affected by democratisation of higher education institutions on the one hand, and an apparent increasingly strong presence of state authority on the other. This illustrates furthermore how the different forms of influence identified in this typology may interact to form highly varied patterns of influence within the policy sector. One important effect of elite structures is to keep up a sharp divide between the fields of academic decision making and government allocations that makes the two fields operate like 'tectonic plates', as pointed out in Chapter 1.

Interest representation and interest politics can be important to many fields of public policy in a double sense. Interest organisations such as employers' associations and trade unions may regard a policy sector as a field that affects them as legitimately interested parties. At a national level major interest organisations are likely to be interested in the matters of a policy sector such as higher education insofar as it affects the labour market. At the same time, higher education has become an important field of work and a major employer. As such it involves the parties on the labour market in questions relating to wages, working conditions, personnel management and workplace democracy.

Similar to elite theorists, corporatists assume that there are a few small groups of power holders who determine political outcomes in society (Cawson 1983; Grant 1985; Schmitter and Lehmbruch 1979). Under corporatism, political exchange is limited to a few participants who are insulated from external pressure. These participants, usually business associations and unions, receive a representational monopoly from the government in exchange for the organisations delivering their members' compliance on government proposals.

The form of corporatism that has characterised Western European countries after 1945 has been portrayed as a form of pluralist politics. Accordingly, concepts such as 'corporate pluralism' (Rokkan 1966) and 'social pluralism' (Schmitter 1974) have been coined to indicate situations where major interest organisations such as labour unions and business associations have access to important decision arenas. However, no one organisation has a monopoly on power so that a measure of competition between organisations exists.

After a period of growth in corporate arrangements and the growing influence of labour unions and employers' associations in a number of countries in central Europe (Austria, Germany) and Scandinavia, the trend was reversed during the early 1980s. The rise of liberalism and managerialism after 1980 has been taken as an indication that the role of corporatist arrangements and the influence of employee interests were weakening. However, the actual role played by corporate arrangements can safely be assumed to vary considerably both cross-nationally and cross-sectorally.

The influence dimension is defined here as a question of what type of actors constitute the network on which the policy regime is based.

We do not presume that the four types of influence are mutually exclusive. Rather we shall ask what types of actors are active in higher education policy, what type of influence they represent and what the relationship between them is. It is of particular interest for us to see whether there have been any changes with respect to influence patterns in higher education during the reform period under study.

COHESION

In the policy networks literature, network cohesion has been an important topic. Van Waarden's (1992) article, the 'Dimensions and Types of Policy Networks', reviewed the policy networks literature and found 38 characteristics that could be used to identify 11 different types of policy networks. These 38 characteristics were extremely difficult to apply in empirical analysis, however, and Rhodes and Marsh's (1992) idea of a policy network as a continuum, with 'policy community' and 'issue networks' at the two opposing ends, gained wider acceptance. The criteria used in this analysis are membership, integration, resources and power. A 'policy community' would thus be characterised by: its limited membership; frequent interaction with shared basic values; all participants having a resource base and the ability to deliver their members' support; and a relatively equal power distribution among the network members. On the opposite end of the continuum is the 'issue network', characterised by: a large and/or wide range of affected interests; fluctuations in contacts, access, and level of agreement; unequal resource distribution combined with varying abilities to deliver members support; and unequal powers among the groups' members.

Cohesion is also an important dimension of policy regimes as we have defined them. Thus corporatist arrangements of policy making can be seen as a type of policy regime most often leaning towards the 'policy community' side of the Rhodes and Marsh continuum. Loosely coupled networks of elite decision makers or autonomous institutions, however, may operate like 'issue networks' and constitute a very different type of policy regime. Considering both the variations across countries and the way in which the relationship between state and interest groups has changed over approximately the last decade and a half, an approach that allows for greater variety in the organisational expressions of such relationships seems to be called for. In the next section we shall discuss challenges to the policy regime concept and attempt to show how the dynamic regime approach can be useful for analysis of the structuring of the English, Norwegian and Swedish higher education policy regimes.

Regime dynamics

Within a policy field the core activities of the field – such as the production and administration of rules, procedures or services – are subject to attempts by more or less cohesive networks of actors to affect and control relevant processes and events. These actors constitute a policy regime that may include local or specialised institutions, interest groups, various elites and central political-administrative authorities. State domination, institutional autonomy, elitism and interest representation constitute attempts at conceptualising different ways in which a policy regime may be structured. Bearing in mind the actor–context model, how an actual regime is structured in this sense does not have to be theoretically predetermined, and the relationship between structuring and policy making constitutes a central part of the empirical analysis. The different types of influence represent ideal typical patterns that are not mutually exclusive. The patterns may thus appear in a variety of combinations depending on the constellation of forces that participate in policy making.

In analysing such forces we shall apply a combination of an actor focused and a structurally focused analysis of actor networks. The question then is to what extent this approach enhances our understanding of how regimes and their policies change. One way in which the problem of change may be approached is via theories of political motivation and rationality. Let us distinguish with March and Olsen (1989, 1994) between two main classes of ideas that, in their reformulation of the Weberian concepts of instrumental and value rationality, can be applied to the study of policy design processes (Weber 1978, pp.24–26). With exchange theories and theories of rational choice, one may assume that policies are the aggregate outcome of interest-maximising behaviour and exchange relationships. Policy characteristics and their implementation may thus be traced back to conscious design and purposive action. Political change is accordingly understood as adaptation to changing environments and as determined by exogenous factors. Different environments typically explain different policy designs in different settings, and internal processes of change become of less interest. How such processes are actually triggered is, by the same token, offered little attention as the answer is implied by the analysis. Political reform and processes of change based on the notion of dynamic regimes would, according to this class of theories, be an outcome of changing relations of power and influence between actors – state authorities, academic institutions, elites, interest groups – with different preferences. Changing resource bases and strategies would be the key to understanding policy change.

By contrast, norm-oriented institutional approaches assume that behaviour is rule driven rather than preference driven. Action is understood in terms of a logic of appropriateness. The logic may be reflected in the structure of rules and conceptions of identities rather than in a logic of consequence that is expressed in exchange relationships (March and Olsen 1989, 1994). Although political change according to this institutionalist perspective might be the result of adaptation to changing environmental conditions, there are several reasons why political change is often better understood in different terms. One main reason is that the concepts of organisation and environment tend to be ambiguous and fuzzy. Therefore, it is often difficult to establish the clear, unambiguous concepts of 'organisation' and 'environment' that are presumed by the rationalist kind of analysis. When this causal knowledge of ends and means is uncertain, policy making may consequently be driven by rule-oriented as well as strategic, goal-oriented behaviour. According to this perspective the following proposition is particularly relevant. Changes in policy design are not so much a question of adaptation to changing environmental condition, as an outcome of changing beliefs about the nature of a given policy field and the way in which it relates to the rest of society. The production and diffusion of such beliefs would make an important focus of the analysis.

Based on the two theoretical positions presented above, the array of possible explanations to policy design may be arranged along a dimension where we find a pure structural, norm-oriented institutional model at one extreme. At the other extreme we find a model based on a purely rational action model and various combinations of the two in between. For our purposes, the recognition of the co-existence and potential tension between these two logics of action will suffice. In the following the possibility that both logics may be operating is taken into account. We thus try to overcome the idea that rational action models and norm-oriented institutionalism have to be treated as mutually excluding alternatives, so that one specific set of factors by definition is given primacy as the driving force in public policy making. Changing policy design may be the result of efficient adaptation to changing environments, in the sense that it enhances the capacity of a policy regime to solve specific problems such as growing numbers of patients within health care or growing numbers of students for the educational system. However, it may also represent shifting conceptions of what are the appropriate university tasks and how they should be solved. Questions such as whether higher education ought to emphasise vocational training or general education, or whether patients should be treated in hospitals or in primary care, may illustrate the kinds of issues where conceptions of appropriateness rather than observed efficiency determine the answer. We emphasise, therefore, the tension between what Becher and Kogan (1992, p.176) call organic growth and radical change (see also Chapter 8). The implication for how we regard policy change is that the notion of consciously designed reforms and radical change needs to be supplemented. We suggest here the idea of gradual change where new structures and values imposed by reforms are grafted onto established arrangements in a process of meandering and sedimentation that gives policies and institutions their character of complexity and ambiguity (Bleiklie 1998). These two explanatory foci may also supplement one another, *ceteris paribus*, in the following sense. The more macroscopic the scope and the longer the time frame, the more relevant are the relatively stable structural arrangements for explaining patterns of behaviour. The more microscopic the scope and the shorter the time frame, the more relevant will be the choices and strategies made by individual actors for explaining the outcome of a given policy process.

The implications of these models as to how policy design may be shaped during the implementation process are pretty straightforward. If rational action is the driving force of the policy process, we assume that policy design takes place under conditions where it is the outcome of power plays among actors who are involved in the process. The outcome depends on the positions they hold, the resources they control, the coalitions they make and the bargains they are able to strike. Policy variation across nations and over time can be explained in this perspective as the outcome of regime variation along the influence dimension, where the preferences of the members of the dominant coalition determine the outcome in each individual case.

If institutionally shaped norm-oriented behaviour drives the policy process, we assume that policy design takes place under conditions where it is the result of a process of adaptation between existing norms and values and new arrangements. The outcome thus depends on what values and norms the actors feel obliged by. Furthermore it depends on what the prevailing authority patterns are like, how the actors shape reform measures to conform with current norms in a mutual process of adaptation and how they reinterpret their values in order to accommodate new arrangements mandated by the reforms. Policy variation can be explained as the outcome of regime variation along the normative (cohesion) dimension where the shared norms defining the community of decision makers determine the outcome.

Bearing this in mind, two kinds of regime change may explain policy design: the constellation of actors and thereby the policy preferences of those actors who make up a policy regime; and hegemonic values and normative conceptions that are shared by all (or at least the dominant coalition of) actors in question. *Actor-preference* driven design processes and *value-structure* driven design processes are not mutually exclusive. We expect that actual policy designs usually do not fall clearly into one of these two categories, but are characterised by some particular mix and tensions that distinguish the process. Although we spoke of a variation along a dimension delimited by the two ideal typical patterns and a range of possible combinations in between, this was meant as an illustration and as such it has its limitations. Actual policy design may be characterised by a combination of strongly preference-driven and strongly value-driven designs. Rather than arranging themselves neatly along one dimension, therefore, we are likely to find that unique combinations of characteristics measured along a number of dimensions can distinguish specific design processes.

The dynamic policy regime approach should demonstrate its empirical relevance in two connections. It should help us to understand policy change and to explain differences in policy design processes comparatively so that we can identify policy variation over time, between policy areas or even different polities. We shall now analyse the changes that have taken place in higher education policy making, particularly with regard to the universities in the three countries.

Changes of the higher education policy regime

In order to understand the policy changes that we identified above we need to look closer at the actors involved, their values and the relationship between them. One implication of the higher education expansion we have witnessed since about 1965 is that the growth of the system in terms of the number of faculty, students and institutions changed significantly the qualitative content, dynamics and conditions of actions for the actors within the system. In the remainder of the chapter we shall explore the changes empirically by way of an analysis of the actors in higher education policy making and their interrelationships.[6]

Actors and influence

In the analysis of the actors and their influence on higher education policy making we shall use the typology of influence and consider to what extent there has been any development regarding the different types of influence during the period considered.

CHANGES IN STATE DOMINATION

England

In the 1980s the central government was characterised by its ability to determine policies and implement them without too much deference to external groups. This could suggest that either the government ministers, or the civil service (Salter and Tapper 1994), had a dominant role in the determination of higher education policies. Kogan and Hanney's (1999) findings suggest that ministers played a powerful role. Thus, the higher education policy regime would be dominated by those largely or partly selected by government, or those acting on behalf of government. Not only was the government the major influence on policy, but it increased the areas over which it was now seen as appropriate for the state to have policies.

However, in the discussion on state domination, a distinction should be made between dominance of the policy-making process and control over the universities once the broad policy framework has been set. The role of the state in the former area undoubtedly increased in England, but the question of its role in the latter is more contested. Certainly in the UK the role of an academic as a loyal civil servant did not arise. Nevertheless Kogan and Hanney's (1999) proposition is that, through various accountability and financial mechanisms and control over the funding councils, there was increased state domination. The latest transfer of research councils to the Department of Trade and Industry illustrated the power of the state to dictate policies and perhaps indicated an intention for the state to have a more direct say over research policy.

Yet, the picture is mixed so far and the Foresight policy (Henkel *et al.* 2000) in the UK testified to the familiar capacity of strong co-opted elites in the research councils to tame and incorporate policies that potentially threatened academic control over science policies.

Norway

Central government higher education policies in Norway were until recently concerned almost wholly with issues relating to access and size and macro structure of the system. They affected only budget size and legislation and to a very limited extent the content of academic studies and research. Although parliament until recently made decisions on detailed matters such as the establishment of new professorships, there were fairly tight informal relations and a common understanding that universities must be granted considerable autonomy in order to function properly (Forland 1993). Higher education policy was and still is defined to a large extent as a matter for the government and academic institutions. According to a former Education Minister, policies were determined within 'the axis' formed by the ministry and the parliament, in particular the parliamentary education committee. As higher education affairs became more politicised, parliament was at times able to affect policies substantially. However, attempts at national higher education policy making were relatively feeble until about 1970 and did not affect the universities in a significant way until the late 1980s.

The question of how the role of government institutions was affected by the events of the reform process is complex for two reasons. First, a number of inconsistencies were built into the attempts by the government to control and direct higher education, as we pointed out in connection with the discussion of authority tools above. Second, there was a general feeling among actors in the field that there has been a clear centralisation trend. However, the role played by the ministry in higher education policy seemed to depend quite a lot on the minister's personal characteristics. In practice two parallel processes seem to have developed. In the first place, the growth and geographical distribution of higher education institutions made the field more interesting for politicians. Furthermore, parliament's appetite for power increased during a fairly long period of minority governments and made itself particularly strongly felt in the area of higher education after 1990. The combined effect was that the stronger central government role in higher education also represented a move from ministerial towards a stronger parliamentary influence. In recent years the stronger parliamentary influence opened up stronger influence by the students and state colleges at the expense of universities and scientific colleges.

Sweden

The central government and its civil servants predominantly determined higher education policy since the 1970s. According to Lane,(1990, p.219): 'The government and its central agencies made decisions in a number of crucial domains including appointment of tenured staff, orientation of the curriculum, construction of physical facilities and student enrolment into screened admission lines of training.' Even the university vice-chancellors were appointed by the government rather than the academic collegium. In addition, the appointment of professors reflected the power of the state, but was based on the suggestion of local faculties at the universities (Svensson 1987). However, it is generally advocated that these state powers did not infringe upon basic academic freedoms. Even so, the Conservative coalition government of 1991–94 was successful in passing legislation that gave the institutions the right to establish professorships (Government Bill 1990/91, p.150). With the arrival of the Social Democratic government (September 1994), this change was somewhat moderated. The government reclaimed its right to establish professorships, stating that it would only exercise this right if there was a need to prioritise a research area of particular concern to the country, or a need to be able to guarantee the availability of scientifically competent researchers in certain fields (Government Bill 94/95, p.100, Ap.9).

According to Bauer *et al.* (1999) the role of central government and civil servants in developing higher education policies changed between the late 1960s and 1970s and the late 1980s and early 1990s. In the former period the voice of the academics seems to have been ignored, whereas academic and institutional input during the later reform process again seemed to be more significant.

CHANGES IN INSTITUTIONAL AUTONOMY

England

The traditional institutional autonomy of English universities could be linked to the view that there was for many decades a strong reluctance by the state to intervene, especially in the supply side of the economy, and a more diffuse feeling that some institutions would do best if not strongly controlled. Paradoxically, it was a Conservative government committed to rolling back the frontiers of the state that came to challenge the autonomy of academic institutions and attempt to harness them to a greater extent to the perceived needs of the economy.

Despite a presumed loss of institutional autonomy in the face of greater state domination, Conservative ministers and departmental officials claimed there had been an increase in institutional autonomy within a quasi-market system, in which the universities were less dependent on the state for their resources. While the ministerial interpretation is contested, institutional leaders undoubtedly became more powerful under the recent reforms, but their space for action was more strongly framed (see also Chapter 5). It is possible that the autonomy of the individual academic was reduced more than that of the institution. However, in gaining their independence from local authorities in 1989, the polytechnics certainly increased their institutional autonomy.

The academic profession saw an erosion of the traditional trust placed in them (Halsey 1992). This fitted a general pattern under the

Conservative government of paying less attention to established producer groups. Such movements can be seen as part of the much broader shifts in the management of public services across the Western world towards New Public Management (Bleiklie 1998; Pollitt 1990) where greater emphasis was placed on accountability, performance assessment and the power of consumers. Part of this proposition was that universities have moved from a position in which they were almost uniquely trusted to run their own affairs to a situation in which they were regarded at times with an element of suspicion, mixed with a feeling of continued respect for the quality of the top research universities.

Norway

Institutional autonomy has been affected by two kinds of developments in recent years. Arrangements that were traditionally regarded as safeguards for autonomy were dismantled. Such arrangements as the incorporation of the universities in a national legislation and planning system were regarded as a threat against institutional autonomy by some critics. Equally important was the internal transformation of the university governing structure that was supposed to guarantee academic authority through academic majorities on decision-making bodies and recruitment procedures designed to guarantee that this authority was based on a satisfactory level of academic competence. In 1989 new legislation mandated a change in the governing bodies that emphasised functional representation by formally equal categories of employees (i.e. academic staff, administrative staff, students, etc.) rather than disciplinary representation, particularly on the university board. Some observers regarded this reduction of disciplinary influence as a threat to university autonomy. From the perspective of disciplinary influence it was also contended that the threat by no means diminished when the 1995 legislation mandated external representation on the university boards. Most university leaders, both directors and rectors, complained about being limited by laws, regulations and parliamentary interference. There was, however, a tendency to point at the ministry as a partner with whom the universities co-operated and to blame parliament as the institution which posed problems to university autonomy.

However, the meaning of the term 'autonomy' was redefined by policy makers and many institutional leaders. Whereas 'autonomy' used to mean both the individual and collective autonomy of a collegium of competent academics to make decisions regarding their teaching and research activities, it gradually came to mean decentralised decision authority that gave university leaders the freedom to make decisions independently of central government authority, particularly in budget matters (see further discussion of this topic in Chapter 4).

Sweden

The notion of the Swedish university as an 'independent' cultural institution was not really evident from the policies implemented during the 1970s and 1980s and even after the 'Freedom for Quality' reform this notion must be questioned. Many reforms during the 1970s were severely opposed by academics and students. The power of the professoriate was weakened by the 1977 reform as outside interests, such as large trade unions and lower level faculty members and student groups, were granted positions on decision-making boards (Premfors and Östergren 1978; Svensson 1987). In 1983 the institutions faced increased outside influence with the passing of a policy which established that one-third of all representatives on the governing boards would be non-academics, representing external interests, and would be appointed by the government (Lane 1990). In the reform of 1993, the Conservative coalition government limited the influence of these outside groups by denying them positions on university boards (Government Bill 1992–93, p.1).

Thus, the varying degrees of institutional autonomy in the Swedish higher education system depended among other things upon how the role of the traditional academic elites, such as the leaders of the 'old' universities in Lund, Uppsala, Stockholm and Göteborg, was mitigated by a corporatist structure of policy making during the 1960s and 1970s. These leaders seem to have been relatively weak in advancing their policy preferences during this time. Most preferences were channelled through the former Office of the Chancellor of the Universities and Colleges, and thus the ability of institutional leaders to act single-handedly in putting forth their views was minimal.

However, as a result of the reforms in 1991–93, the role of individual institutions as well as their leaders seems to have been strengthened. During the consultation process in connection with these reforms, many hearings were held by the Minister of Education in order to receive directly the suggestions of the academics. In relation to the new freedoms that the institutions were granted by the state authorities, many new responsibilities were delegated to the institutions' leadership (vice-chancellor and pro-vice chancellor). Thus we observe one parallel to the Norwegian case in the sense that autonomy was redefined as a value for the institutional leadership, possibly to the extent that it weakened or infringed upon the powers of the professoriate and faculties.

CHANGES IN ELITE MEDIATION

England

The range of academic elites in England has been characterised as to some extent non-coterminous. They played a variety of roles in relation to policy formation. In some cases, such as decisions about what is to be regarded as high status academic work, elites within disciplines played a dominant role. The leaders of the elite institutions, such as Oxford and Cambridge, seem not to have been involved in many issues, but were influential in defending college fees at their own institutions (which were over and above the payments common to all institutions). Although the academic elites as a general class were not influential in government policy making, many of the most powerful co-opted elites were at the same time members of the 'real' academic elite. Within the broad policy framework, substantive decisions affecting institutions or academic subject resources were delegated to bodies allocating teaching or research monies. These bodies consisted of 'co-opted elites', which became increasingly important in the implementation of quality assessment policies and the research selectivity exercise carried out by the UGC, and the successive funding councils. This policy involved the grading of the research performance of university departments and selectively funding them according to such grades.

There had always been some overlap and extensive networking between the subject elites and the co-opted elites on the research councils and the UGC and its sub-committees. According to Becher and Kogan, (1992, p.59) these arrangements provided a well-functioning link between academic judgements and allocations, between the normative and operational modes of working. With the research selectivity exercises, however, some of the academic decisions may have become more formalised in the decisions of the co-opted elites.

It is not clear, however, whether the co-opted elites directly affected policy making as opposed to its implementation, although in the case of research selectivity a few leading individuals were involved in creating the policy, which proved to be acceptable to government ministers and officials and to the academic elites, although not in its detailed application.

There is a clear overlap between elites and interest groups in the academic world; furthermore the links between academic and political elites are complex and intertwined. Traditionally, they may all have been seen as part of the establishment. A key feature of the Thatcher style of government had been that individual academics, without necessarily occupying key roles within established groups, were influential in networks involving right-wing think-tanks, though this has been less a feature of higher education policy than of other fields. An important contrast here is the influence exercised by the less prestigious polytechnic directors. They effectively persuaded ministers and succeeded in securing seismic changes in structure (see our discussion of changes in interest mediation below).

Norway

The function of elites in the Norwegian higher education system must take into account the small scale of Norwegian society and the intimacy of a system where top civil servants in the ministries and university professors knew each other personally. They belonged to the small civil service elite that in a not too distant past, during the better part of the last century, made up the ruling elite of the country and dominated parliamentary, administrative and university life. Although the system had grown, it was still relatively homogeneous. However, status differences between universities and individual academics were relatively negligible. Recruitment to national decision-making bodies was primarily determined by considerations of representativeness across institutions, disciplines, regions, gender and so on. Individuals such as Gudmund Hernes, while an education minister, might play important parts for extended periods of time, but their power was based on formal position rather than membership of an elite group. It is hard to discern any co-opted elite, a group of power holders that stood out in contrast to the powerless, in the context of higher education policy making.

In the Norwegian study we drew conclusions that were shared by the major players in Norwegian university politics:

1.   There was no national higher education policy elite.

2.   To the extent that there were integrated groups of powerful actors in higher education policy making, they are local or specialised.

3.   The groups were often relatively loose, temporary person- or issue-based networks.

Thus the university directors tended to establish personal networks of contacts among members of parliament, civil servants and local allies, such as other higher education institutions in the region. The purpose of these networks was always to promote the interests of a particular institution or occasionally of groups of institutions within a particular region. The Norwegian University Council might be considered a potentially influential elite group.[7] However, it was not considered a powerful player in policy making. Rather than acting collectively within a common framework like the Council, the institutions operated individually or regionally. In certain instances, such as the establishment and location of new institutions, ad hoc groups of business people and politicians were active as lobbyists.

Sweden

The role of academic elites and their possible co-option in the Swedish higher education regime are difficult to discern for primarily two reasons:

1. The Swedish university system was based on the notion of equality of institutions across the country. Thus a *clear recognition* of an institution as 'elite', or the members of that institution as 'elite' individuals, was not very common.

2. There was a long tradition of 'expert' involvement in the policy process through the use of government commissions.

Furthermore, participation in such a commission did not necessarily mean support for the government's plans and policies, but could reflect a desire to ensure that the views of academia as an 'affected party' were put forth. This was especially highlighted by the fact that members who disagreed with the results of a commission could and must state their reservations and remarks in written form as part of the commission's final report; otherwise their support for the conclusions of the commission was assumed.

Comparing the individual actors who comprised the leadership of the two major reform commissions, U68 and Högskoleutredningen 89, Bauer *et al.* (1999) noticed quite a significant difference in background and areas of expertise. The U68 Commission was headed by the Under Secretary from the Department of Education, Lennart Sandgren, with the other key members all representing central government positions, such as the head of the Swedish National Labour Market Board, the head of the National Board of Education, the current and former university chancellors. The key members of the Högskoleutredningen 89 were all academics, headed by the vice chancellor from Lund University. Thus, it appears that academic elite persons played a much more salient policy-making role in the late 1980s and early 1990s. Whether this amounted to the emergence of a co-opted academic elite is difficult to judge. However, centralisation tendencies from 1994 on made such a development unlikely.

CHANGES IN CORPORATIST MEDIATION

England

Overall the role of the corporatist actors is difficult to detect, although certain actors who may be members of interest groups intersect with those admitted to decision making as co-opted elites. The interest group representing the university leaders, the Committee of Vice-Chancellors and Principals (CVCP), often encountered difficulties in representing the collective voice of institutional leaders who valued institutional autonomy above agreeing to a common line, even if some chairmen of the CVCP often had good relations with the Secretary of State for Education. The CVCP was able to lobby powerfully and with some success in parliament – especially the House of Lords, where some academics sat. It was strongly opposed to the cuts of 1981 onwards, but with scarcely any success. Part of this proposition is to point the contrast with the situation described by Kogan (1975) in which the central government department had continuous and systematic negotiation with the local government association on key policies for schools.

Previously, corporate interest-based networks existed in certain areas of higher education in the form of policy communities with stable, limited and consensual membership. One example was the National Advisory Council for the Supply and Training of Teachers on questions of teacher training policies in the 1950s, 1960s and 1970s. A second example was the former National Advisory Body (NAB) for public sector higher education funding, although this existed only for eight years in the 1980s.[8] Finally, the UGC may be considered an interest group. The policy community it formed with the government not only demonstrated characteristics of stability, limited membership and agreement, but also, during much of its history, the idea of networking through trusting relationships was particularly important.

To the extent that interest groups played a part in England, they may have played their most important part in the period after elite structures started to disintegrate and before relatively stable policy communities shifted towards a larger issue network. The latter development characterised the 1980s, as the rapid number of large-scale policies were discussed in a fluctuating, episodic system of communication with varying agreement on policy alternatives. The predominant model was consultation rather than negotiation, although the consultations have not always been as widespread or systematic as is typical of an issue network. Thus we may say that the influence structure in England moved from implicit consensus between universities and government to governmental framing of policy without too much heed to established interest groups except where their interests were clearly aligned to current policies. The success of the polytechnic directors in bringing about an end to the binary structure is a case in point.

Norway

Norway has traditionally been counted among those countries where interest organisations and corporatist institutions have played an important part in national politics (Olsen 1978; Rokkan 1966). In the past 15 years Norway experienced increased competition among interest organisations, primarily on the union side, and a reduction in the number of committees and boards that traditionally constituted the corporate channel of influence (Christensen and Egeberg 1997). Simultaneously there was an increase in parliamentary lobbying, indicating a shift in the forms of state–society interaction away from corporatist arrangements (Rommetveit 1995).

The teachers' unions were traditionally influential political actors in education politics on the primary and secondary levels. In higher education the situation was different. Although most university employees were unionised, their unions were not influential. The exception were the traditional domains of labour unions such as working conditions and wage negotiations. To the extent that such issues interfered with other aspects of higher education policy, however, corporatist arrangements might make themselves felt. The following example from a study at the University of Bergen aptly illustrates the point (Aarre 1994). The attempt to differentiate professorial wages, by opening up for wage hikes based on individual performance, was deeply affected by the unions' success in negotiating a list of performance indicators so long and diversified that seniority in practice became the best predictor of individual wage increases. In general the field of work environment and the detailed regulations in that connection might in principle make the unions important and influential players, but in practice they did not seem to have exploited this potential.

Sweden

The corporatist tradition in Sweden was evident during the late 1960s and the 1970s in the strong representation of the trade unions, industry leaders and local government officials in the policy process.

The policy network certainly leaned towards a type of policy community, with a limited number of powerful players having a 'reserved place' at the negotiation table with consensus prevailing. During this time, the National Swedish Labour Market Board had a special role in the formation of higher education policy, given the goal of the welfare state to connect higher education to job purpose and job creation. As a result, all the major trade unions acted as representatives to the U68 Commission, and were primarily positive to the view of higher education as an instrument in providing full employment and social equality. However, the union which represented the university educated, white-collar workers (SACO) was critical of one major aspect of the reform, the internal governance policies, and was unsuccessful in getting its points across.

During the 1990s, a shift from this 'policy community' style of policy making to an 'issue network' seemed to have occurred. A wide variety of interest groups and organisations were involved in policy making. Of particular interest is the involvement of the national student union (SFS), the union of university teachers (SULF) and business leaders, as well as academic elite groups (such as the Royal Swedish Academy of Sciences and the Royal Swedish Academy of Engineering Sciences). The focus of the major reform (Prop. 1992/93: 1, 'Freedom for Quality') on issues of a pedagogical nature might have reflected the strong student and teacher input, and the reform on research quality and competitiveness (Prop. 1993/94: 77) might reflect the business and scientific communities' interests.

In discussing Swedish policy making it is important to note the traditional goal of reaching consensus through negotiation and consultation, among government, labour and employers, which has been prevalent in corporatist arrangements. During the recent reforms, the policy-making process occasionally broke with this tradition. For example, the Högskoleutredning report mentions that for certain areas they felt it was necessary to put changes in place quickly, without the typical consultation process (Statens Offentliga Utredningar 1992: 1, p.325). Compared with the corporatist regime before the early 1990s, the 1993 reform process was characterised by a shortening of the policy process, often skipping the traditional consultation process (remiss) which may have reduced the chance for some groups of fully expressing their policy preferences.

Actor networks and cohesion

Whereas the basic characteristics of the three higher education policy regimes seemed relatively unchanged during the first half of this century, unprecedented growth and successive waves of reform policies introduced a new dynamism from the 1960s on. These waves broke up established structures and reshaped fundamental aspects of the regimes and the relationship between the actors within them. Thus all three countries underwent broad processes of structural change that had a number of similar characteristics.

First, the size of higher education until the 1960s was by and large relatively stable; it was exposed to fairly modest demand and its political salience was low. The growth of the system made it much more politically important and the prevailing notions changed as to what the university does and its relationship with the state. Until the 1960s the prevailing view of university research was still as the location of a small-scale intellectual and culturally important activity, whose autonomy should be protected by the state. With regard to education, utilitarian concerns in the Scandinavian cases shaped the programmes and degree system. Today it has come to be conceived as a high-cost, large-scale research and educational enterprise, an economically important activity, the cost of which it is a state responsibility to control and the results of which it is a state responsibility to exploit. As higher education grew it became more interesting to the politicians. It was gradually lifted out of the purely elite, administrative sphere, where top ministry officials and university professors prevailed, and into the political sphere of a wider network of actors such as parliament and interest organisations. Higher education thus became more exposed to various 'external influences' and the wider political agenda of central governments. Economic policies, in particular labour market policies, thus increasingly influenced relations and decisions in higher education in all three countries.

Second, although the co-ordination of higher education institutions traditionally turned on the relationship between the state and the institutions, the institutional side changed considerably. The systems evolved from relatively few universities and national scientific institutions into much more comprehensive systems. Binary systems were developed from the 1960s in all countries, but have been or are currently about to be dismantled. This meant that a large number of institutions competed for resources, academic privileges and students. They were not only concerned with absolute growth of their budgets, but also with how they fared compared with other institutions. Thus the network of actors involved has increased and their interrelations have changed. As higher education became politicised, relations became formalised and affected by the attempts of central government authorities to direct, integrate and control the costs of the higher education sector.

An appropriate overall characteristic seems to be that the regimes changed from cohesive, transparent networks of few actors – mainly the leaders of a few academic institutions and top civil servants – to a wider and more politicised network. Compared with present times, we may say of all three countries that when the expansion started in the 1960s the higher education systems were small and policies were often made within what today appear as intimate, community-like and informal settings where the actors knew one another personally. As the system grew it become more formal and arguably less transparent. Management based on informal knowledge and personal relationships within relatively homogeneous elite groups gave way to political-administrative processes embedded in formal structures and based on formal positions. The new networks of actors were more opaque and politicised. There was a stronger focus on the competition between institutions, the needs of the students and the labour market. The process of politicisation also contributed to integrating higher education policies with welfare state and labour market policies.

Although the regimes of the three countries originally had elitist features, it is important to bear in mind the differences between them. First of all, whereas English universities were considered self-governed corporations supported by the state, Norwegian and Swedish universities have always been part of the civil service. Whereas in England academic elites appear to have been self-governed, it is harder to distinguish between the state and the academic elite in Norway and Sweden. Furthermore, comparing the two state systems, corporate actors were more influential in Sweden than in Norway.

However, both the informal cohesive community-like actor networks and the wider formal actor networks were different. In England there was a movement from an independent academic elite to a wider set of actors in which central government through ministerial influence was a particularly influential actor. The changing actor constellation in Norway went from a situation in which a state civil service elite encompassed the academic elite to a situation where central government influence manifested itself as a more politicised and parliamentary influence through which regional interests were able to influence policy making. Finally, in Sweden a state civil service elite influence first transformed into a network characterised by corporate influence and then into a wider and looser network in which 1990s academic elites, business groups and party politics played more important roles.

Conclusions

Change and regime dynamics

Over time, say the latter half of the last century, there has been a tendency to use a growing array of policy instruments. Traditionally, public policies typically relied upon the use of authority tools and symbolic tools. An increasing diversity of public tasks and growing responsibilities during the era of public expansion until the mid-1970s made capacity and incentive tools more important. Particularly important in this connection were welfare state services and various productive tasks, in some countries also active labour market policies and comprehensive macro-economic planning. The policy shifts during the last decades, including the rise of neo-liberalism, led to changes in the directions of the use of policy instruments. The use of incentives in general and incentives directed at individuals in particular grew, as did the use of learning tools. The latter typically manifested itself in the form of the growth of evaluation within public administration. These were all policy shifts common to the three cases. They underscore that actor strategies and their impact must be considered against a backdrop of structural change which we find in all three countries.

In addition to the focus on policy change over time, the dynamic regime approach directs our attention to cross-national and cross-sector comparison between countries and policy sectors. Let us briefly try to sum up and draw some conclusions from the observations of higher education reform in the three countries. First of all it demonstrated that reforms espousing similar ideologies varied considerably, both with respect to how radical the reforms were and how stable the policies were (Bleiklie *et al.* 1997). Although the reforms meant an increased use of incentive and learning tools in all three countries, they were used quite differently. The reform patterns had some striking differences that seem clearly related to general system characteristics of the three countries. These processes suggest that regime characteristics may be linked with policy design in different ways. The three patterns make up three types of policy styles that may be used as an aid for further studies into the relationship between institutional design and policy design.

In spite of the fact that the countries apparently moved in the same direction, they did so in manners which were characterised by different national points of departure and which to some extent seemed to sustain national peculiarities. Thus the 1977 reform gave Sweden a point of departure that was different from England and Norway when the reforms of the late 1980s and early 1990s where conceived. Having introduced reforms in the 1970s that significantly

reduced institutional autonomy, and tailored the educational programmes to national labour market planning, the latter reforms were
considered to move higher education out of the grip of central government and closer to traditional academic values. In England and
Norway the reforms were regarded as moves in the opposite direction
as the state tried to gain control of higher education in order to control
costs and use it in the service of general economic policy goals. In
addition the politicisation of higher education meant different things
in the three countries. In England the influence of education
ministers seems to have been particularly strong. In Sweden party
politics have influenced policies and in Norway MPs have acted as
representatives of regions and their local state colleges rather than as
party members. English reforms were comparatively centralised,
radical and relied more on tougher measures in order to discipline
non-compliant institutions. Once introduced, the policy was pursued
rather consistently. This pattern illustrates the confrontational style,
but also the relative stability that is the aim of the Westminster style of
'winner-take-all-democracy': what we may call a *heroic style* of policy
making. Actor preferences and their strategies were important for the
initial policy change during the 1980s. Since then a new consensus
seems to have emerged and the process has been more value-
structure driven, characterised by a relative consensus under which
the New Labour government that came to power in 1997 did not significantly alter the policies of its Conservative predecessor.

The Norwegian reforms, however, were less radical. In a comparative perspective they evolved gradually in a value-structure driven
process with considerable local variation as to how the reforms were
implemented. The pattern illustrated the decentralised, steady and
consensual political *incremental style* characterised by Olsen (1983) as
'revolution in slow motion'. Although the policies were formulated by
central government, individual institutions had considerable leeway
as to how the reforms were implemented, but most importantly
incentives were used to reward those institutions and individuals who
performed well.

Swedish reforms were characterised by a more confrontational
style than those of Norway, but also by less political stability. Government changes led to policy changes and a varying central government
control in terms of authority tools and use of incentives vis-à-vis educational institutions. The Swedish experience thus illustrates what we
may call an *adversarial style* of policy making in the sense of an uneasy
tug-of-war between two major political blocks with two very different
visions of higher education. These policy shifts indicate that actor

preferences and the tension between them have played a more important part in Sweden than in the other two countries.

Notes

1   Earlier versions of the approach, called a dynamic network approach, were developed together with Susan Marton and Steve Hanney from the Swedish and British research teams within the collaboration of the International Study of Higher Education Reform (Bleiklie 1998; Bleiklie and Marton 1998; Bleiklie, Marton and Hanney 1995, 1997).

2   According to Webster's unabridged dictionary (1981), a 'regime' may refer both to 'a method of ruling or management', 'a manner of administration' and 'a form of government and administration'. The concept of a regime refers to a formal aspect, a form of government and a procedural aspect, a manner of governing, and thus comprises both the structures and processes of government.

3   We have thus preferred this definition to the alternative in the literature where policy design is regarded as rational process where policy makers are regarded as architects or engineers and public policy is seen as the mechanical application of means in order to realise given ends. When we chose to define policy design as a set of characteristics it is because this definition does not presume a rational actor model or any other specific explanation, but is open to alternative explanations.

4   Heclo and Wildavsky (1974) originally used the depiction to characterize British public administration in general.

5   It should be noted that the 'same' instrument such as money may be used both as a capacity tool and as an incentive tool. How it is classified in each instance depends on what behavioural assumptions about target groups its application is based. The purpose of capacity tools then is to enable rather than motivate target groups.

6   The analysis is based on personal interviews with politicians, civil servants, university administrators and elected officials in addition to relevant policy documents and other written material.

7   The Council of Norwegian Universities is a body for co-operation between universities and scientific colleges, that was based on the former Rectors' conference and is charged with the co-ordination and promotion of national level initiatives by the institutions.

8   The policy network term might be more appropriate to describe this body and the proposals made during its creation than Salter and Tapper's (1994) depiction of it as pluralism, because the groups represented came almost entirely from the education world.

Chapter 4

The State and Higher Education

Maurice Kogan
and Susan Gerard Marton

Changes in the role of the state and the place of the universities within it

In this chapter, we take up the implications of those aspects of policy that can be interpreted as theories of the state and of the university and their role in society.

The starting point for our three national projects was the evident changes in the role of the state promoted by national governments. As major public institutions, universities can be considered either as subsystems of the state or as independent institutions that nevertheless are strongly affected by the nature of the state. A primary task is therefore to locate universities among the range of public institutions, and to assess how they can be related, if sometimes uncertainly, to a continuum of views about the appropriate role of the state. Therefore, much of our analysis in this book considers whether, if the discretion allowed to universities and the academics who constitute their working base has been increasingly circumscribed, the central tasks of universities (i.e research and teaching-learning) remain the domain of the prime practitioners, rather than the governing structures.

Taking the UK case first, viewed as a set of public institutions, universities have held a particular place, shared by only a few others, within the range of British governmental arrangements. The British state mediates its policies through what can be described as an organisational zoo in which the different species can be typified in terms of the functions they perform, the power or authority characteristics and the forms of control and dependency which they employ, and the kinds of knowledge on which they depend for their functioning.

At one end of the spectrum of state mechanisms some public institutions, such as the armed forces, the tax authorities and social security, have direct lines of command to a national authority. This hierarchical structure may be mitigated by the use of wide discretion, as with tax authorities, but, essentially, such organisations act within legal and managerial structures which can be fashioned to meet exclusively policies which are determined on high. Then there are those in an intermediate position, the most obvious of which are local authorities, which are intended to carry out national policies (which have become increasingly prescriptive in the UK since the early 1980s), but with regard to the wishes of their local electorates and on the basis of a high component of professional judgement. At the furthest end of the spectrum are charter institutions which include the BBC, the national museums and the universities. Their status has been that of almost wholly independent institutions but deferring to public policies that largely constitute the conditions under which the bulk of their resources have been secured.

In Sweden, the situation is significantly different. The civil service's relationship to ministers is unique in a comparative perspective. With a tradition dating back to the 1600s, the Swedish public administration is organised on the basis of independent civil authorities. There is a division between the minister (and the Ministry of Education, run by the ruling government and civil servants) and the independent civil authorities (run by general directors and bureaucrats). Thus there is no direct hierarchy, or chain of command, from the minister to the various general directors. Steering of the public service is achieved by decisions in parliament and resulting instructions from the government (where the decisions are made on a collective basis, i.e. the individual minister is not responsible on his own). As Petersson (1993) has indicated, such a system has led to much discussion as to what extent the ministry has a right to try to influence the civil authorities.

The range of institutions covered by the spectrum of state mechanisms in Sweden is not as wide; there is no equivalent institution to that of the British 'charter institution'. Many scientific and cultural public authorities have, however, received greater independence from the parliament and government through new laws, yet their status as 'public authorities' is maintained. Most closely related to the British 'charter institution' is possibly the Swedish *stiftelse*, or foundation, which does have a high degree of independence. This institutional structure is quite rare in Swedish public administration; the change of two universities to this type of status invoked extensive political debate in the early 1990s. (All other universities and colleges in Sweden are 'public authorities'.)

Under the Norwegian ministries one finds different types of institution: directorates, government enterprises, government owned corporate enterprises and independent foundations, and other government agencies such as universities and state colleges. The universities are formally government agencies under the Ministry of Education. The degree of autonomy enjoyed by the universities must be seen in a wider public administration context where the question of independent professional judgement has been an important issue since the latter part of the nineteenth century. It has affected the relationship between the ministries and subordinate agencies (in particular the directorates and professionally run agencies like those within the national health service). Thus there is a constant tension between the principle of professionally independent judgement and the principle of subordination to superior popularly elected political authorities.

As with the range of institutions, so normative accounts of the appropriate extent of state action, or the values and purposes of the state, can be placed on a spectrum. This goes from the minimalist position advocated by Nozick (1974) in which the state does no more than protect the natural rights of individuals, through more traditional liberal and conservative thinking, to the maximalist communitarian or absolutist views, both of which grant maximum authority to the collectivity. Arguments about higher education's autonomy may have, indeed, not been too far from the Nozickian view in that they have sometimes included demands for complete freedom from public control, to the extent of arguing for exemption from public audit of the funds originating from the national purse (Kogan 1969).

Recent UK Conservative governments adopted a neo-liberal rhetoric about the desirability of limiting the role of the state. However, this was not entirely consistent with previous conservative thinking; it is worth recalling Scruton's (1980) statement that 'the conservative is recognisable as a political animal by his reluctance to effect complete separation between the state and civil society, and that it is as deep an instinct in a conservative as it is in a socialist to resist the champions of "minimal" government' (p.48). This ambivalence is reflected in, for example, the fluctuations of policy on the extent to which research should be funded from the public purse and directed into 'economically useful' areas.

In Sweden, the Conservative coalition government (1991–94) also espoused this neo-liberal ideology, strongly advocating that the universities needed to be freed from the grip of the state (the Conservative party had been arguing this since the 1970s). It advocated the freedom of the universities in the quality debate, although it did apply detailed regulation in attempts to evaluate and preserve quality, often justified under the principles of New Public Management. A similar trend was evident in Norway, but not nearly as strongly based on neo-liberal ideology, but more on the need for renewal of the civil service. Strong arguments for increased decentralisation were combined with more policies for accountability, standardisation and stronger administrative influence.

Views about the appropriate arrangements for specific institutions are not always consistent with opinions about the degree of state action that is appropriate in the society as a whole. In general the particular nature of higher education, or higher education essentialism, means that in most societies universities have a rather special place.

This has given rise to different models of higher education government. The classic model has been that of the self-regulating higher education institution which sustains its own values and ways of working. The contrast is that of the dependent institution, characterised by higher degrees of dependency and sponsorship and whose objectives might be set externally. It is possible to strip down these models by contrasting their dominant values and client groups and from there educe internal and external governmental structures.

First, on values, the choice is between those arrangements which lay claim to the disinterested search for truth and those that espouse responsiveness to social and economic needs. Neither value position is exercised absolutely. Ultimately, both models may lay claim to serve the whole society – truth being an indispensable commodity in civilised and efficient living together. The classic model places its boundary in order to safeguard teaching and knowledge generation that show a respect for demonstrated logic and evidence. The dependent institution in claiming to speak of the truth brings in reference groups and definitions beyond the academic.

From modes of knowledge, for example, that which aims at 'the disinterested search for truth' as against 'social and economic responsiveness', we can make connections with modes of power. If good academic work requires freedom to pursue knowledge without deference to outside users – the claim of blue skies research in the hard sciences and of scholarship in the humanities – it follows that governmental arrangements must be minimal, and subject to minimal external pressures. The collegium is a minimum device for asserting standards and sharing out resources. It does not seek to manage academic work, if by that is meant requiring acceptance of institutionally drawn up objectives. Thus the social arrangements meet the needs of the task. The raison d'être of the socially conditioned or dependent institution is that it will read the needs of its client groups and fashion knowledge to meet them.

From these intermediary steps, the ideal patterns of government become clear. On the one side the collegium rules. On the other, the

dependent and interactive institution works within a frame set up by
society at both the national and governmental levels. Throughout the
whole spectrum of HEIs, however, there is negotiation between and
mixtures of the two positions.

We can fill in this exercise in modelling by noting the range of relationships between government and higher education institutions.
They go through the range of self-regulation and exchange relationships with sponsors to sponsorship dependency and hierarchical relationships with sponsors.

It would be facile to assume simple correspondences between these
different sets of characteristics though some seem to follow quite
easily. Thus self-regulation goes fairly comfortably with colle-
gial-professional modes of government. Modes of operation which
stem from modes of government can be multi-valent. For example,
evaluation can choose between a host of intentions, value positions
and modes: formative/summative; managerial/developmental;
internal/external. So can the market, that often is used to mean no
more than the use of contractual mechanisms specifying quality,
timeliness and cost and which may be free of profit connotations.

On the bases of these ranges, we can generalise about the functions
undertaken by government. There have been changes in all three
countries, but not all in the same direction. An extended version of
this list will be used in Chapter 8 when we consider the extent to
which changes have resulted from reform policies:

- between the enabling and the evaluative
- between the facilitatory and the interventionist (Neave and
  van Vught 1991)
- between the providing and the regulative
- between the welfare, deficiency funding and the market
  driven
- between the decentralised and the centralised
- between the professionally and the managerially led systems
- between control by the political and administrative laity and
  the academic professionals.

Normative theories of the university

Of all public institutions, the university has been subjected to most
analysis of its idiosyncratic nature. In the theory of the independent
institution, albeit in receipt of substantial subventions from the public
purse, institutional and professional freedoms are regarded as essen-

tial for the pursuit of its purposes. We shall analyse the position of the universities in the light of two different approaches. First we shall use Burton Clark's (1983) triangle to identify co-ordinating forces within higher education systems. Then we shall look at some dimensions of the concept of autonomy that can help us locate variations in university autonomy across countries and over time.

Clark's triangle refers to the way in which higher education systems are the resultant of a triangle of forces: professional–collegial; governmental–managerial and market. Becher and Kogan (1980), adapting Premfors, added a welfare state force. This could also be expressed as a civil society force which might accommodate community, distributive and other welfare functions of higher education. An important subset of Clark's hypothesis is that academics have a dual accountability to their invisible colleges of fellow academics and to their institution.

On the basis of this heuristic it is possible to compare systems and, at any one time, to denote the extent to which one force, e.g. managerial as against collegial, or civil society as opposed to market criteria, is driving a system at any one time. In the UK, power seems to have shifted from the level of the working academic to that of the institution, the national authorities and the market. This irregularity of pattern in itself demands explanation (Figure 4.1). The UK began at an opposite corner of Clark's triangle from that of its continental counterparts. It is shifting towards state control, while other systems are moving in the opposite direction. In Sweden, given a perspective of over twenty years, it seems that the academics never had much power in policy making. The shift of power in the late 1980s and start of the 1990s was primarily from the state to the institutions, operating in a quasi-market. Norway, with its previous system of central author-

State authority

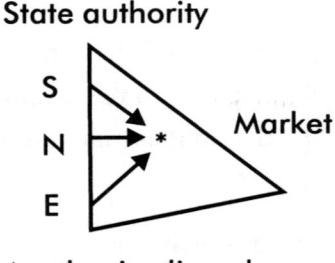

Academic oligarchy

* Represents a point towards which all three nations may be propelled.

Figure 4.1 Applying Clark's triangle

ities negotiating with the academics at the individual universities, is now aiming at the market with the university seen as a 'corporate enterprise in the knowledge industry' (Bleiklie *et al.* 2000).

Clark's triangle does not, of itself, entail particular normative positions, but his general corpus of writing falls in with the position taken until recently by that of virtually every other scholar in the field. These entail the socio-technological assumption (Woodward 1965) that the primary modes of production in higher education determine the social, and hence governmental, arrangements for that field (see Chapter 1). If we follow this view, since higher education's main activities – research, scholarship and teaching – are essentially individualistic, and depend on the expertise and commitment of creative individuals, its governmental arrangements fall best within the collegial format. A collegium is a minimalist organisation constructed to control standards of entry, to allocate essential common tasks and to distribute resources to its members while avoiding control over the amount and nature of the work to be done. By contrast, managerial and hierarchical arrangements assume that there will be policies and objectives set on high which will be disaggregated by academics to whom tasks would be allocated. The professionally led model assumes that collegial arrangements, in which authority and power are shared by academics, are the appropriate way to organise universities. 'Many special characteristics of academic organisations are rooted in the structure of academic work ... the parts of academic systems have grown to be quite fragmented and independent with extreme division of labour and complicating mutual influences on each other' (Hölttä 1995, quoting Birnbaum 1989 and Clark 1983).

Clark extended these assumptions to his account of the change mechanisms of higher education. These are driven by the way in which knowledge is produced through ever changing and increasing specialisation which constantly generates new forms and boundaries, subdisciplines and domains. This all happens with scant regard to national government or institutional management. Institutions may develop their own portfolio of values and lay down their own criteria of excellence (Becher and Kogan 1992), but more salient are the criteria and judgements of the international disciplines or the national guilds to which academics belong. Hence process determines structure.

Much the same themes are celebrated by a succession of authors on the organisational and decision-making characteristics of universities. The diffusion and complexity of patterns of authority give rise to the dominant organisational models which accompany the normative political theory of higher education. Collegial, bureaucratic, political and organised anarchy models 'are found in universities, but in different parts, different issues, and at different points in time' (Hölttä 1995). The collegial model is compatible with the model of disciplinary self-governance. In it decision making is characterised by consensus. The bureaucratic model, in which the institution creates rules, regulations and hierarchies to regulate procedures and processes which might assure accountability for the performance of public purposes, is also present in virtually all higher education institutions. Within the political model however (Baldridge 1971), the university is assumed to be fragmented into specialised groups with divergent interests and preferences and the system therefore depends upon mutual dependency groups and on social exchange. The organised anarchy model (Cohen and March 1974) predicts that organisational action at university is virtually unintentional. Decision making and organisational choice are characterised by the 'garbage can' model (Cohen, March and Olsen 1972). The choices available are determined by the use of the garbage can into which various problems and solutions are dumped by participants. Decision making is individual rather than organisational. At the same time, a university behaving on the model of organised anarchy 'also has formal structures, roles, and eternal regulation mechanisms for educational and administrative activities' (Hölttä 1995). Garbage can processes are embedded in institutional contexts which affect their outcomes (March and Olsen 1989). Against this traditional normative model we can increasingly set models derived from managerial concepts of higher education, from the pursuit of social concerns derived from access or lifelong learning policies or from the burgeoning quality industry. These find expression in some of the prescriptive literature on quality assurance and on effective management on institutions.

It is not easy to distinguish normative from empirical statements in this area. While many of these (mainly American) statements were intended to be analytic descriptions of the nature of higher education based on their understanding of the governmental arrangements demanded by the essential nature of higher education, the analysis usually started from acquaintance with the most prestigious research universities and did not encompass the 'less noble' forms of higher education, such as teacher training institutions or military academies, also usually but not always defined into higher education. The analyses also tended to understate the extent to which some basic units in some subjects were led in hierarchical and even authoritarian ways. It would not be unfair to say that the collegial or anarchic models were based as much on wished-for states as on states that were discoverable in the whole range of institutions. They constituted ideal pictures.

At the empirical level the nature of higher education institutions has, however, seemed to justify unique relationships with the state and perhaps to strengthen the case for claiming a degree of higher education exceptionalism. These features include the central role of knowledge generation and transmission in higher education institutions. We have already noted that the basic argument for autonomy is that the very nature of knowledge generation requires freedom from direction if it is to result in the disinterested and critical search for knowledge. The disinterested search for knowledge also reflects the role of the university as a provider of critical viewpoints in a democratic society: 'The underlying dynamics of knowledge organisation are difficult for the state to contain' (Clark 1983, p.179). However, it is also argued that new forms of knowledge generation increase steerage opportunities (Gibbons *et al.* 1994), although an earlier tradition of 'finalisation theory' (Van den daele, Krahn and Weingart 1977) maintained that the willingness of a field to be steered depended on the paradigmal stage that had been reached.

Further claims for exceptionalism rest on the long history of some of the institutions which pre-date the existence of national states. This provides them not only with an historically-based assumption of the right to autonomy, but also considerable immovable assets which provide a degree of protection from state control. In many societies links between universities and other elites defend them from lay interference. There is the perceived importance of higher education to the success of modern economies and the resulting pressures on institutions (see, for example, Becher and Kogan 1992; Salter and Tapper 1994). Some outputs are used directly as consumption benefits and others as part of the production process (Cave *et al.* 1997). Higher education can thus be seen as contributing to both production and consumption as used in Cawson's (1986) model of corporatism. The increasing emphasis on the role of graduates in the economy means that higher education can be increasingly seen as part of the supply side of the economy.

But many of these arguments are two-edged. Thus the very importance of universities to the economy favours a stronger degree of public policy influence. Arguments derived from the nature of knowledge production work in favour of autonomy, and arguments from its use argue in favour of state intervention. Moreover, arguments over control need to have some appeal to their political constituencies. In the UK the political constituency coming to higher education's aid and arguing its case for continued protection has been weaker than for the top US universities, which seems to imply that exceptionalism is not entirely carried by force of moral argument but also by the characteristics of the political environment.

Analysts of higher education government must, in fact, look out for a range of normative theories which will develop and change in response to changes in higher education tasks. New Public Management and the Evaluative State start with largely managerial preoccupations. Assumptions about governance connected with powerful drives towards lifelong learning and wider access can be expected to develop and contest the space hitherto occupied by the traditional academic-professional theory.

As we noted above, comparisons of the state's role in relation to higher education in different countries follow closely the style of Clark's triangle (e.g. Frederiks, Westerheijden and Wensthof 1994). Analysis of the grip of the state has also utilised Neave and van Vught's (1994) continuum which has a controlling role for the state at one end and a more liberal supervising role at the other (Richardson and Fielden 1997). These international comparisons usually suggest the UK still gives more autonomy to its universities than most other countries. Historically, we can discern contrasts between the liberal anglophone and the continental regimes.

Normative theories can be applied to an analysis of traditional university autonomy in different countries and how the position has changed. Meanings vary according to historical and national perspectives and to the level of the system at which the analysis is being applied. Berdahl (1977) noted that academic freedom and institutional autonomy are not the same thing. This distinction is borne out by some of our interviewees who believed that the power of the institutions has grown at the expense of individual academic freedom (see also Tapper and Salter 1995). Berdahl distinguished between academic freedom which belongs to the individual academic, substantive autonomy which is the power of the institution to determine its own goals and programmes, and procedural autonomy which is the power of the institution to determine the means by which its goals and programmes will be pursued. The extent of autonomy can be identified by analysis on several dimensions (Frazer 1997). These include:

1. *The legal status of an institution*: Is it recognised as a separate entity? Is it free to own property?

2. *Academic authority*: Can it make academic awards?

3. *Mission*: Does it determine its own goals?

4. *Governance*: Who appoints its governing body?

5. *Financial*: Is it free to make expenditure decisions?

6. *Employment*: Does it employ its own staff?

7. *Academic decentralisation*: Does it determine student admissions? Must it seek approval for courses? Does it determine its own curriculum and has it freedom to pursue research?

Frazer points out that autonomy must be qualified by some attribute of the institution. Thus in some systems it will be the faculty rather than the institution that possesses the autonomy.

Substantive autonomy can be thought of in terms of a dimension labelled 'purpose', i.e. what the role of higher education in society is or should be along a continuum based on either cultural or utilitarian values. Cultural values would emphasise the disinterested pursuit of knowledge, given the understanding that in such pursuit the goals of society are best met in the long run. Utilitarian values would, on the other hand, emphasise that knowledge should be pursued for the purpose of meeting socially determined goals. Thus cultural values promote some form of autonomy, whereas utilitarian values promote heteronomy in the sense that the pursuit of knowledge is subordinated to some other societal goal.[1]

Using Frazer's dimensions of autonomy listed above as a point of departure, it is clear that autonomy is intimately related to the distribution of authority from the national government to the institutions, which we will call the 'authority dimension'. In the light of such an authority dimension we may distinguish between universities as state institutions and universities as formally independent charter institutions. These principles constitute two main versions of the European university tradition. Within the continental tradition epitomised by the Humboldtian university, the autonomy of the university is guaranteed and supported by the state mechanisms of ownership and control. In the liberal Anglo-Saxon tradition, autonomy is guaranteed by keeping the universities out of the reach of public authority, but with access to public funding.

By analysing the concept of 'institutional autonomy' within the space constituted by these dimensions, it becomes evident that the degree of institutional autonomy varies among them. Thus, they add depth to the institutional autonomy concept, moving beyond the common conception of institutional autonomy as just related to the vertical shift of authority from a state model to a liberal model (van Vught 1988), or the conception of institutional autonomy as being related only to the purpose of the university (Tasker and Packham

1990). Rather, institutional autonomy is intricately tied to under-standings of both the purpose of higher education and the way in which the state exercises authority.[2]

The two dimensions of purpose and authority constitute a space within which we may position and compare specific university systems and map their development over time. The Humboldtian model represents the combination of a state model and a cultural purpose. Cardinal Newman's idea of a university combines a cultural purpose with a liberal model. Bernal's (1969) notion of a university in the service of the people within a socialist political order represents the combination of a utilitarian purpose and state control. Finally, a completely customer dependent, market-controlled university offering whatever prospective buyers want represents the combi-nation of utilitarianism and a liberal model (Figure 4.2).

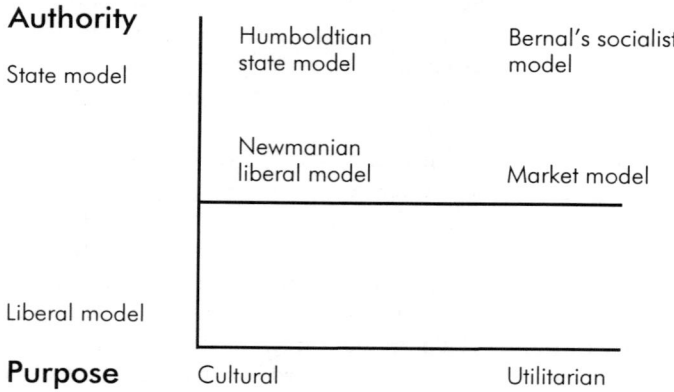

Figure 4.2 Four types of institutional autonomy

Universities in Britain, Sweden and Norway: Their position and autonomy

On almost all criteria of autonomy, UK universities have scored high. The concepts of academic freedom and institutional autonomy, as exemplified historically by the role of the University Grants Com-mittee (UGC), were strongly embedded in the British political culture. The traditional autonomy of UK higher education was bol-stered by thinking from a wide range of positions on the extent of appropriate state action.

The traditional liberal view of restricting the role of the state in fields such as higher education was stated by John Stuart Mill who claimed the 'most cogent reason for restricting the interference of government is the great evil of adding unnecessarily to its power' (1962, p.244). Even for the conservative Scruton, with his belief in a role for the state, it is important that universities are autonomous and 'focused on internal aims' (1980, p.160). Elsewhere in this book (Chapters 6 and 8) we describe the strong links between universities and other bodies in which members of elites can be found, such as those existing between the UGC and the Treasury. This played an important part in bolstering the autonomy of universities. Another aspect of this that is seen to be stronger in Britain and other Westminster systems than elsewhere, is the role of buffer bodies standing between the state and the universities.

These considerations form part of a general assumption about the role of the UK state. In the UK there existed a broadly held view which regarded education 'as ill-served by state intervention' (Neave 1986, pp.109–124). Instead there developed the idea of the facilitatory state which would provide resources to universities whose freedom would be enjoyed within an area of negotiation largely controlled by themselves. The resulting autonomy was both institutional and individual and embodied in charters and collegial self-government. More recently, the authority of the state was strengthened by its policies and by the comprehensive use of legislation which before the 1980s was hardly part of the UK scene.

Swedish higher education from the 1970s to the 1990s underwent changes as the overall governance model advocated by the state shifted in ways which significantly made an impact on institutional autonomy.

Changes which primarily characterised the shift in purpose were the emphasis in the 1990s on the needs of a broad 'knowledge society' rather than the needs of a narrowly defined job market, along with relinquishing the use of the higher education system to reform society, and instead a focus towards the various market demands and the need for 'academic excellence'. In the 1970s, the higher education system was intricately involved in building the Swedish welfare state. This was reflected in the division of undergraduate education into five major occupational groupings, with a 'study line' system which was to prepare students for the job market (with a heavy emphasis on careers in the public service). In the early 1990s, this line system was abolished (replaced by a new system of degrees) and the strong central-level regulation of course curriculum was significantly lightened. The previously centrally planned curriculum was seen as causing lower competency levels in the Swedish workforce. Thus it was now time to increase the offering of courses to meet the needs of the private sector and business. Other problems cited by the Minister of Education included the low number of employees in business with academic degrees, the difficulty in transferring research results to high-tech businesses, and the changing composition of the job market, with less than 20 per cent of the workforce employed in industry while the service sector was dramatically increasing. To foster more co-operation between the higher education institutions and the business community, the Minister proposed that the universities and colleges be able to conduct research in the form of companies, receiving start-up capital from the government.

The shift in authority between the state and the institutions was primarily characterised by the move from a utilitarian state model with centrally regulated and steered institutions to more autonomous institutions, led by powerful institutional leaders who were now to compete in an education marketplace. Interest representation for trade unions and political authorities was no longer dictated by central regulation. The Minister declared: 'My principal view of the universities and colleges stems from the traditional meaning of the concept of university: an autonomous academy composed of students and teachers who freely choose each other' (Gov. Prop. 92/93: 169, p.93). This shift in the distribution of authority between the state and the institutions naturally brought about a change in the authority of the central bureaucracy, with a new emphasis on accountability rather than on planning and managing the system. With the transfer of authority from the central bureaucracy to the individual institutions, the tasks of the university boards changed radically from those of the 1970s when their primary task was to implement centrally determined goals and manage the allocation of resources as prescribed by the central government. Now, increased local freedom to determine the administrative composition of the rector's office at each higher education institution was also stressed, with long-term strategic planning declared as this office's most important task.

Believing that competition would improve quality, one of the most prominent policy changes occurring in the early 1990s was the introduction of a new resource allocation system. The universities now compete at the undergraduate level for students (within the boundaries of top limits still set by the government) and are allocated money based not just on student enrolment but also, as we have seen, on the semester-based study results of the students.

Having described these changes along our two dimensions, it becomes evident that the Swedish higher education system has moved from a 'state-utilitarian' governance type towards a more cultural purpose and more market-liberal authority type. Although there has been some retreat from the original intentions of the 1993 reform with the election of a new government in 1994, significant changes in internal organisation and in resource distribution are still making a strong impact on the system today.

The position in Norway was historically different from that in Britain (though somewhat similar to historical development of the Swedish system). Until the post-war period, universities in Norway were essentially directed towards training for the public services, particularly teaching, but much of their post-1945 history has been that of evolving into the more general liberal assumptions of the purposes of universities.

As mentioned previously, Norway had quite a different arrangement for the authority relationship between the state and the higher education institutions, with each institution having its own laws which were negotiated with the central authorities. In the 1990s the universities were incorporated under national legislation for the first time. Yet this did not entail a fundamental shift in the power of the state over the universities, but rather a new increased authority in the administrative management at the universities appeared. Decentralisation measures left more budgetary power to the universities themselves, but as an expanded university bureaucratisation occurred, the influence of the disciplines waned. In meeting the needs of the welfare state, Norwegian universities had also been seen as an intricate component of national employment policies. In order to meet the goals of full employment, the universities had been increasingly regulated by the state in terms of student places. Yet in the 1990s, the proposals from the Hernes Commission broke with this principle and advocated the use of the higher education system for long-term, strategic needs in the face of international economic competition.

There also appeared to be a shift in the ideas on the purpose of the university in Norway during the 1990s. Moving away from the previous view of the university as a cultural institution, it was now seen more as a 'corporate enterprise' – where emphasis was to be placed on efficiency, consumer orientation and personnel management. There was evidence of greater ambitions to steer research, as basic research funds were increasingly allocated to research programmes. In addition, the power of the discipline-based units probably diminished as governing bodies (in 1990) were to recognise equal categories of employees (academic staff, administrative staff, students, etc.) and external representatives were mandated seats on the university boards (1995).

Structures operationalising relations between the state and higher education

Only in Norway did the state work directly with universities. In the UK and Sweden there were formalised intermediary or buffer bodies: national agencies, funding and research councils, and quality assurance bodies. In all systems, if in differing degrees, the state depended on co-opted elites to provide the academic judgements on which allocative decisions on status or resource could be made. However, as pointed out in Chapter 3, the latter was true for Norway only to the extent that institutional leaders were considered members of such an elite.

Different models evolved with the changing relationships with the state. Members were appointed by ministers, unlike in Germany where members of research councils are elected. This need not affect academic power; the UK's University Grants Committee consisted almost entirely of professors, but appointed by the minister. In the UK, they shifted from being largely academic controlled to being increasingly dominated by governmental interests. They used to be mechanisms for reconciling government's policies with academic development. Now they served mainly to recruit academic expertise to the implementation of government policy.

Most funding in Norway and Sweden went directly from parliament to the universities; there were no funding councils. The budgets for research councils were also determined by parliament. The Swedish Higher Education Agency had no funding functions but was concerned with quality assurance, juridical functions, making investigations and building up information. In the 1990s, the Conservative coalition government created private research foundations, using public funds (called the 'wage-earner's funds', Bauer *et al.* 1999, Chapter 3). Their budgets were a percentage of the funds invested in the stock market. When the Social Democratic government returned to power in 1994 they changed the articles of incorporation for these foundations so that appointments to the board would be carried out by the government. As a result, the chairmen of the boards of these seven foundations were replaced so that six were led either by politicians or high-ranking bureaucrats and one by a professor. New appointments as members of the board allowed increased representation for parliamentarians, bureaucrats and labour union representatives. This trend of increasing political representation on the boards was evident not only in these research foundations, but also in some of the national research councils (Rothstein in Fridlund and Sandström 2000).

Conclusions

Explaining higher education relationships as the state transforms

The role of the state changed in all three nations, reflecting ideas about the appropriate level of state intervention in general, and specifically, impacting on the relationship between the state and higher education institutions. The prominent change in the role of the state in Sweden was the move from social corporatism to a more neo-liberal state. In England, while also adopting neo-liberal rhetoric, governments seriously reframed the chartered autonomy of universities and 'nationalised' them. In Norway there was also a reframing of institutional autonomy, in the sense that the state showed a more active interest in the efficiency and economic usefulness of higher education.

In explaining these changes in relation to the model in Chapter 1 depicting change between T^1 and T^2 we can discern two primary changes in terms of the shared values that became institutionalised. In all three countries there was widespread support for New Public Management and the shifting conceptions of the type of knowledge needed and the role of knowledge in modern society. This would have to do with, for example, in Norway, the belief that more knowledge, basically of almost any type, was always beneficial, and in Sweden the similar idea that we were living in a 'knowledge society'. In the UK, the 'knowledge society' appeared late in political rhetoric, possibly with the arrival of the Labour government in 1997, although the Foresight initiative and the 1993 White Paper aims centred on the exploitation of knowledge. In the 1980s it was skills that were highlighted.

If we look at the other main explanatory variable of the actor–context model in Chapter 1, we may raise the question of the role of 'bounded rational actors' and preference-driven behaviour. The Swedish case displays this type of preference-driven behaviour, in particular on the policies relating to quality – which were connected to which political party was in power. Changes that occurred did so because of party politics. In England, more than elsewhere, ministers and a few other actors adopted a heroic role. Similar individual cases can be identified in the other countries, although for the most part policies were value-structure driven. Some ministers decisively moulded policy and in doing so only consulted those interest groups that had adopted positions broadly in line with their own preferences. In Norway, policies evolved more consensually and gradually.

As already demonstrated in Chapter 3, higher education policies and the changes in them are not the result of one or the other of preference-driven or value-structure driven processes, but rather the interaction of the two.

Some questions for further exploration

Elsewhere (Chapter 7) we consider the impact of reforms on knowledge creation and control. Here we conjecture that there are relationships between the types of knowledge generated and the higher education organisation required to sustain them (Becher 1989; Bernstein 1963). Forms of knowledge, hard or soft, the collected or the integrated curriculum, affect and are affected by its social or organisational forms. It may not be fanciful to assume that if certain types of knowledge are promoted by government, that will affect the nature of government itself.

Thus the 'collected' curriculum is likely to be regulated by less hierarchical structures than would be the 'integrated' curriculum. Where a form of knowledge is provisional or contestable (soft) and not based on pyramids of paradigms and clear evidence (hard), the system governing it will be less determinate. The movement away from disciplines towards areas of study weakens subject boundaries and the forms of academic control over them. It follows that higher education organisation, such as decentralisation, binary systems, more power to rectors, are/should be determined in part by the extent to which they are applicable to the knowledge structures implicit in teaching and research.

The assumption, taken from Geertz (1964) and Archer (1979), that forms of knowledge, feeling or value become shaped and structured into procedures, processes and structures, supports the traditional theory of higher education. The basic generative process in higher education thus links the relative freedom of the individual academic to follow their own curiosity and exercise their own expertise, with institutional requirements for collective decision making and rule setting. Henkel *et al.* (2000), in their evaluation of the Foresight initiative in the UK, have noted how government-steered science policies had in the past often been met with academic scepticism on the grounds that they conflicted with the norms of scientific activity and with well-established beliefs about how science works (Polanyi 1962).

Scientists, philosophers of science and economists tend to stress the logical relationship between epistemologies, the values of scientists and other academics and the distinctive organisational structures within which they work (Polanyi 1962; Dasgupta and David 1994; David 1996). Sociologists of science, though initially promoting these ideas (Merton's classic statement, 1973), later emphasised the influence upon academic values and agendas of dominant societal values and of authority and power and reward structures (Mulkay 1977).

It could be assumed, therefore, that government preferences for particular kinds of knowledge – that which is useful and likely to appeal to the market – will also affect its view of its relationship with universities and how they should be organised. If the government expects universities to be visibly and calculably productive, its perception of them moves from that of the chartered institution driven by intellectual curiosity, and either towards a more hierarchical model of relationships with the state and a managerial view of university internal government, or in the other direction to more market styles of activity and organisation.

Current emphases on particular policy dimensions – lifelong learning, internationalisation and the like – illustrate how the governmental agenda may differ from those of the ablest academics. If the positions were negotiable, there would be no harm in both sets of perspectives coming to the fore. But the increased power of government makes that unlikely.

A further area on which our three national projects did not make a systematic attempt was an assessment of the impact of changes on the machinery and functioning of government itself. We regard this, however, as an important task for political science. Here we merely note our own largely conjectural assumptions in the hope of opening up the subject for future research and analysis.

As governments change to a more determined role, whether facilitatory or command in purpose, this will produce a problem of governability, even when most of the strain is taken by intermediary bodies. It would follow that the assertion of determined policies should require a growth in government's capacity to know the characteristics of the system, its costs, accesses and outcomes.

In fact, government does have more data now because evaluation, quality assurance and selective research allocations entail a growth of knowledge seeking and using capacity. If so how do we typify the kinds of expertise grown by government, if any? What are the backgrounds, expertise and attitudes? How is governmental knowledge distributed, used and organised? Answering these questions in future research projects should shed some light on the changing role of the state in higher education policy making.

Notes

1   These dimensions are a modified version of Susan Marton's model of state governance (cf. S. Marton, forthcoming, *The Mind of the State: The Politics of University Autonomy in Sweden, 1968–1998*, Göteborg Studies in Political Science, Göteborg University).

2   It is important to recognise that although these four types are based on concepts of higher education systems as observed in locations such as Europe, Scandinavia and the USA, they are however theoretical models. The range of theoretically possible choices has been narrowed down to exemplify and epitomise different logics favoured by different systems – but not absolutely or essentially exclusive logics. We recognise that within the same state governing system mixtures of these models may exist at the same time.

Chapter 5

Higher Education Institutions

Berit Askling and Mary Henkel

Introduction

Governments have changed their relationships to the institutions and formulated new kinds of expectations on institutional governance, management and leadership (see Chapter 3). As discussed in Chapter 4, various buffer organisations have been established to bridge governments with institutions. Thus, both government and buffer organisations are framing the space of action for the institutions, both normatively and more directly through changing the nature of regulatory control. This may mean either a tightening or loosening of central control.

There are some striking phenomena in the transformation of higher education systems in our three countries which indicate that institutions in recent years have taken a more central role than previously in the process of transmitting political intentions to academic processes and outcomes.

These phenomena are in part linked with national visions of the function of the higher education system in their societies and with political assumptions about what is required to ensure those functions are fulfilled. As we have seen, such assumptions, in their turn, can be related to concepts of institutional governance and their implications for change processes.

Institutional leaders and managers can be considered mediators between policy and practice. In higher education systems, they can be looked upon as potential agents of change. They form the preconditions and define the space of action for academics' work and perhaps too for their norms and values (an issue to which we will return in later chapters).

The increased authority of higher education institutions, various forms of pressure upon the institutions to become more autonomous (or at least financially independent), the elements of accountability and external control of efficiency and quality, and the expectations of a more pronounced and evident institutional leadership and management seemed to give the institutions quite new roles and functions as public institutions and academic organisations in the higher education systems of today.

In all three countries, the 1990s seemed to represent a period of experimenting with new forms of public control. Buffer organisations were established or reformulated, or closed down and replaced. We identified many instances of *ambiguity, uncertainty* and *conflict* in our studies, as political intentions and expectations were transmitted through the instructions and activities of buffer organisations and then met by steps and measures of institutional governance and management.

Our main questions are: how did the institutions meet the expectations of executive leadership and internal devolution of authority and how did they operationalise their own functions and purposes in domains of knowledge, in academic 'production' and in their concern for quality? The main purpose of this chapter is to analyse our findings on the following issues:

1. The 'normative space' given to higher education institutions in the reforms and their implementation (Bleiklie 1998).

2. The implications of this framing and the institutions' own responses.

3. The 'normative functions' executed by the higher education system – as they might be interpreted from the various manoeuvres and measures of the institutions.

We raise these questions before we return to our basic issue of change: how can we understand the changes that have taken place at the institutional level? What is the role (impact) of these changes in the overall process of transformation in the three countries?

The normative space given to higher education institutions in the reform and their implementation

Although the national contexts differ, there are many elements in common in the national definitions of autonomy (see Chapter 4). There is strong influence from new normative theories of the state, made explicit in notions of New Public Management (Pollitt 1995) and self-regulation (see Kells 1992; Kells and van Vught 1988; van Vught 1989).

However, as elaborated in Chapters 2 and 4, our three country studies show that each national context forms its own framework for the adoption, interpretation and implementation of such ideas. As we have seen, in all three countries the state took on a more controlling role, either through a strengthening of the functions of intermediary bodies or through the strengthening of accountability and quality assurance as enunciated in New Public Management. In Norway, universities were incorporated even more firmly into the Civil Service.

A number of institutional measures directly influenced by this policy were introduced, such as structural reorganisation by mergers of departments into bigger units, the introduction of activity planning and evaluations, and finally the decentralisation and strengthening of leadership on all levels of the university organisation. It led to extensive programmes of measuring individual and organisational performance through national evaluations of programmes and a few extensive evaluations of entire university institutions. One of the characteristics that distinguished this policy from previous policy formulations was the attempt to make academia more transparent through the application of formal and standardised criteria. Such transparency made it possible for non-experts such as university administrators to dominate the evaluative process.

In Sweden, as in England and Norway, the ideological impact of New Public Management was evident when the Conservative government formulated its higher education policy in the early 1990s: a focus on evaluation and control (of quality and efficiency), competition among the institutions and demands on strong institutional leadership. Already in the 1980s, and in response to the increasingly difficult economic situation, public administration was subjected to a decentralisation policy accompanied by a 'management by objectives' philosophy. The Conservative coalition government of 1991–94 accelerated the transformation of the public sector and also the application of the ideas within the higher education sector.

However, after the change of government in 1994 and also in the measures taken by the buffer organisation (the National Agency and its predecessors in the 1990s), the application of the New Public Management policy became less obvious in the official rhetoric. Instead, in the argument for a change from the long tradition of a uniform, public, centrally regulated higher education system to a more autonomous one, 'the self-regulative model' of governance (with its more dialectical relationship between the components in the system) was emphasised.

The role of the state – and its buffer organisation – as a controller and evaluator of the institutions was suppressed and the supportive, encouraging and assisting role of the Agency was reinforced, aimed at helping the institutions to become partners of learning organisations in a self-regulative system. However, this dual role of the Agency has been questioned (Askling and Bauer 1997, 1999; Bohlin and Elzinga 1998; Franke and Frykholm 1998), most recently by the Audit of the Swedish Parliament (1999), which recommended the Agency to concentrate on its evaluative and controlling activities.

Our studies show that in none of the countries did the state manage to keep strictly to the role it gave itself vis-à-vis the higher education institutions. Irrespective of which model of state governance they espoused, and irrespective of their own references to autonomy and freedom, from time to time they broke their own promises and intervened.

Following Maassen (1996) and Maassen and van Vught (1994) the two strategies of state governance, New Public Management and self-regulation, represented alternatives to former models of governance. They differed in at least one important aspect: the underlying assumptions about decision making. Maassen and van Vught distinguish between models of rational planning and self-regulation. The former is based on rational decision making while the latter bases decision making on cybernetic principles.

'The New Public Management ideology is ridden with tension.' When this ideology is to be put into action, it will, accordingly, give rise to quite diverse consequences, depending on how its tensions are balanced in practice. Bleiklie (1998) identifies two kinds of tension:

- the tension between the twin ideas of 'management by objectives' and 'decentralisation'

- the tension between the emphasis put on efficiency and quality.

The self-regulative model of governance is also ridden with tension. Kells and van Vught admit:

> The strategy of self-regulation in higher education has two different faces. It is a combination of two fundamentally different theoretical conceptions ...Aspects of the classical model of central planning and control are combined with aspects of the natural selection model. The result is a hybrid which may be interesting to watch in practice, but which is not very clear from a theoretical point of view. (Kells and van Vught 1988, p.28)

New ideal models of institutional governance

Within the theoretical framework of one or other of the two ideals of state governance, or as efforts to bridge the gap between their contradictory elements, an array of normative models of institutional governance has been launched, such as corporate enterprise, entrepreneurial university, adaptive university and learning university. The models are examples of efforts to find a proper balance between centralisation and decentralisation, between internal (academic) influences and external (corporate and/or market-dominated) influences, between organisational stability and flexibility, all in order to maximise the capacity for institutional development within a frame of state control. They differ not only in their theoretical underpinning, but also in the consequences for the institutional leadership and for the academic staff. They are also more or less congruent with system characteristics in the nations' educational systems.

One model is the university as corporate enterprise. This concept tends to undermine the claims of universities to be exceptional institutions and to perceive the challenges facing them as broadly similar to those of a range of public service agencies in the late twentieth century. It assumes that the solutions are to incorporate modes of working or tools from private sector management theory and practice. As a corporate enterprise a university consists of a strong centralised leadership and different functional (academic, technical and administrative) staff groups which offer public service:

> Since the late 1980s there has been a tendency to emphasise *quality* as a fundamental objective of the corporate enterprise, an idea that apparently is well attuned to more traditional notions about the cultural mission of the modern university. However, the most important expectation confronting the corporate enterprise is *efficiency*... the university as corporate enterprise is a producer of educational and research activities. It is based on the set of ideas that under labels such as 'The New Public Management', 'Management by Objectives' and 'Managerialism' have served as ideological justifications of several public administrative reforms internationally as well as in Norway in the last 10 to 15 years. (Bleiklie *et al.* 2000).

In England, the idea of the university as *corporate enterprise* was directly advocated in the Jarratt Report in 1985 as an alternative to traditional diffuse decision making in universities and departmental (academic) autonomy. Thus, in England and Norway, the corporate enterprise model was advocated as the logical consequence of the New Public Management policy.

Due to environmental complexity, higher education institutions are confronted with external as well as internal challenges. In the metaphor of the *adaptive university*, the need to adjust to a more dynamic and competitive environment is a crucial issue. Institutional governance, management and leadership are considered important elements of the institution's capacity to interact successfully with its environment (Sporn 1999).

In his study of how five European universities which classify themselves as innovative have changed their character in order to become more adaptive, Clark (1998) uses *entrepreneurial* as the key term for characterising the institutions as social systems (p.3). 'An entrepreneurial university, on its own, actively seeks to innovate in how it goes about its business' (p.4). Institutional autonomy, a certain space of action, is in itself not sufficient: 'Autonomous institutions become active institutions when they decide they must explore and experiment with changes in how they are composed and how they react to internal and external demands' (p.5).

Clark emphasises collective actions on all levels as being essential for the transformation processes. Such processes do not reduce the academic legitimacy of the institution. 'Rather [they] can provide resources and infrastructures that build capability beyond what a university would otherwise have, thereby allowing it to subsidise and enact an up-market climb in quality and reputation' (p.5). Yet the entrepreneurial university implies strong leadership which devolves authority while paying respect to academic collegiality.

In many countries the development of quality assurance policies assumes that universities not only adapt to external environmental factors, but also accumulate their own experiences and acquire new knowledge about them, thus becoming *learning organisations.* Dill (1998) takes the organisation as the learning subject and argues for a collectively shared knowledge base of knowledge about the organisation and its purposes, processes and outcomes. In this respect his argumentation is close to Clark's. Senge (1990) focuses more on the individual staff member in his encouragement of organisational learning and development. In Senge's terminology, a learning organisation is an organisation where people at all levels work collectively to enhance their capacity to create things they want to create (Ramsden 1998, p. 118).

This concept has mainly found expression in theoretical writing, but our project found traces of its adoption by the Swedish system and some institutions. In Sweden, the learning organisation model provided the frame of reference for the National Agency's audits. The learning university metaphor is a logical consequence of a self-regulation policy, in which 'the logic of the cybernetic perspective in decision-making is reinforced, and the principle of feedback is emphsasised' (Bauer *et al.* 1999, p.184).

The models mentioned above are introduced and argued for, or recommended, in many national contexts as expectations are placed on institutional governance, leadership and management. They have been introduced as modifications of collegially-based models of institutional governance within the framework of changing forms of state governance. Another common element is the emphasis on strong institutional leadership. One main difference between the models is how much a collectively shared knowledge of the institution itself and its goals, processes and outcomes is emphasised as a precondition for successful implementation. Another difference is to what extent external pressure or internal capacity is emphasised as a point of departure in the argumentation.

The idealistic stance of the models, the duality of leadership and collectivism and of autonomy and external control have contributed to the sense of uncertainty, and sometimes confusion, we noted in all three countries among leaders and staff members when the institutions tried to shape their own models of institutional governance. In addition, what is lacking is critical empirical analysis of how they fit one particular national context and structural characteristics of the institutions, such as size, number of schools and faculties and historical preconditions (Askling and Kristensen 2000).

The institutions' responses on leadership, organisation and internal relationships

In all three countries the tendency towards a 'centralised decentralisation' at institutional level was evident, although, as pointed out in the previous section, the underlying normative assumptions about state–institution relationship differed, as did the choice of the model of institutional governance. There was tension between management for control and management for innovation, management for quality and management for efficiency, bureaucratic or more democratic management, managerial and academic values, academic criteria of quality or more market-defined criteria.

Institutional leadership

A key element in the new models of institutional governance was the strengthening of institutional leadership. In all three countries the power of the university boards also increased, as did the proportion of external representatives. The expectations of strong institutional leadership had implications for individuals in leadership positions, for the allocation of authority and decision-making power and for the organisational structure of the institutions.

The simultaneous expansion in student numbers, restrictions in funding and dependency on additional and external sources of funding propelled institutional leaders to become spokespersons for their institutions with the state, and also brokers in various new areas, as well as internal negotiators between different parts of the institution, although this was always true in the UK (Becher and Kogan 1980).

In England, the Jarratt recommendation was that vice-chancellors should be chief executives and thus be in charge of a hierarchy of academics rather than leading a collegium. Deans and heads of departments would report to the vice-chancellor as line managers. Vice-chancellors moved from the role of academic leadership to that of institutional management, although, as pointed out in a recent study of vice-chancellors, 'academic leadership remains an ambiguous yet vital component of executive leadership' (Smith *et al.* 1999, p.304).

In Norway, a main objective of reform was to change the way in which institutions were governed. As a consequence of the adoption of the New Public Management policy with its tools of governance (management by objectives, activity planning and performance control), the leadership at all levels of the university organisation was to be strengthened.

In Sweden, too, the rector had to shape a new style of academic leadership and establish a new and unfamiliar kind of relationship to the university board and to academics in order to meet the expectations of leading an expanding, innovative, quality-minded and self-regulated institution. At the same time, the government's role changed. The state retired (although not always in a predictable manner) from being the monolithic commissioner, planner, provider and protector of the higher education system, its institutions and its staff members. However, it left the institutions – and thus also the rectors – more exposed in an arena in which the state is just one (although the major) actor.

The relationship to members of the academic community also changed. Formerly, the ideal university leader was a collegial co-ordinator who claimed authority in his or her capacity as a member of an egalitarian and autonomous disciplinary community. Institutional leadership was now seen as a task radically different from research and teaching. 'One of the genuine challenges for any head of institution is to ensure there is a balance between managerial accountability and giving a say to the academic community' (Kogan and Hanney 1999, p.195).

The Swedish study tells us that the devolution of authority to the institutions was positively received by the institutional leaders. However, many leaders found that they were not prepared for the complexity of tasks and the intense tempo of the job. They were left to themselves in defining the rules of the game and in formulating their own roles, with no earlier models from which to get guidance. Although an initial key word of the change was 'freedom', many of them found that the word 'responsibility' was more appropriate.

The traditional sets of rituals and properties which helped their predecessors to overcome initial insecurity apparently lost their magic in a landscape of internal and external negotiations and lobbying. Neither the honour of being elected as a *primus inter pares* nor recognition of the generosity involved in doing a duty or 'community service' generated enough support to carry the institutional leader safely through his or her term of mandate. Many institutional leaders felt that, although their positions were temporary, when their term of office (mandate) came to an end they would probably have changed so much both personally and professionally that there would be no return for them to their former life as an academic. It is however too early to draw the conclusion that a new career ladder has opened.

Again, however, we must note differences between the UK and the other two countries. The vice-chancellors had always been a kind of public notable, and this partly reflected the incorporated or chartered status of the institutions they led. They were also appointed, not elected, until retirement. Now their role was further reinforced with executive power and the enhancement of existing privileges of pay, car and house which constituted a definite pulling away from the professoriat.

There were indications in the three studies that the changed rector's role also had an impact on appointment procedures. Criteria for the election or appointment of academic leaders shifted from the procedural ('now it's the turn for a person from the Faculty of Law to take over the responsibilities of a rector') towards the more individualistic ('we need a person who is a visionary and strong leader'). The internal hierarchy, based on scholarly reputation, was replaced by a more unofficial institutional hierarchy based on a personal reputation as a dynamic and successful research manager. Such attributes as leadership and management skills were now of at least equal importance as academic reputation and a distinguished appearance.

Internal devolution of authority

The increase in institutional responsibilities called for measures to strengthen their central executive capacity. Some rectors began to build senior management teams around themselves, or to introduce vice-rector positions and form advisory groups with a predominance of academics. In Sweden, at some of the large universities, a delicate question was whether power was to be concentrated at the top of the entire institution, at the rector's office or with deans of faculties.

The new model of governance brought about an increased and heavy administrative workload at all levels within the institutions. Responsibilities expanded and administrative tasks became more complex and challenging. Academics themselves spent more time on developing and complying with procedures and rules, as well as on data collection and transfer for institutional purposes. In British universities, 'the earlier simple diarchical assumptions of how institutional tasks are performed, however, no longer hold. Academics move into system management, and administrators increasingly help create the policy and procedural frames for academic work' (Kogan and Hanney 1999, p.197). The same statement also held for Norway and Sweden.

In all three countries, from the perspective of the academics, concentration of power, either with the institution or the faculty or schools, was often interpreted as an increase in bureaucratisation, irrespective of whether the bureaucrats were academic colleagues or administrators (Kogan 1999). This kind of bureaucratisation implied a form of transparency of academics' work. In particular, the many elements of accountability, assessment, evaluation and control contributed to the negative attitudes to 'bureaucratisation'.

Accountability had in some respects been made clearer. In the UK, it was linked most directly to financial delegation. Budgets were devolved and deans and heads of department were made accountable for the management of resources, as faculties and departments were designated, variously, cost, budget or resource centres. However, they were not necessarily allocated the income that they had earned or, if they were, they were not necessarily given total freedom to decide how to spend it.

In Sweden, financial responsibilities had also been devolved to different levels. However, because of gradual reduction in the unit of resource since the mid-1980s, those given these responsibilities felt that financial control simply meant dealing with deficits.

The internal organisation

To the growing bureaucratisation (in terms of a concentration of power to executives, who might be recruited from academics or from the professional administrators) must also be added the tendency (at least at the large universities) to create special support units. These were sometimes staffed with highly specialised academics (teaching/learning centres, research policy centres, quality development centres, evaluation centres, centres for external affairs). Sometimes, however, administrators moved into these roles. Such units formed a new kind of inter-faculty network organisation crossing the traditional hierarchical academic line structure (faculty–department–basic unit). The units also illustrated another trend, namely that the traditional division between academics and administrators, and between academic tasks and administrative tasks, had become an oversimplification.

Such cross-cutting units were looked upon with scepticism by many academics, who believed that a disproportionate level of resources was spent on these new bodies, as compared with the small amount allocated to the departments and basic units 'where the real work is done'. They felt, too, that institutional policies and 'solutions', rather than the academics' own values, guided the decisions which were taken.

Another kind of extraordinary unit was also emerging for entrepreneurial reasons. These were to make it easier for teachers or researchers to respond to external opportunities to mount profit-making activities by freeing them from bureaucratic practices and chores. They represented the organisational and value tensions with which academic institutions were now working.

A significant feature in all three countries was the merging of departments. Small departments were vulnerable in the context of external assessments and internal planning and efficiency criteria. In Norway mergers of university departments (one of the key elements of the New Policy Management policy) were proposed by the Minister of Education and actively promoted by the university leaders. The idea of economy of scale gained wide acceptance, in spite of some research evidence that economies of scale were not always secured (Kyvik 1991).

The normative function of the higher education system: institutional intepretations

The quality issue

The drastic expansion of student numbers and institutions, in combination with restricted economy, led to a political concern for quality in almost all European countries. We have also seen that quality aims and definitions easily become displaced by efficiency in certain conceptions of higher education institutions.

Until the 1980s, it had been assumed in all three countries that quality was a matter for internal regulation by academics, who in turn took for granted what quality meant and that its sustenance was inherent in academic values and modes of organisation (e.g. Scott

1994). Here we consider to what extent higher education institutions had installed it in their policy and management agendas, how far this was reflected in institutional structures and processes in the 1980s and 1990s and, to the extent that it was, how far this was a function of state policies. We will also review the balance between the influence upon institutions of informal judgements of quality and formal measurements of quality that might elide into measurements of efficiency or output.

England moved rapidly from a position in which the state had virtually no direct interest in assuring quality in universities to one in which quality requirements were imposed by law. If the justification for the extensive use of quality assurance procedures lay in the massification of higher education, it was also strongly associated in the UK with government efficiency and public accountability goals for higher education.

The British experience was that quality assurance was the most potent of the change agents among the elements in the New Public Management policy. A major reason for this was the external, transparent and compulsory nature of the quality assurance policies established. Quality assurance of institutional policies and structures remained in the hands of the quality council (HEQC) formed by the institutions themselves, but even the exercises (or 'academic audits') conducted under these auspices were experienced as external. However, they had neither the significance nor the publicity attached to the Higher Education Funding Councils' assessment of research (RAE) and teaching quality (TQA). In the case of both these forms of assessment, peer judgements were converted, along with other quantitative measures, into published gradings of subject groups or departments in all institutions. These in turn were incorporated into public, albeit unofficial, league tables and widely recognised markers of institutional reputations within and beyond the higher education system. The academic quality of institutions and departments became transparent and open to external interpretation in a way that was without precedent and could affect institutions' entrée into a range of markets.

Assessment of the quality of teaching was mandatory for all subject providers in higher education, although the systematic link with funding intended by government had not been made by the end of the century. However, participation in the RAE was a condition of eligibility for the receipt of research money from the Funding Council and the amount of this money was tied to the RAE grading.

It was, therefore, not surprising that quality assurance (particularly in the field of research) was among the most important drivers of the policies and structural arrangements of almost all higher education institutions. Senior academic management made direct interventions into faculty and departmental strategies for quality assessments. Committee structures, support units and institutional review arrangements were established with a view to maximising the institutions' and departments' performance in external quality assurance exercises. Academic recruitment, reward and conditions of service policies were increasingly influenced by the RAE.

The RAE, and TQA too, made individual and departmental performance transparent within as well as outside the institution. This meant that institutions had new bases from which to make judgements about the relative quality of their departments and the contribution they were making to the institution. In some cases, they could mean that traditional pecking orders were brought into question.

In a sense it could be said that quality judgements were converted into quasi-performance indicators and became among the most influential of such indicators within institutions. Performance indicators had, as we have seen, been incorporated into higher education in the UK with the Jarratt Report in the mid-1980s. However, whereas, like quality assurance, they were originally associated with government's aims to exert greater control over higher education in the name of economy, efficiency and effectiveness, by the mid-1990s their main value had come to be regarded as tools of internal institutional management (Cave *et al.* 1997; Jarratt 1985).

In Norway, the Hernes Commission tried in 1988 to introduce a policy in which academic quality was clearly emphasised in addition to quantitative dimensions, such as student numbers and number of institutions. Although the origins of this policy lay in a media controversy provoked by Hernes' criticism in 1987 of Norwegian higher education as mediocre, the proposals of the Commission were welcomed in academia. Quality improvement was also to be supported by an increase in resources. However, the student influx fundamentally disrupted this policy.

Instead, as we have seen, there was a strong emphasis in Norwegian policies on mechanisms associated with New Public Management, management by objectives, academic activity planning and evaluation against pre-set goals, and the use of performance indicators. Potentially such developments could make the institutions vulnerable to increased external control, again through the power of transparency and the potential linkage between performance and resource allocation. They certainly provoked debate in the universities, some of it on these lines, but it was organised round different issues. In Oslo, objections focused on questioning whether universities should formulate goals at all or on the issue of who would be qualified to evaluate how far the goals of an academic institution had been achieved. In Bergen, the debate centred on externally defined performance indicators and the dangers of defining quality in administrative terms.

However, so far, neither performance indicators nor activity plans seem to have given rise to the drastic consequences that some opponents feared. Activity plans were considered a time-consuming administrative ritual rather than a control instrument representing a threat to academic freedom. Meanwhile, although performance indicators were developed and some were linked to funding, it was felt that because some, at least, were conflicting, it was not too difficult to maintain a rather diffuse picture of performance.

In Sweden, concern for quality was a central constituent (and became almost the central one) in the reform of higher education at the beginning of the 1990s and was firmly associated by the policy makers with freedom for the institutions, rather than control. Each institution was required to develop its own system for quality assurance and, as in England, this stimulated the development of new internal structures. Committees were established at the centre of the institutions and responsibilities for quality assurance devolved in varying degrees to faculties and departments in different institutions.

However, that did not mean a simple shift towards professional co-ordination of quality, as against that of the state or the market. Originally, students were meant to become a strong market force through their free choice of programmes and institutions. This intention was hindered by restricted admission. It had, however, become an important driver for academic development in institutions in the form of curriculum development. In Sweden both undergraduate student numbers and graduation rates became performance indicators on which resource allocations were based. This proved an effective incentive for institutions to devise new interdisciplinary programmes thought likely to attract good students.

The Conservative government also proposed originally that five per cent of resource allocation to institutions should be based on quality. This was abandoned as impracticable and a new proposal calling for audits of the institutions' quality development programmes was accepted. As mentioned earlier, they were put into effect in a way that respected the idea of a self-regulative system, the learning organisation model and the need for internal systematic quality assurance and self-evaluation programmes. So far, there is much yet to be accomplished in that respect in Swedish universities. There are still signs of a predominantly individualistic view of quality, which might reflect a lack of awareness about and perhaps ignorance of the requirements of self-regulation.

It therefore remains to be seen whether the policies in Sweden based on trust and self-regulation can be more successful in embedding quality assurance into institutions and integrating it into academic conceptions of core values and activities than policies based on financial incentives and on managerialist and coercive strategies. This issue will be pursued in Chapters 6 and 7.

Towards uniformity or differentiation in aims and functions?

In England, the activities of intermediary bodies, in particular the funding councils, created pressures towards conformity and competition between institutions within defined parameters. However, at the same time, the institutions were encouraged to operate in less bounded areas, a key driver being income generation. New partnerships with the private sector were encouraged and new levels of collaboration and partnership were opened up in research and education programmes. Many institutions saw the development of taught postgraduate programmes as an area in which there was more freedom for new initiatives than in undergraduate degrees, which were subject to government control on frequently shifting principles.

The abolition of the binary divide, together with the massive increase in student numbers in the 1980s and early 1990s, meant increased diversity in higher education in the UK, but within a system that was always informally highly stratified and had now become more explicitly so. Institutions varied widely in the extent to which they could take control of their destinies. This was partly a matter of whether they had adopted the kind of active innovative strategic management identified by Clark (1998). However, it was also a matter of the intellectual and physical capital accrued by different institutions. Some could exploit new and lucrative markets or funding opportunities, confident that they could subsume them within their own academic agendas and cultures. Others might find their choices more restricted.

In Norway, the strong binary divide between universities and state colleges was beginning to weaken. It is to be expected, however, that, as in England, informal stratification might ensue with degrees of research selectivity being applied. This might be mitigated by regional disposal of research funds.

In Sweden, after the radical deregulation of 1993, the higher education system was moving towards increased variation in students, programmes, teaching tasks, research activities, knowledge areas and additional assignments. The renewal of programmes and courses reflects a substantial shift from a disciplinary to a more inter-disciplinary structured education. A substantial number of interdisciplinary and interfaculty activities were introduced. The number of external funders was increased.

Not only did systems become more diversified, but so did variation between faculties, departments and groups of academics. As the departments were encouraged to extend their activities to new markets and new funders, the successful strengthened their position vis-à-vis the institutional leaders. Appeals to institutions to improve their academic quality and increase their external incomes also brought about tensions and imbalance between successful and less successful faculties and departments.

Increased market dependency might also cause internal tensions and raise the temperature within the institutions, as 'the market' is not a uniform phenomenon acting in a uniform way on the entire institution. On the contrary, different parts of an institution interact with different kinds of markets and different kinds of external actors (public and private). An active interplay with external markets can provide such faculties as technology and medicine (and individual departments) substantial extra income for teaching and, not least, for research, while such faculties (schools) as divinity and education obtain only a percentage of their total income from external sources, mainly in terms of contract teaching and in-service training for the public sector. Thus, behind the facade of the institution as an entity, the economic power is unevenly distributed.

Conclusions

The reconstruction of intermediary bodies in our three countries during the 1980s and 1990s reflected a search for an adequate balance between institutional autonomy and governmental control, and between internal (academic) initiatives and external (state and market) influences.

In England and Norway, differing components of New Public Management, with all of its ambiguities, challenged previous state–institutional relationships, as did the corporate enterprise model affect institutional governance and organisation. In Sweden, the ideas of self-regulative governance and a perception of the ideal institution as a learning organisation were adopted. However, in all three countries, as noted earlier, irrespective of the model which they adopted, reactions of ambiguity, uncertainty and conflict at the state and institutional top level, and (as will be evident in the following chapters) among the academics, were evident when increased autonomy was to be exercised by the institutions.

How can we explain the differences between England, Norway and Sweden in the choices of strategies and models of state governance?

One explanation may be the overall structures of the higher education system. Although both the Norwegian and Swedish higher education systems developed in the continental tradition with strong governments and strong faculties, they differed in two main respects. Like England, Norway had a diversified higher education system in which the differences between institutions were not concealed but, on the contrary, considered an important element of its regional policy. In Sweden, the national equivalence of all higher education examinations was a core characteristic ever since the first universities were established. The adoption of New Public Management also implied acceptance of the notions of evaluation and control, which would reveal inequalities between institutions, whether signalled in quality terms or not. In Sweden, as we have seen, the government and the National Agency hesitated in this respect. The political intention to guarantee national uniformity and equivalence prevented the Social Democrat government and the Agency from a straightforward implementation of evaluative measures which might allow for institutional ranking and simple benchmarking.

Another explanation focuses on the different traditions of evaluation and assessment. In both England and Norway external examination was a regular constituent. In Norway that tradition probably contributed to the readiness for the recent emphasis on evaluation of various kinds (a strong element in the New Public Management policy). In the UK the polytechnics were already subject to rigorous evaluation and this might have made it easier for it to be imposed on the universities with which they drew level in status. In Sweden there was no tradition of external evaluation and assessment, as extensive central planning activities and firm regulations were considered a guarantee of national equivalence (Askling and Bauer 1999).

The role of the intermediary bodies and how data from their evaluative activities were used in the allocation of resources also differed between countries. In England, data from the intermediary bodies were linked directly to allocation of resources. In Norway the activities of the institutions became more transparent. Evaluations and annual reports were used in the annual negotiations between government and the institutions (although in a soft and formal manner), while in Sweden the government did not explicitly refer to data from the National Agency's evaluations and audits when it allocated resources.

The effects of quality assurance on institutional behaviour were marked. In Sweden it pointed the way to self-evaluation, if precariously installed, and the notion of the self-learning organisation. In the UK, it strengthened the power of the institution and influenced the criteria by which academics were judged and made judgements. The power of evaluation was particularly reinforced in the UK where the link between research assessment and selective funding was strong. In Sweden, the rewards attached to graduation rates encouraged new forms of curriculum development.

A particular source of governmental ambivalence might have had its roots in governments' deliberate efforts to use the higher education system as a tool for welfare policy (to increase the total number of student enrolments and at the same time recruit new – non-privileged – categories of students). At the same time, governments relied on the innovative capacity of the institutions and their academics for the necessary renewal of programmes and courses to meet the demands of the knowledge society. The first intention was best supported by central regulations, the second one by devolution of authority. In this respect, the Swedish government was less confident in its self-regulative model of governance than the governments of England and Norway, who were more consistent in their reliance on New Public Management policy or other measures of control.

Thus, historical and present contextual conditions influenced which national policy was launched, what particular policy instruments were selected and what measures taken.

How can we explain the ambiguity and uncertainty of some institutional leaders and the many examples of tensions and conflicts within the institutions when institutional autonomy is to be put into use?

The change in the relationship between the institutions and the state was probably greater in Sweden than in either Norway or England. Institutional leaders in our Swedish interviews admitted how badly prepared they felt for their new role and how they also noticed that they changed perspective during their period of duty. They witnessed an initial lack of knowledge about how their own organisations worked and were intended to work in their higher education systems – and, referring to academics in general, a kind of ignorance about how thoroughly the whole situation had changed in the last ten years. Institutional leaders in Norway and England may also have experienced some unexpressed difficulties, but the transitions they were required to make were somewhat less drastic.

However, the challenges facing all of them were considerable. They had to find ways of enabling much enlarged institutions, unused to developing generic, institution-wide policies, to become sufficiently strong and coherent entities to manage new demands. At the same time, they had to ensure that their institutions were intellectually stronger and more ambitious than in the past, in cultures where a primary belief was that intellectual power was rooted in individual academic autonomy (see Chapter 7). In some instances, institutional leaders were required to steer their institutions through a change of status, which implied the adoption of a research culture in what had been an educational culture.

As Dill (1998) put it, although universities had long experiences as centres for knowledge creation and application for the larger society, they had not seen the necessity for developing and transferring knowledge for improving their own basic processes.

Overall, our study suggests that the consequences for the institutions of the changed relation to the state have, at least from the perspective of many institutions, been an overlooked aspect of institutional autonomy.

PART III

Academics in a Context of Policy and System Change

Chapter 6

Policy Change
and the Academic Profession

Roar Høstaker

In this chapter we will discuss the consequences of the policy changes for the academic profession in the three countries. An important starting point is to analyse the differences in the constitution in the three countries. We can also ask whether the notion of 'academic profession' is a viable one. Hence the weight is given to analyses of integrative and disintegrative forces of the profession. The main focus is what sort of common markers and points of identification are constructed within the profession and what relations may weaken the strength of such common points of identification. The first part of the chapter sketches the historical constitution of the academic professions in each of the three countries leading to the eve of the reforms in the 1980s and 1990s. The second part presents the main lines of reform policies with reference to the conditions of the academic profession in each country. A closer look at certain effects of the reform policies is taken in the third part of the chapter in which we discuss changes concerning hierarchisation within the profession, divides between disciplines and becoming an academic.

In many ways the academic professions in England, Sweden and Norway may be said not to be fully professionalised. In the literature on professions it is usually emphasised that in order to be useful as a concept, there should be some characteristic that distinguishes a 'profession' as an occupational group from other closely related groups. There must be some sort of cohesion between the members of the group. Usually groups such as the Anglo-American professions of doctors and lawyers serve as master templates for what to look for: common educational background, autonomy in professional questions, protection through certification, a strong professional association and a common occupational ethos (Abbot 1988; Erichsen 1997; Johnson 1982; Parsons 1939; Torgersen 1994; Wilensky 1964).

Compared with such classical professions as doctors and lawyers, the notion of an academic profession may be problematic. It is important to see this notion in our context more like an open question or a regulative idea for our investigation. Professional and disciplinary allegiances may represent alternative points of identification for university teachers that impede the emergence of a specific academic profession. An academic profession must somehow be united across disciplinary boundaries and extramural professional obligations. Integrating forces may emerge from the fact that academics are situated within the same type of institutions and therefore have many relations in common. The nature of these relations and the extent to which they promote cohesion and common points of identification are the topic of this chapter.

Status before the reform periods

Until the early 1980s academics in England may be seen as the one most closely resembling the classical professional ideal (cf. above). Universities were governed by academics as self-governed corporations. Historically, endowments had been the main source of income, but since the 1920s grants from the state became more and more important and by 1980 the major part of university incomes were such grants. This system relied upon a sort of contract with society (a corporatist bargain in Cawson's 1983 term) in which universities gave young people an education and made research for the benefit of all, while the government supported those activities. The allocation of funds were made by the UGC as an intermediary body controlled by academic representatives.

The professional ethos of the modern English academics was formed in the nineteenth century and centred around the gentlemanly amateur. This was an ideal derived from the social classes that sent their sons to university at the time: their sons were usually expected to complete their training as self-sustained gentlemen, not to learn a trade. General education was preferred to specialist training for a specific occupation. This ideal was coupled to pedagogic practices of small group tutoring and a continuation of the guild tradition of students living at colleges or residential halls under the supervision of their teachers. Universities attempted to continue these professional ideals and practices through the expansion of the universities in the late nineteenth century ('redbrick' universities) and after World War II (the 'greenfield' universities). This continuation of ideals was maintained through the employment of mainly Oxbridge graduates as teachers and academic leaders. Although universities established after World War II were less well endowed than the older ones, they attempted, at least to a degree, to attain some of the same ideals of small-scale teaching and communal living (Halsey and Trow 1971). The Robbins Report of 1963 initiated an increased expansion for universities, but also a redefinition of their clientele. Higher education was supposed to be open to all who were qualified for it. This pledge for open access was seen to be the universities' contribution to a democratisation of education [1]. The main effect on the profession was to change its outlook from being private, elite and eclectic to becoming more open and socially responsive by 1970 (Becher and Kogan 1992, pp.32–33). Another interpretation of this development is that of proletarianisation of a professional group (Halsey 1992). A historical decline of status and wages throughout most of the twentieth century gradually forced the profession to find new social alliances. This alliance was in Halsey's view formed when the major teacher union, the AUT, joined the TUC (1992).

The basis of the academic professions in Sweden and Norway was quite different from the English one. In both cases universities followed the continental pattern of being state institutions. Their raison d'être was to educate civil servants for the state and the professoriate, who until the 1950s represented the majority of university employees. Their professional activities were regulated by ordinances concerning the institutions, degree structure and exams and the general legislation concerning civil servants. Within this framework, however, there was considerable leeway for autonomous decision making and self-regulation. In the Norwegian case, academics have not been seen as a separate profession, but rather as a part of the university-educated class (*Akademikerne*) which in the nineteenth century was almost synonymous with the civil service class or estate (cf. Aubert *et al.* 1960, 1962). This educated class was subdivided into each of its disciplinary professions: medical doctors, theologians, jurists, engineers and lecturers in upper secondary education [2]. For most of the nineteenth century this educated class also remained the political elite in Norway, which gave it a prominent place in the political and social development of the country.

The pedagogical ideals of Norwegian and Swedish academics were quite different from those of the English. The ideal of the self-sustained gentleman had no influence and the main purpose of attending a university was to learn a trade. Compared with English universities there was little teaching and scant attention given to the students' written work, except at the advanced stages. In accordance with the continental university model, teaching was mainly given as lectures in auditoriums and assessment of students concentrated on examinations. While small group teaching and writing of essays were central to the English system, the continental model in its Swedish and Norwegian form was concentrated around the syllabus. The syllabus may be seen as a contract between teacher and student, and the function of the examination was to test whether the student had read and understood the syllabus. The teacher was, however, constrained by the syllabus in the formulation of examination questions and had to remain within its boundaries in order to keep his part of the contract (cf. e.g. Øverland 1988). Between the time the students started to study a certain topic and the *dies irae* of the examination day, they remained in a sort of limbo with few, if any, signs of how they were living up to the expectations of their teachers. A certain level of failure was expected in such a system and it was common for some students to take exams more than once to improve their results.

From the 1950s the overall characteristics of the academic professions in Sweden and Norway started to diverge, as universities and the state chose to meet the expansion of student numbers in different ways. From the late 1950s and through the whole of the 1960s the number of students increased significantly. The initial response to the growing demand for teaching was the same in both countries – to increase the number of teachers. Here the similarity stops. In the same way as Finland, Sweden introduced a large number of adjunct teachers and lecturers during this period. This situation led to a division of labour within the academic profession between those academics who do undergraduate teaching (lecturers and adjunct teachers) and those whose main task is to do research and teach at graduate level (professors, research assistants). Lecturers and adjunct teachers had few possibilities to undertake research as their teaching loads were heavy. At the same time there was a substantial increase in external funding for research. For those academics who primarily wanted to do research, external funding was a way to avoid too much teaching. In this way two different career patterns developed among Swedish academics; one oriented towards teaching and one for research. The latter often included periods of external funding in order to qualify for a professorship.

The Norwegian academic profession developed in a pattern closer to its Danish counterpart and went through a process of homogenisation and equalisation of status and working conditions. By the 1950s there were demands that the different categories of the 'middle group' of the positional hierarchy, amanuensises (sciences), prosektors (medicine) and lecturers (arts and sciences), should have the same opportunity to do research. Lecturers had at the time more teaching than members of the other categories, but many of them managed to pursue a considerable amount of research. At the same time the holders of research positions of prosektor and amanuensis also taught. It was seen as 'natural' that the duties of the categories should be equalised, with about half their work time devoted to research and the other half to teaching. During the 1960s a homogenisation of work conditions according to the principles of a 50–50 partition of work between teaching and research de facto took place in many departments. In 1969 some of these changes were taken into the regulations concerning these positions.

The homogenisation and equalisation of status and work conditions did not stop at the level of the middle tier, but also engulfed the professoriate. Radicalisation of both students and the middle tier from the late 1960s led to demands for democratisation of university departments and faculties. Norwegian universities were at the time based upon the principle of the professor governing a department. The faculty board mainly consisted of the chairs of each department and the university board consisted of the deans from each faculty and the university leadership. The chair governed the department on behalf of the university board. Already in the early 1970s the authority of professors to make recommendations on appointments of middle-tier staff (and in fact to control them) was thwarted by the introduction of multi-member assessment committees, and from 1975 the chair became an elected office. The boards at department level, faculty level and university level became representative organs in which all tenured staff became one of several groups represented [3]. The tenured staff jointly controlled over 50 per cent of the seats to all boards. This election system added to the homogenisation of the profession by making it clear that only co-operation would secure common interests, and at the same time the main status divide in the profession became between those with tenure and those without. The gradual homogenisation of the profession also effaced formal workload differences between the professoriate and the middle tier and a professorship became formally attainable for all middle tier personnel by becoming a title open for promotions according to qualifications in 1991 (Overland 1988, Chap.9).

The development of the academic profession in Norway from the 1960s to the 1980s may be characterised as an ascent of the middle tier, and the profession itself was the main policy maker in this process. Many professors supported the middle tier and even took part in their own 'downfall' (Overland 1988, Chap.9). In Sweden educational planning and politics were much more centralised and professional wishes in favour of research opportunities for lecturers were not heard.

The divide between teaching and research was strengthened by the 1977 reform in which undergraduate education was taken out of the control of the disciplines and departments. Undergraduate education was subordinated to professionally oriented and centrally defined study tracks. These tracks had their own boards (*linjenämnder*) and administrative personnel. The boards had representatives from the relevant departments, but also from students, non-academic staff and the professional field relevant for the track. Although the authority of the professoriate was thwarted at undergraduate level by this dispersion of powers, the governance of departments and at the graduate education level still retained many of its traits from the chair-faculty system.

In England and Norway the departments and disciplines retained control over undergraduate education. In England undergraduate education was, in many ways, seen as the core activity of an academic group at a university. When it came to governance English university departments were traditionally less centralised around a chair holder than on the continent, and individual members enjoyed a greater degree of autonomy (Neave and Rhoades 1987). The traditions of the universities varied. Halsey and Trow (1971, Chap.14) point to the redbrick universities as following a much more continental pattern as late as the 1960s. There may also have been differences between the disciplines in this respect. Nevertheless, the higher degree of equality among members was probably one of the reasons why the English academic profession, aside from politicisation in the 1970s and a more socially responsive attitude, was less changed as a result of the expansion period of the 1960s than was the case in Sweden and Norway. While the Swedish university department modified its chair-faculty structure, the Norwegian department saw a lapse into a situation with little formal academic authority whatever. All tenured staff could be elected head of department[4] and the task mainly entailed administrative work. An evaluation of the position of Norwegian department chairs from a British perspective was given in the NAVF[5] evaluation of English studies. The evaluators concluded that 'there is a lack of good basis for leadership within the department given the short span of office'[6], and the function of the chair is often 'as a committee leader without much accepted authority' whatsoever[7].

The academic professions on the brink of the political reforms of the 1980s and 1990s were thus very different. The divide between teaching and research was well established in Sweden, while the same divide largely followed institutional status in Britain and Norway. The academic professions on the brink of the political reforms of the 1980s and 1990s differed greatly.

From 1966 a new sector of higher education was constructed in the UK led by the polytechnics governed by local councils and regulated by the Council for National Academic Awards (CNAA). These were institutions in which the staff were not expected to do research (Becher and Kogan 1992: pp.29–32), although it was not formally restricted. Similar developments came in Norway as professional colleges (teacher training, nursing, social work, etc.) were upgraded to higher education standards in the 1970s and early 1980s. A specific case is the new institutions of district colleges. These institutions were supposed to offer teaching at undergraduate level and not engage in research. Many of the academics in these institutions managed a considerable amount of research and gradually their terms of employment, i.e. their opportunity to do research, became equal to those of university academics (Jerdal 1996). The line struck between teaching and research institutions thus to some degree eroded.

The reforms

The reform processes in the UK from the early 1980s and in Sweden and Norway, both from the late 1980s, diverged in many aspects. Compared with changes in the condition of the academic profession in England, the reforms in Sweden and Norway only scratched the surface. The reform period in the UK may be said to have started in 1981 when the UGC was left to handle a severe cut in funding and chose to reduce the number of places at universities by 20,000 students instead of reducing the unit of resource for each student. This happened at a time of peak demand from school leavers (Becher and Kogan 1992, p.42; Kogan and Kogan 1983). This decision forced many universities to lay off teachers.

Further cuts were imposed on the universities in the years to come and left many of them with few alternatives to increasing their student numbers, while staffing ratios decreased, and to seek alternative incomes from contract research, consultancies and by enrolling students from non-EU countries. There was a dramatic increase in students and a simultaneous fall in staff–student ratios, especially in the years from 1988 to 1995 . During the same period the *per capita* funding of students was reduced (Fulton 1999). These changed circumstances had dramatic effects on the working conditions of many English academics, but these were unevenly felt between universities as each had different options available to them to counter the cuts in grants with incomes from other sources such as endowments (especially Oxford and Cambridge), research funding or from selectively allocated core funding.

The government's policies were not to reduce quality at universities, but to get value for money and to make universities more fit for different purposes. Increasing division between teaching and research was often a consequence, and the polytechnics were favoured by the government as they were more responsive to its wishes for occupationally relevant teaching. While the government tried from the mid-1980s to increase its direct hold on universities by better control of the financing bodies and through common legislation, the policy changed in the late 1980s to a stronger strand of marketisation. All institutions should compete for the same resources on the same market and would thereby be able to strengthen their specific qualities (Fulton 1999). A logical conclusion of that policy was to elevate the polytechnics to university status in 1992 (the 1992 universities) and to integrate them in the same funding system under the HEFCE. From 1985 the universities had competed for research funding through the RAE in which they were graded according to quality (cf. below). During the 1990s the distribution of research grants was to an increasing degree to the benefit of those universities with the highest grades. Most of the 1992 universities did poorly in the RAE and gained very little research funding. The ratio between teaching and research grants from the HEFCE differed between universities from 267:1 at one extreme to 0.72:1 at the other for the allocation for the academic year of 1999–2000 (Fulton 1999, pp.5–6). These numbers indicate the huge differences between universities in their rate of funding and their opportunities to combine research and teaching.

For a foreign observer it is striking to what degree all sorts of decisions in English universities are made with reference to financial considerations. This 'financialisation' of academic relations may be a particular trait of the development of the academic profession in England. It reflects not only the pecuniary problems of English universities, but also the new corporate bargain between universities and the state. The possibility of the state to regulate relations at universities by decree is quite limited, and the government has to use indirect measures linked to financing to succeed. Academic strategies are thus formed according to the possibility of achieving financial rewards or of avoiding financial punishments.

The reform processes in Sweden had much less dramatic consequences for the academic profession than in the English case. The major aim of the Swedish reforms has been twofold: to reduce centralised governance of university relations; and to increase the quality of teaching and research in higher education institutions. Both of these issues for the most part concerned academic leaders and administrators who were now left more to their own initiatives and had a greater responsibility than before. The quality systems were also to a large degree managed by them and only indirectly impinged on the work relations of 'lay' academics (cf. below). Aside from the fact that both the number of students and the responsibility for them increased and the teaching–research divide was softened, the reforms in Sweden may be characterised as a reform of leadership and administration (Askling 1999).

Similarly, the reforms in Norway mainly concerned delegation of responsibility and increased emphasis given to quality management. The results of delegation of powers were much less dramatic than in Sweden as institutions already enjoyed a high degree of autonomy. The government, however, to a minor degree governed by decrees in relation to universities. Through general policy statements, incentives and partial decisions aimed at changes in an indirect manner (such as formalisation of institutional management) it was able to influence the sector. This mode of governance relied upon local initiatives and thus the results varied between institutions.

For several years the quality issues were subject to public deliberation but, as noted earlier, they disappeared in the tremendous increase in students between 1988 and 1995. Universities concentrated their efforts on meeting this challenge and all discussions of teaching quality became discussions of how to attain higher throughput (Høstaker 1997). The sudden increase in students also highlighted the inability of universities to control their environment. Free admission traditions within the humanities, social sciences, law and sciences made them victims of great fluctuations. Yet when the institutions took measures to regulate their intake of new students, parliament and the government acted against them in order to decrease youth unemployment and to maintain education for everyone as a welfare right. This policy was not met with hostility by academics because, until the mid-1990s, universities were compensated in the form of higher grants and more academic posts. The early 1990s was marked as a period of great strain on academic staff, while one of the more permanent features was a higher teaching load at graduate level as a larger proportion of students continued beyond their basic training (Høstaker 1997).

Consequences for the academic profession

Since the university systems, the policies and historical traditions of the academic professions in the UK, Sweden and Norway are very different, it is neither possible nor desirable to make sweeping conclusions of any kind about the effects on the professions. It is more relevant to discuss different aspects of the professions' condition in relation to changes within academia, and a starting point may be to discuss integrating and disintegrating relations. While there are forces that may threaten to tear apart all kinds of unity, there is clearly also a basis for unity based on common points of reference among academics. Some processes engender a higher degree of unity and strength on the part of the academic profession, while others may split it into fractions or change its face fundamentally. In this section we will concentrate on the following broad topics:

- hierarchisation within the profession
- divides between the disciplines
- how to become an academic.

Hierarchies

Hierarchies within academia affect relations within the academic profession in many different ways. The hierarchies we will address in this context are, first and foremost, those between universities and academic positions. As we will see, the different types of hierarchies have different consequences for academic work relations and hence also for the potential unity of the profession.

While hierarchies between universities are of little significance in Norway and Sweden, they are an important element in the UK. Traditionally the academic precedence of institutions was given to universities according to age. Oxford and Cambridge embodied the traditional ideals of universities as selective elite institutions with close teacher–student contact. These universities were central in the reproduction of the academic profession as their graduates occupied university posts around the country. However, before the introduction of research selectivity this hierarchy had few material repercussions, with the exception of rich endowments at Oxbridge colleges and some other institutions (Becher and Kogan 1992). All teaching staff at pre-1992 universities were expected to both teach and research and universities were given block grants to fulfil this task. With the introduction of selectivity in the 1980s this hierarchy became much more important. The results of the RAE substituted the traditional hierarchy and to some degree confirmed it, as its apex comprised the 'the golden triangle' of Oxford, Cambridge and London, but also included about twelve other universities. These universities now supply the model of excellence as they have been able to maintain high research activity, and attain high research and teaching evaluation scores. These universities have also been able to continue traditional forms of teaching such as single-subject undergraduate degrees (as opposed to the wider modular options available to students in lower status institutions) and a high degree of selectivity of students on entry. They also have a low proportion of older and 'non-traditional' students and little provision for part-time study and lifelong learning schemes (Bauer and Kogan 1997; Fulton 1999).

These institutions have been able to steer their own course to a greater degree than many of the other universities. One of the interpretations of the effects of selectivity and the increased importance of the university hierarchy is the uniformity of what is seen as excellence (Fulton 1996). In the previous condition the universities were to a much greater extent able to diversify and gain credit for it, while in the present condition diversity of offerings to students is seen, by some, to be opportunistic deviation from the ideal. Such 'opportunistic' moves to attract students or to handle greater numbers of students included increased provision of taught masters' degrees, modularisation, part-time schemes, prepackaging of courses and IT-based teaching (Fulton 1999); although many of these changes were under way before pressure was placed on institutions (Boys *et al.* 1988). Similarly research assessments penalised applied research and multi-disciplinary work and exerted an important influence on what types of research were laudable or not (Bauer and Kogan 1997).

The basic effect of this development for the academic profession in England was increased diversity both in working conditions of academics and in the academic recognition of their work. This description also holds if we exclude the 1992 universities from the equation. While teachers in the more highly esteemed universities might have maintained a considerable degree of professional autonomy, teachers in the lower levels of the hierarchy could be subject to prepackaging and close monitoring of their courses. At the top end of the hierarchy there may be available research money for topics of the academic's own choice, while other institutions depend to a higher degree on external contracts with 'users'. These variations in working conditions led to great differences in the experience of being an academic at English universities. Evaluations assessed their work as being of a different worth. The stratification of universities in a hierarchy was thus also a stratification of academic experiences.

In Sweden and Norway the hierarchy between institutions is less pronounced and more a question of the line between traditional universities (and specialised university colleges) and other higher education institutions. This division has in Sweden been softened by the elevation of some former state colleges to university status, and a similar development will probably take place in Norway. The absence of hierarchies between universities in these two countries was connected to the traditional task of the state as a guarantor of quality and provisions. Relatively uniform standards of work relations, wages, admissions and offerings to students were enforced across the board. The state as guarantor and standardiser gave few possibilities to develop hierarchies, with the exception of those between professional fields and along the binary line.

The main effects of hierarchy in Norway and Sweden were connected to relations within departments. In Norway the development of the positional hierarchy towards equality of working conditions led to a dissolution of formal academic authority in departments during the 1970s. The chair of department became an elected office that tenured teachers had to fill when their 'turn' came. The most important status divide within the academic profession became that between tenured academics and non-tenured junior academics qualifying for tenure. One of the results of the dissolution of academic authority was that tenured teachers faced few demands regarding the quality of their teaching and research efforts. This led to a system of collegial relations which gave few indications to the individual academic whether his or her work really was of any value. The exceptions were the few crucial moments when work was assessed by an appointment or promotion committee. A person who passed some of these hurdles was seen, by definition, to embody a high level of quality. Although there always existed an informal hierarchy of intellectual renown, the absence of expectations and demands fostered a belief in a general level of quality that protected mediocrity (Høstaker 1997, Chap.4). The most recent reform process in Norway started with a newspaper debate in 1986–87 on the quality of universities. One of the main reactions was that quality of teaching or research at universities was no problem; universities were, by definition, institutions of high quality (cf. Høstaker 1997 and Chapter 5).

Although many of the structural features of Norwegian university departments have not been shaken, the increased weight given to departmental governance, planning and reporting and to the doctorate has in many ways countered this view. In many disciplines in the humanities and social sciences there was an increased emphasis on the need to publish research, which was something seen as less important earlier (Høstaker 1997). The need to make both teaching and research visible in some way (cf. below) made the university organisation much more transparent and the differences between academics open for all to see. Some of the effects of the dissolution of academic authority were thus counteracted through both self-regulation and administrative visibility. Yet the basic status of the academic was still unshaken, as there was still little monitoring and few administrative sanctions available against substandard performers.

While the problem of hierarchy in Norway was its dissolution, the Swedish situation was quite different. The division of labour between researchers (professors, research assistants) and teachers (lecturers, adjunct teachers) was a major structural trait. The professors were still those expected to lead the discipline and the departments and this hierarchy was reinforced by the privilege of leading research groups and controlling graduate education. The latter activity was also under academic control, while basic undergraduate education was subordinated to bureaucratic regulation. The reforms tried to loosen this situation by giving the disciplines more control over undergraduate education and introducing a new career ladder. This ladder was intended to make all positions open to promotion. Outstanding qualifications in teaching or research might lead from the position of adjunct teacher to lecturer and to professor. The consequences of this reform were twofold: first, pedagogical qualifications became more important in appointments or promotions; second, adjunct teachers and lecturers must be offered opportunities for individual competence development (Askling 1999).

The research of Bauer *et al.* shows that the Humboldtian ideal of a unity of teaching and research was still alive in Swedish academia (1999, Chap.3). The reform attempted to make the distribution of opportunities and duties more even between academic staff. All academic staff were now supposed to contribute to the development of their institutions and department and all lecturers were expected to do research (Askling 1999). Nevertheless, the situation in Swedish universities was quite different from the one previously found in the pre-1992 universities in England and in Norwegian universities. For most normal teaching posts in these universities, research was a part of both the duties and entitlements of academics, and the institutions allowed time and resources for the employee to fulfil this obligation (Fulton 1999). It was unusual for the institution not to fulfil its obligations or for the academic not to perform as expected. In England the introduction of the RAE was confirmation that academic work also consisted of research. The situation in Sweden was the reverse: a lecturer or adjunct teacher undertaking research as part of his or her normal work was 'bought free' from teaching either by external finances or by institutional funds. Research time was thus no entitlement, but a limited benefit open to institutional wrangling (Askling 1999). One of the reasons for this situation was that the maximum teaching load fixed for each category in the hierarchy was often interpreted as a minimum teaching load. Any deviation from teaching was seen as out of the ordinary (Askling 1999).

However, both in England and Norway the entitlement to research changed in the 1990s. In many ways the three university systems converged in their methods of allocating research resources. In England the greater financial differentiation between high scorers and low scorers in the RAE in the 1990s led to sharp variations in funding for research to the pre-1992 universities. This development erased the entitlement to research resources in many departments and, if the department chose, there might be great differences among colleagues in the same department (Fulton 1999, p.11). While most university academics in Norway had contracts that both obliged and entitled them to research, a development more like the current Swedish system was not unlikely with the integration of the state college system into a unified higher education system

One of the similarities between Norway, Sweden and England was the system of promotion to professorship. The handling of promotions diverged between the three nations and within the English system between the different traditions of the old and new universities. In Norway the homogenisation of work conditions and duties rendered the professorship a category that only signified a personal qualification and, unlike Sweden, entailed relatively few particular duties or privileges. [8]

The professor category was also freed from previous attachments to quotas between the different categories in the positional hierarchy and promotions were not tied to financial considerations of the institution. The result of this policy was, as in Iceland, a considerable increase in the number of professors[9]. In Sweden, until the recent reforms, the number of professorships were kept low [10] by the government, while the institutions could only regulate the pool of teachers by appointing lecturers and adjunct teachers. In recent years the areas with a high percentage of external finances have been based upon both research and curriculum development – something that will probably increase the number of professors in all disciplines (Askling 1999).

At English universities the proportion of professors among academic staff was also quite low[11]. The share of professors among staff, in contrast to Norway and Sweden, has not been subordinated to public policies, but to institutional policies and professional self-regulation. The institutional policies varied between the former binary line. Normally a person would have to have a distinctive research reputation to be appointed professor in one of the pre-1992 universities, while many of the 1992 universities gave professor as an honorary title to managers or for curriculum development. Others might award the titles of professor or reader based on personal achievements, as in the pre-1992 universities, but here the promotion carried no extra salary (Fulton 1999, pp.20–21). The main career grade for teaching staff in English universities was lecturer without any entitlement to move beyond this point. Lecturer was also the entry grade and the pay scale distinguished between lecturer A and lecturer B. Promotion to lecturer B was liable to an internal review and failure at this hurdle was normally an inducement for a staff member to leave. Senior lecturer and reader were promotion titles at the same level, but with different demands attached. Reader was mainly a research-based promotion, while senior lecturer also included teaching achievements. In some of the 1992 universities the title of principal lecturer was at the same level, but was connected to a specific post with particular responsibilities (Fulton 1999, pp.20–21). The positional hierarchy in England was thus not as unified and codified as in the state-owned institutions in Norway and Sweden, but is liable to institutional policies, traditions in the old and the new universities and professional self-regulation (ibid.).

Divides between the disciplines

One of the questions in this section is to what degree the division into different disciplines influences the viability of a notion of an academic profession. This division of labour within universities is not only reflected in the organisation into faculties and departments, but forms the experience of being an academic through intellectual polarities and through different extramural obligations to professional groups in society. Another concern in this section is whether or how the current reforms in higher education in the three countries have influenced these relations.

Tony Becher has developed the notion of research mode to analyse how intellectual principles are grounded in different practices in academia and hence into different experiences of being an academic. A 'research mode' may, in its basic meaning, refer to the way in which research is done. It also refers to the social relations and policy formulations of the various disciplinary groups (Becher 1985, 1989). Becher offers a general classification of research modes along two dimensions: 'hard' vs. 'soft' and 'pure' vs. 'applied' research. The first distinction refers to research methods and may be loosely illustrated by the distinction between those fields that depend on experimentation or systematic theories and those fields that rely upon interpretation and *Verstehen*. The second distinction refers to the difference between pure basic research that has no other purpose beyond the development of knowledge and research that aims at achieving results that can be applied for other practical purposes than knowledge formation itself. These distinctions are not meant to reproduce the administrative divisions within universities, e.g. natural sciences (hard/pure), medicine (hard/applied), humanities (soft/pure) and law (soft/applied), nor do they necessarily coincide with the boundaries which various disciplines draw between themselves. Different research modes may be found in many disciplinary fields, as distinctions between the different disciplines in the same field or even between disciplinary specialities or sub-specialities. A discipline or speciality may even change research mode during its development (ibid.).

A hallmark of the harder disciplines is that complex problems may be divided into simpler ones and there is also a clear hierarchy of relevant research problems. Especially in the purer fields, certain research problems may be congested with researchers and the investment in instruments and laboratories may be huge. In the softer fields the number of research problems may be seen as unbounded and complex research questions cannot be divided into simpler ones. Complexity is, on the contrary, acknowledged as an integral part of research. Due to this complexity the number of researchers for each research problem is low and the most sought after resource is time, while the harder fields are more dependent upon manpower and equipment (ibid.). The formulation of needs and policies may differ greatly in the two research domains because the research process and the challenges that face researchers are different. The 'harder' disciplines usually rely more upon external research grants for finance than do other areas. In many ways the disciplines develop different relations to different sections of society depending on who finances their research (Høstaker 1997, Chap.5). In our context it is important to emphasise that different research modes render different social experiences of being an academic. The 'seed of discontent' within the academic profession thus lies at the core of the intellectual activity and the actual organisation of academic relations into disciplines, departments, faculties and extramural professions reflects the centrifugal force created by the intellectual division of labour.

What impact did the reforms in the three countries have on the relations between the different disciplinary fields? Since the seed of discontent is grounded in the intellectual activity itself, policies had mainly indirect results on these relations. One of the major transitions of the 1980s and 1990s in all three countries, although to different degrees, was the shift to more applied research funded on a competitive basis. In the UK all state funding of research was liable to competition. While funding based on the RAE is formed as block grants to the institution, other types of funding are disseminated by the research councils through open competitions. Many achieved funding in this way and thrived, but the consequences of this system were quite uneven across the disciplines. Since 1992 departments sought grants for research equipment by competitive bids to research and funding councils; and most of them failed to do this with detrimental effects mainly for the natural sciences departments. This situation increasingly restricted not only the research effort but also the ability of these departments to teach PhD students. At the same time public grants did not, in these fields, meet the real costs of PhD programmes. Some of the strongest research groups opted not to train research council funded students but to rely on other sources with more adequate funding levels.

The system of funding thus led to a centralisation of the research effort within the natural sciences in the UK. Since the early 1980s this has been seen as inevitable and also desirable by leading circles in the natural sciences. The combined effects of limited state resources and growing costs and complexities of science were to force through a concentration of research to a reduced number of university departments. The current system of financing had the opposite effect, however, on some of the less capital intensive disciplines. The eligibility to enter the RAE of the new universities from 1992 meant some potential for research funding, although the grants have been small in absolute terms due to low grading. For some departments in the humanities this extra funding meant a major difference in income and the capacity to pursue research, and the incentives to enhance the research profile were substantial. A whole range of new possibilities opened up for academics in these universities, including postgraduate education.

The current system of funding in the UK thus led to the development of the disciplines in two different directions: a strong contraction of resources and manpower in the harder disciplines and a diffusion of resources in the softer ones, especially in the humanities. These developments have had certain consequences for the possibility of establishing oneself as a research-active professional in the different fields since the hurdles to get over are higher within the sciences.

In the Swedish case, changes in the structure of financing might lead to centrifugal forces within university organisation. With the reforms in the 1990s, funding for research at universities was reshaped. Direct state funding for research went through cuts while the Wage Earners' Funds were transformed into research foundations. The total amount of research financing was increased in this way but became much more oriented towards applied fields. The departments to a higher degree than before depended upon external competitive bids for their total funding. The result was a great variation in the level of funding, leading to 'rich' departments that brought money to the institution and 'poor' departments which depended on their institution for their own survival. The latter group often could not pay for their share of common facilities like libraries, IT services, etc. Some departments in the natural sciences, medicine and technology received more than 80 per cent of their total funding from external resources (Askling 1999). Their feeling of dependence upon and obligation to the institution were comparatively lower. This was a major challenge to Swedish universities. Due to the previous centralisation of powers to the state agency UHÄ, the university level was relatively weak, as the state agency negotiated directly with the faculties. The decentralisation of powers to the university level during the early 1990s meant that the universities themselves had to cope with the tensions between different faculties and disciplines. Differences in funding levels could possibly lead to a climate of protection and mistrust between faculties which called for strong, and hitherto unfamiliar management by university leaders (Askling 1999).

The devolution of powers to the institutions, faculties and departments, together with the changes in financial structure, led to a situation in which some departments might cling to the institution as their saviour while others will claim independence. This situation of unevenness was recently aggravated by the low priority given by the government to the social sciences and the humanities for research financing in the coming years (ibid.). The financial structure of research funding in Sweden produced great differences in the situation of academics of different disciplines within the same institutions. The level of external financing influenced the possibility of promotions to professorships, the amount of teaching for lecturers and adjunct teachers and also to what degree it was possible to pursue research at all.

The Norwegian case was again in contrast, as the political dynamics of higher education were different. Universities were generally financed by the government through block grants that did not divide teaching and research. In addition there were grants from the research council that were open to competition. The great inflow of new students from the early 1980s to the mid-1990s was followed by compensations in the form of more teaching positions. Most of these positions were in categories that included both teaching and research, and in this way the amount of basic research funding increased in Norway during the first half of the 1990s. However, there was in the same period a restructuring of the research councils into one council with a higher emphasis on applied research and with priorities given to the natural sciences and technology. These diverging developments were due to different political logics operating independently. While labour market policies governed the admissions of new students, especially to 'low-cost' fields like the humanities and the social sciences, economic policies governed the priorities of the research councils (Askling 1999).

The comparison between the three countries shows that the policies had different effects within each one along the institutionalised divides within academia. These divides are both translations and confirmations of the intellectual polarity within academic work and form what we have called the 'seed of discontent' within the academic profession. The unions organising university teachers in the three countries only managed to bridge the gap between the disciplines to a limited degree. In a broad sense the unions have limited their core activities to wages and work conditions which may be seen as a sort of least common denominator for all university teachers. In both Sweden and Norway the major unions in the university field, SULF[12] and Forskerforbundet[13] respectively, were parts of confederations consisting of unions for other university educated groups. Each member might hold double membership in the university teacher union and the extramural professional union (cf. Askling 1999). By this division of membership academics maintained both professional bonds with fellow professionals outside the universities and at the same time had a specific organisation to represent their interests towards their employer. Double membership thus represented a sort of division of tasks between unions by which the university teachers' union mainly took care of the material interests of its members, while one of the tasks of the professional unions was to develop the standards of the professionals. This division of tasks thus reproduced and confirmed the division between disciplines found in the academic organisation.

A similar division of tasks is not found in the English unions, but the Association of University Teachers, the major union in the pre-1992 universities, seems to have been struggling with a double claim to authority. On the one hand it tried to uphold the image of university teachers as members of common corporations and bearers of professional authority. In this model conflicts should be solved by collegial compromises. On the other hand they claimed authority as representatives of their members' material interests. In this case industrial action might be one means to achieve results. The major union in the 1992 universities, NATFHE[14], does not seem to be in doubt over its mainly trade union function (Fulton 1999, pp.15–17). Despite these differences both the major unions concentrated their activities around wages and conditions of service, a sort of common ground on which all academics could meet.

How to become an academic

One of the major potentials for the creation of an academic identity across disciplines is the standardising effect of common professional trajectories. The academic career may be seen as a series of more or less narrow gates through which the university educated person has to pass in order to become and stay an academic. The common experience of these stages in intellectual and professional education is not only part of academic folklore or simply rites of passage, but also signifies transformations in ascribed 'inherent' qualities. The constructions of academic trajectories differed among the three countries as they also differed between academic generations and between disciplines. In this section we will concentrate on the degree of standardisation of academic trajectories provided by graduate education and by important hurdles like obtaining the first job and a permanent contract.

The UK probably saw the greatest changes in the work conditions of academics and also in career expectations and career tracks. These changes were due to general cuts in funding, but also to changes in public and institutional policies. Henkel's research shows that the experience of young academics must have changed significantly since the 1970s. While young aspiring academics in the expansion periods of the 1960s and early 1970s obtained teaching posts relatively easily, this came to an abrupt end with the general contraction of this labour market from the early 1980s. The competition for most positions was fierce and the introduction of selectivity in research financing underscored that appointment policies in departments could also affect future research gradings. Financial insecurities led many universities, especially the pre-1992 universities, to use fixed term contracts for junior teaching staff (Fulton 1999, p.23). The mounting pressures on junior academics led to much more conscious career planning on their part. They became less inclined to engage in activities that would not enhance their careers. Career planning already started at PhD student level, as some supervisors would try to let their students get a head start in the job market with an early co-publication (Fulton 1999; Henkel 2000).

In the 1980s the PhD became the standard entry requirement for lecturing staff in most disciplines within the pre-1992 universities (Fulton 1999, p.22). Historically the PhD was connected to research training in the natural sciences, while in the humanities and social sciences lecturing staff came into teaching at an early stage after their master's degree. Some completed their PhDs after obtaining their first position, while others had very little if any intentions of completing a doctorate. In some disciplines there were even notions that the best people never finished a doctorate. In addition, graduate education for a long period occupied a residual place both in public policy making and in departments. Teaching in departments had always been concentrated at the undergraduate level and research training was usually a sort of apprenticeship in the sciences and an individual quest in the humanities and social sciences (Becher, Henkel and Kogan 1994).

In the early 1980s there was a change in public policies in this field. The teaching of PhDs was redefined from being a function necessary for the reproduction of the academic corps to a necessity for the economy and society in general. The research councils that paid for studentships and supported PhD programmes redefined the objectives of the PhD in less ambitious terms and also wanted to broaden the inculcation of skills in order to make doctors more relevant for a broader labour market (Becher *et al.* 1994). Later the conditions for studentships were sharpened as research councils tightened the demands for certain timed degrees. The English PhD was defined to consist of a year for a master's degree and two additional years for the PhD (Fulton 1999), although in practice this policy proposal did not take hold. The reallocation and concentration of funds made studentships much more difficult to obtain from research councils and many universities appointed PhD students as teaching assistants in order to finance their studies. However, the hierarchical differences between universities also intervened in the financing of graduate education. It was common for graduate students at Cambridge and Oxford to receive funding in addition to a studentship from a research council, amounting to a total period of seven years' preparation for the PhD.

The increased weight given to graduate teaching at universities, a common public policy in this field, together with the propensity of universities to make the PhD a point of entry to the first normal lecturing position, undoubtedly had a standardising effect on academic trajectories in the UK. It was, however, a standard of the natural sciences that was imposed across the board. This standardisation was possible partly due to indirect financial sanctions and by making the PhD thesis less demanding for the student in the humanities and the social sciences (Fulton 1999). Similar standardisation took place in many European countries and for most of these reforms the American PhD with a course component and a researched thesis was the model. In Sweden graduate education was restructured in 1969 and both the doctorate and the licence degree (*licensiatgrad*) were replaced by a new doctoral degree supposedly similar to the PhD. The licence degree had had the function of an obligatory exam before the student could start on the solitary ordeal of writing the thesis for a doctorate[15] (Ståhle 1996, pp.257–259). During the 1960s many natural scientists worked for a similar solution in Norway, and from the mid-1970s until the early 1980s new doctoral degrees were introduced in all disciplinary fields. This did not happen without resistance and the older doctorates were kept for those who wanted to take a less structured trajectory for their degree. This doctorate did not include any course component and, historically, graduate education in Norway in the fields of natural sciences, humanities and the social sciences has been connected to the *hovudfag* level of the candidate degree – a sort of two-year master's degree – or the *magister* degree. Most Norwegian academics have received their basic research training working for these degrees and in many disciplines the *hovudfag* students still have an important function as unpaid research workers (ibid.).

Both in Sweden and Norway the intention of standardisation was only in part followed through by organised courses and grants to doctoral programmes. In Sweden the rate of awarded doctorates fell during the 1970s as a result of this situation and only at the end of the 1980s did the rate of completion reach the level of the 1960s (Ståhle 1996, Chap.6). In Norway the first serious attempts to organise doctorate studies came within the fields of the natural sciences and technology, while in other fields the traditional doctorates even strengthened their positions as the total number of completed doctorates increased during the 1980s. In most fields the new doctorate did not have any prestige compared with the older one. One of the main political objectives of the Hernes Commission of 1988 was to get all the new PhD-like doctorates to function properly and, aside from the incorporation of the doctorates into organised studies, the Commission wanted to make the doctorate a requirement for a permanent position at universities (NOU 1988, p.28).

In Sweden the position of the doctorate has historically been, and still is, central to appointments. It is a requirement for professors, research assistants and lecturers, but not for adjunct teachers (Askling 1999). In Norway during the 1960s a doctorate was a *de facto*, and not *de jure* requirement for leading positions like professors and readers, and before that often seen as a requirement for any permanent contract. The devolution of academic authority from the late 1960s also hit the doctorate as one of the epitomes of the bourgeois university. The expansion of the number of university teachers and the homogenisation of the academic corps in many ways made the doctorate irrelevant for an academic career. It was not usually needed for the achievement of a professorship in the 1970s and the 1980s (Høstaker 1997, Chap. 7). A statistical survey from 1985 found that only 38 per cent of all academic staff held doctorates (Olsen 1988, p.48). The lowest percentage was found among the humanities and social sciences teachers. Medicine was the only field in which the doctorate had maintained its status as an obligatory requirement (ibid.). The policies from the mid-1980s made the doctorate more important as an academic distinction and from 1990 the doctorate or similar qualification was made into a sine qua non for all permanent positions at universities. In practice this change in regulations has made the doctorate the only gate of entry for junior academics (Høstaker 1997, Chap. 7).

From an historical perspective the standardisation of graduate education according to the ideal of the natural sciences is a common trait in the three countries. Predictably the policy influences in the UK were indirect through financing bodies, while in Norway and Sweden changes in this field were much more based upon direct interventions. The actual layout of doctoral education is quite different in the three countries, mainly due to the differences in the place of the doctoral student within the university system. The greatest difference was between Norway and the two other countries because a doctoral student is a member of the academic staff and paid a salary comparable with what he or she would expect outside academia. Historically, students at doctoral level in Norway were not students at all, but seen as 'research recruits'. They were needed to reproduce the academic corps and this view still informs much of the policy making in this field. Despite the 'studentification' of doctoral students from the early 1990s, there were rigorous demands for a financial plan in order to be admitted to a doctoral programme and it is not possible to study for a doctorate as a part-time student (Høstaker 1997).

In Sweden the graduate student started by taking courses and gradually became a part of the academic staff when appointed to a 'doctoral position' (*doktorandtjänst*), which might be financed externally or by the institution. The level of external finance often decided the possibilities of students to complete their degrees, and many students remained in a state of limbo after the course period. One of the results of this situation was a low rate of completion[16] (Ståhle 1996, Chap.6). Lately universities have been met with demands that no student should be admitted without a complete financial plan (Askling 1999). In the UK the policies introduced in the 1990s required postgraduate students to start with a master's degree. This was to provide a filter for entry to doctoral studies. Typical of the English system was closer monitoring of the progress of the student, and the department decided at the end of the first year whether the student should continue with the doctorate or settle for the less ambitious MPhil. Due to the policies of the research councils on the question of timed degrees, the ability of students to complete their doctorates on time was a matter of importance for departments and not solely a personal question for the student. A way to sidestep the rigour of this system was to take the PhD on a part-time basis (Becher *et al.* 1994).

An important difference between the UK and Sweden and Norway was that newly awarded doctors were regularly older in the latter two countries (cf. Ståhle 1996, Chap.6) and their career expectations were higher. The reasons for this are many and we will only mention two of them here: expectations of the quality of the thesis have been decreased reluctantly, if decreased at all, and doctors were also supposed to be qualified for employment in teaching and research. In England, however, a PhD was the point of entry for the lowest level on the pay scale of lecturers. While academics in the social sciences and humanities might achieve a first teaching job with a PhD, this was usually not sufficient in the sciences. Henkel found that it was not uncommon for science doctors to work for ten years as researchers in order to achieve an appointment to a teaching post, and the risks of failure were considerable. An important difference between Norway and the two other countries was that a Norwegian doctoral student would be a member of the academic staff and paid a salary comparable with what he or she could expect outside academia.

The way academic careers were constructed was also different between the UK and the two Scandinavian countries. A distinct feature of both Sweden and Norway was that most careers were made at the same university and even in the same department in which an academic took his or her higher exam or doctorate. Usually this question is addressed in the literature as a matter of low mobility (Askling 1999; Johansson 1989; Tvede 1992) and may be a result of the small sizes of the university systems. This absence of exchanges of personnel between universities has in many ways impeded a proper labour market within academia. All hopes of being recruited to an academic trajectory and later to the advancement of a career were connected to a rather small number of senior academics. This situation lay open, of course, to patronage and favouritism (Høstaker 1997, Chap.4). Such relations, however, are difficult to document beyond statements of interviewees. One of the few well-documented cases of outright favouritism was made within the medical field in Sweden by the immunologists Wennerås and Wold (1997). They found that the assessment and ranking of applicants to postdoctoral fellowships at the medical research council to a great extent depended upon the applicant's sex and/or whether the supervisor of the applicant sat on the assessment committee[17].

These patterns of internal recruitment of staff or auto-reproduction of academic groups are a distinctive mark of Swedish and Norwegian academia. The effects of this pattern are not fully researched, but evidence from the humanities and social sciences in Norway suggests that within these fields one effect might be a strong localism in the development of the disciplinary traditions (Høstaker 1997, Chap.4). In the UK junior academics usually had to seek employment at other institutions and they depended to a high degree upon 'invisible colleges' of peer groups and conference attendances to get the first appointment and later to publish their work. Many academics seem to have settled early at a university for most of their careers. This latter pattern, however, seems to be changing as one of the long-term effects of the RAE has been a higher mobility of senior academic personnel in order to build up research profiles at certain departments (ibid, Chap.5). To a greater extent than in the Swedish and the Norwegian cases it is possible to talk about academic labour markets in the UK. One of the effects of the RAE was to produce a general standard of what to expect from an academic in the different disciplines and those who lived up to this standard were in demand in specific academic labour markets.

One of the general traits of the developments in the three countries has been that of increased standardisation of academic trajectories. This standardisation has taken place with reference to the existing system of relations within each country. The university systems have not converged, but within each system the career expectations, the gates to pass in order to succeed and the matter of what success is all about, have become more standardised. The research practices of the natural sciences and the research policies emanating from the scientific field have served as the master patterns for much of this standardisation process, including the RAE in the UK. These processes are important as academics were forced to relate to them and form common points of identification around them. The doctorate, for instance, may be seen as a social marker of what distinguishes academics from other professionals.

Conclusion

It is quite clear that the three academic professions in England, Sweden and Norway respectively led quite different 'lives' during the reform periods of the 1980s and 1990s. This was due not only to differences in policies between the three countries, but also to quite different traditions in higher education. While universities in the UK are chartered semi-independent institutions, universities in Sweden and Norway are state owned and the teachers are civil servants. The mode of regulation and state influence were thus different, as direct intervention is much easier in a state-owned system, although the reform policies in both Sweden and Norway involved devolution of power to the institutions.

Although the development of the three university systems was quite different during the period, it is possible to identify some common dimensions that either standardise the experience of being an academic within each country or, in contrast, divide this experience into particular points of view. The most important of the latter kind was clearly the 'seed of discontent' connected to the intellectual activity itself. All reform policies seemed to benefit or disadvantage different groups along the disciplinary divides. Similarly the hierarchisation of academic institutions in the UK and the divide between teaching and research, in its different manifestations in the three countries, all gave different experiences of being an academic. Nonetheless, there were strong tendencies towards certain standardisations of academic experience connected to graduate education, academic trajectories and accountability in universities. One of the strongest forces of standardisation in the UK seemed to be the RAE, which has come to define the rhythm of much academic life. The importance of such standardisation is that it may provide common points of identification for academics. In order to be able to state what an academic profession is, one must start with these common markers connected to common experience. Perhaps the definition of an academic is just this heterogeneous collection of points of identification. This may be a strange profession in the views of professional theory, but it leaves us with more than a nonentity.

We may conclude that the academic profession experienced considerable structural changes in terms of growth, differentiation and standardisation between T^1 and T^2. The profession as such did not play the role of an actor in the three countries. To the extent that we find actors at this level, they were representatives of academic disciplines rather than the profession as such.

Notes

1   Before before the expansion of the 1980s and 1990s universities still enrolled only 6 per cent of each age group and the whole of higher education 15 per cent of each age group.

2   Medical doctors and jurists were state professions in Norway. The health service was a concern for the state from the early nineteenth century and jurists dominated the ministries. Theologians were also usually civil servants as the church was part of the state.

3   The others were non-tenured staff, technical staff and students.

4   Our case study from Bergen shows that the vast majority of all tenured staff (in all position categories) had been head at some time during their career (Bleiklie *et al.* 2000, Chap.8).

5   Norsk allmennvitenskapelige forskningsråd. Until 1995 Norway's research council for basic research.

6   NAVF; Evaluation of English Studies 1991, p.42

7   loc.cit.

8   Except a pay rise and the opportunity/duty to assess others to the same qualification.

9   Between 1997 and 1993 the number of professors (Professor I) increased by 25 per cent in both universities and colleges. At universities the share of professors of all teaching and research personnel at universities was 21 per cent in 1999. (*FOU statistikk og indikatorer* 1995; *Det norske forsknings- og innovasjonssystemet – statistikk og indikatorer* 1999).

10   In 1997 about 10 per cent of all full-time equivalents in teaching or research at Swedish universities belonged to the professor category (Askling 1999).

11   The Carnegie Report found that 15 per cent of academic staff at universities were professors in 1992, while 3 per cent were professors in the polytechnics (Fulton 1996, Table 10.5). Since then the new universities have appointed more professors and the Dearing Report found that for the whole of the UK 11 per cent of academic staff at the pre-1992 universities held professorships compared with 9 per cent at the 1992 universities (Fulton 1999, p.21).

12   The Swedish Association of University Teachers.

13   The Association of Researchers.

14   National Association of Teachers in Further and Higher Education.

15   The opportunity to take the licence degree was reopened in the early 1980s, but was not made compulsory.

16   Ståhle claims that less than 50 per cent of all graduate students complete their doctorate in Sweden, but he admits that these figures should be taken with a serious health warning (1996: 311).

17   Female applicants were disadvantaged in the assessment as well as those applicants, both male and female, who did not know anyone on the committee. The gender 'handicap' could be evened out by having the supervisor on the committee. Very few women could rely solely upon their publication record (Wennerås and Wold 1997).

Chapter 7

Academic Identities

Mary Henkel and Agnete Vabø

Introduction

Our central concern in this chapter is to examine the implications of policy change for academics in England, Norway and Sweden in our chosen period. We thus seek to extend our analysis to encompass the individual actors in the basic units of higher education institutions, who create and recreate the experience of higher education and its contribution to societies in their working lives. How far did academic values, self-perceptions and modes of working shift in the face of the political and institutional transformations that we have described? In short, how far did policy change permeate academic identities?

Throughout this book we have sought to identify patterns of change and responses to change across differences of national histories, institutions and cultures in which higher education has accumulated different configurations of meaning and purpose. We have seen in the previous chapter how these differences informed and shaped the academic profession in three countries over time. The national histories of higher education had resulted in different divisions of labour, different understanding of roles and different self-images on the part of academics. Academics were working in systems of quite different scales. In England, the 'golden triangle' of Oxford, Cambridge and London universities continued to dominate for most of the century. However, stratification was embedded in the whole system and the inter-institutional differences of resource and reputation were taken for granted by academics (Halsey 1992). In both Sweden and Norway, there were strong assumptions of inter-institutional equality, as far as the universities were concerned. The different political responses in the three countries to the idea of 'the knowledge society', as it emerged in the 1980s and 1990s, may in part be explained by long-standing differences of belief as to the contribution of advanced knowledge to national goals and differences in the value accorded intellectuals.

At the same time, we have noted the divisions within the academic profession that transcended national boundaries and so constituted a significant paradox. The disciplines and the specialised communities within them that made for divisions within academic institutions and created uncertainties about the idea of an academic profession could also generate transnational identities.

Any analysis of higher education at the level of the individual and the basic unit has, therefore, to take account of the intricate web of heterogeneity and homogeneity in the academic profession. Caveats about the possibilities of generalisation must be particularly strong. Our approach to this chapter reflects our awareness of this need for caution.

We will frame our analysis with an understanding of academic identities. Concepts and theories of identity provide insights into the stabilities at the core of academia, in the production, reproduction and negotiation of conceptions of knowledge and programmes of work over time within relatively bounded institutions. Such stabilities make it hard to change academic practice by the imposition of new purposes and structures from different policy and cultural arenas, even if periods of reform give the impression that it is possible.

Within theories of identity, values, interests and beliefs, self-images and reputations are central. They are the products of interaction between individual histories and choices and the workings of key communities and structures: disciplines, departments and institutions. More than the abstract and generalised construct of academic profession, they provide the structures, processes, rewards and sanctions that in turn reinforce academic values and beliefs and establish academic identities.

We will first elaborate more fully this conceptual framework. We will then briefly draw attention to the major challenges to academic identities implied in the transformation of higher education in our three countries, as they have emerged from our book. These can then be set against the dominant academic values and beliefs identified in the study.

However, we have chosen to concentrate our analysis in two case studies of academic responses to change, the policy of merging departments in Norway and the development of quality policies in the three countries. We believe that a case study approach makes it possible to address some of the complexities involved in analysing how policies with both different and similar meanings in the three countries were perceived by academics with both shared and distinctive identities. Our choice of cases reflects some of the national differences of context to which we have already referred: policies had higher profiles in some settings than others. It also enables us to focus our analysis at different levels. Concentration on specific disciplines and a specific institution in the Norwegian study makes it possible to examine sources of stability and change in academic identities at quite a deep level. The quality study places more emphasis on comparative analysis across the countries and illustrates some of the ambiguities in the meaning of policies for academic identities.

Conceptual framework

By the late twentieth century, idealist concepts of identity, centred on an essential self, had become discredited. However, the ideas of individuation, uniqueness and continuity remain, within a sense of self not as essence but as a project, 'a reflexively organised endeavour... which consists in the sustaining of coherent, yet continuously revised, biographical narratives' (Giddens 1991, p.5). This formulation incorporates both the future orientation of identity and its continuity with the past, the notion that all individuals have their own narrative history, which they can construct for themselves and present to others as a coherent account of a whole human life.

This is one facet of the concept of identity developed within the communitarian tradition of philosophy, on which we draw heavily here. Communitarianism contains paradoxical but mutually reinforcing ideas. In addition to embracing sameness and difference, individuation and identification, future and past in identity, communitarian philosophers also stress the dynamic between individual and collective. MacIntyre (1981, p.206) argues that the individual is embedded in and emerges from a history. 'What I am is in key part what I inherit... I find myself part of a history... one of the bearers of a tradition... A living tradition is an historically extended, socially embodied argument...in part about the goods which constitute that tradition.'

Taylor (1989) emphasises the importance of 'a defining community' in the formation of identity. One function of such a community is that it provides the language in which individuals understand themselves and interpret their world. However, in Taylor's view it goes beyond that. Being initiated into a language entails 'entering into ongoing conversations between ... people with a particular role or status in the web of relationships that make up [the] community' (Mulhall and Swift 1992, p.111). Through such conversations, individuals learn not only a language but substance, the ideas and experience expressed in that language.

Taylor also introduces a set of spatial metaphors in the form of horizons and frameworks, which constitute a bounded and defining space within which individuals forge an identity. For him these frameworks are moral. 'To know who you are is to be oriented in moral space, a space in which questions arise about what is good or bad ... what has meaning and importance to you and what is trivial and secondary' (Taylor 1989, p.28). He contends that morality has three dimensions: obligation to others; fulfilment or meaningfulness; and a range of notions concerned with dignity, respect and self-esteem. These ideas can be linked with the achievement of the goods which you value and which, in turn, may make your sense of identity more tangible.

Individuals in this mode of thought enter into argument with their significant communities, as well as being in some degree shaped by them, as far as their values and beliefs are concerned. They are both distinctive and 'embedded within a normative order' (Chapter 1). They are distinctive, in that they are each the subject of a unique narrative history, each located in a chosen moral and conceptual framework and each identified by the goods he or she has achieved. At the same time they are embedded, emergent from, working within and making an individual contribution to communities and/or institutions with their own languages, conceptual structures, histories, myths, values, practices and achieved goods. Communities and institutions provide the bounded space within which the individuals work and carry a range of social roles.

Insofar as communitarian philosophers suggest that individuals live their lives within a moral framework, their ideas have strong affinities with normative institutionalists. Individuals, in this perspective, may pursue goods that enhance their own lives as well as, or even more than, those of others, but they cannot be confined within the rationalist definition 'utility maximisers'. We suggest that the literature on higher education predominantly reflects the normative view: the universal, idealistic values of the academic community rather than the pursuit of interests by individuals and collectives. However, our comparative analysis, based on our empirical findings, will show that academics are driven by both values and interests. Deeply held values, sometimes expressed in the form of myths, may at times be used to reinforce or change the balance of power. But power may also be perceived as essential for the sustainment of values.

Identity and academia

Identity has been of central, symbolic and instrumental significance in the lives of individual academics and in the workings of the academic world. Traditional academic reward systems reflect the cultivation of an institutionalised individualism within a community or communities of peers. They bring together the goals of an individual sense of uniqueness and a public reputation

In the literature on higher education and science, the discipline is generally assumed to be the primary organising influence upon academic working lives, through which rewards are allocated and values reproduced, although in the sociology of science the broader framework of science is also important (e.g. Merton 1973; Polanyi 1962). Constructs such as disciplines and fields, science, social science and the humanities are understood as having both epistemological and social or cultural meaning.

Bourdieu (1975), writing within a conflict-oriented perspective upon science, portrays scientists as driven not only by intrinsic interest in research but even more by ambition. He defines the fields in which they work as 'loci of competitive struggle'. The achievement of identity in the field is critically important to them. They have both to distinguish themselves from their predecessors and rivals and to integrate the work of these groups into a construction that transcends it.

Clark (1983), Geertz (1983) and Becher (1989) perceive disciplines as cultures, centred round different knowledge traditions, which shape how individuals define themselves. These cultures are seen as generating individual identities that can be more powerful in the lives of their members than any other influence. According to Geertz (1983), disciplines constitute 'ways of being in the world'. High energy physicists and historians of the crusades, for example, 'inhabit the worlds they imagine'.

Välimaa (1995) broadens the concept of culture, in emphasising how different contexts shed light on different aspects of academic identities, the discipline, the profession, the institution and the nation.

Clark (1983) goes on to define academic systems in terms of matrix structures formed by the cross-cutting imperatives of discipline (the primary force) and enterprise (the university or college): it 'must be centred in disciplines, but it must simultaneously be pulled together in enterprises'. Discipline and enterprise are, in turn, perceived as coming together in the basic units: 'the department ... or the institute is simultaneously a part of the discipline and a part of the enterprise, melding the two and drawing strength from the combination' (p.32).

We also define the discipline, the enterprise and the department as the key communities or institutions in which individual academics engage in the project of identity building. However, they form an asymmetrical and incommensurate triangle or framework of influences. The dominant, cosmopolitan but diffuse power of the discipline is, in part, embodied in local and tangible form in the department that derives from an institutional and, indeed, a national context. Membership of a department can influence individual orientations to the discipline, through the media of collective responsibilities and day-to-day dialogue. At the same time, departments are constructs of the enterprise, as well as being critical to their wellbeing. Both departments and enterprises, as local and defined entities are, arguably, more open than the invisible colleges of the disciplines to the influence of other bodies with their own agendas. They might, however, derive power from those other bodies.

The question whether and how academic identities are likely to be affected by institutional and policy changes in higher education is, therefore, complex and bound up with change in the interplay between and the relative power of disciplines, departments and higher education institutions.

Policy change and the challenge to academic identities

The transformations in higher education described in this book for the most part implied or derived from changes in the relationship between higher education and the state, and had some implications for the dynamic between institutions, departments, disciplines and individuals.

Historically, there were substantial differences of emphasis in the three countries in the aims they espoused for higher education, as between the provision of liberal education for an elite, preparation for public service, the redistribution of welfare, cultural transmission and the advance of research and scholarship. By the end of our period there was strong convergence towards defining the purposes of higher education primarily in terms of national competitiveness in the context of a global economy. Academics and higher education institutions were increasingly expected to develop different forms of collaboration with industries and businesses of all kinds and to meet their educational and research needs. Graduates must be equipped for the more flexible labour markets of knowledge societies. Basic research continued to be encouraged by governments, but for its ultimate utility value rather than as an intrinsic good.

As we have seen, all three countries had experienced huge growth in student numbers by the mid-1990s. Lifelong learning policies had different histories and different meanings in the three countries. They also tended to be diffuse and ill-defined. However, they entailed demands across the countries for education to a more diversified population, at multiple levels (above and below that of the undergraduate programme) and at different stages in the careers of the learners. At the same time, the unit of resource had been reduced in all three countries, although more severely in Sweden and England than in Norway. All the above developments meant growing emphasis on integration, efficiency and quality in higher education.

The other key issue was that of control. There may have been profound differences in the degree and directions of change in the three countries as far as autonomy was concerned. However, we have seen that governments in all three were seeking new mechanisms of control in the public sector, and were to varying degrees influenced by the ideas loosely brought together under the heading of New Public Management. All advocated some combination of centralisation and decentralisation of authority in higher education and promoted the virtues of strong leadership, management by objectives and strategic planning in institutions. All introduced evaluation, performance measurement, greater transparency and some forms of performance-related resource allocation as modes of steerage or control. In all countries there were shifts towards co-ordination of higher education by the market and principles of competition and consumerism.

Whether higher education institutions acquired more freedom from state control or became more constrained by it, as we saw in Chapter 5, they became pivotal organisations in the implementation of policies. All assumed more explicit functions relative to their basic units and the academics working in them. Increasingly they became sites of struggle for academics competing for authority and resources, and mediators of external mechanisms of control. They also took on tasks such as planning for academic development, which implied a shift in authority from the discipline to the enterprise.

Dominant values of academia

Before directly addressing this question, we first review briefly the dominant academic values, as identified in the literature on higher education. Much of this literature is based on relatively elite institutions. However, our fieldwork in all three countries, although more broadly based, demonstrated the influence of these values upon academic perceptions of themselves, their motives and their roles. The reflection by individuals on their working lives, their own aspirations and the implications for these of policy changes were strongly informed by values and beliefs, often expressed in the form of academic myths. The concept of myth as used here is not intended to convey a sense of untruth, for instance a false representation of a historic reality. Rather, myths are understood as a simplified representation of a complex reality (Bailey 1977). The power of these expressions will be explored more fully in the first of our case studies.

The dominance of a certain set of academic values can, in part, be explained by the way in which academics are inducted into the profession, normally within a disciplinary culture mediated through particular kinds of institutions. A high proportion receive their postgraduate as well as their undergraduate education in a prestigious institution, either in a university at the top of a national hierarchy or in one of a small number of universities with equal status in a smaller country (Becher 1989; Geertz 1983). Postgraduate education is also a research education. During that period of induction, individuals can have an intensive exposure to the culture of a discipline through interaction with their research supervisor, with members of their research group, with fellow students and with other members of a department.

It is, therefore, hardly surprising that dominant values are knowledge-led, deriving largely from academic definitions of the distinctive mandate of their specialist and strongly bounded sector of society: to develop and control the creation and testing of new specialist knowledge and to ensure that this knowledge and the norms and values regulating academic practices are transmitted to the next generation. The knowledge and values are resources for society but independent of it. The link between the mandate and the values of structural independence, self-regulation and the freedom of individuals to determine their own agendas is central, even if, as we have seen, the distinction between individual and institutional autonomy is not always kept clearly in mind. Academic freedom, in turn, rests heavily on other values, such as integrity, respect for evidence, reasoned argument and critical thinking, which are developed through engaging with a discipline.

According to Bleiklie (1994), the dominant social science perspectives on universities have derived from two theory traditions – German idealist and American functionalist. They have much in common as far as the institutional and behavioural norms and values they embody are concerned, although in one tradition they are self-justificatory; and in the other they serve an instrumental purpose: they are seen as ensuring the best research. In Europe idealist conceptions of universities and higher education have been dominant, although, as we remarked in Chapter 4, they have taken different forms in different national contexts. The Newman ideal placed more emphasis on the social and moral value to individuals of a liberal education, while the Humboldtian ideal centred upon the engagement of students with professors in the process of new learning within its own terms and for its own sake. The inheritors of these traditions have, however, broadly shared the ideal that a university education is grounded in academic responsibilities to sustain the connections between research, learning and teaching within the framework of the discipline.

However, the development of more differentiated systems of higher education meant that, while this ideal remained dominant, there were other perspectives. They might be centred on the student rather than the teacher, focusing on their aims and objectives, on their modes of learning and on what departments or institutions might do to enable them to reach their goals. They might be focused on labour markets, how they were changing and how higher education could best meet their needs. Such alternative beliefs fed on traditions developed outside disciplinary communities and enabled them to become more elaborated and to generate their own modes of enquiry and the more effective transmission of their own values and practices.

We will now present two case studies of systematic attempts at reforms designed to reach into the core structures and activities of academia. We examine how these affected individual and collective academic identities and the institutions and communities in which those identities were developed.

Case study I: Merging university departments

Introduction

Despite great resistance, in 1989, the council at the Faculty of Arts at University of Oslo, Norway, decided to merge the existing approximately 40 departments into 10 larger units. The merger process challenged the disciplinary identities of the members of the various departments. By treating the traditional departments as if they were equal, the reform functioned as a catalyst for myths about disciplinary distinctiveness and differences in the field.

Disciplinary identity is shaped, in part, by socially constructed beliefs and myths about disciplines. In the academic fields, myths and symbols not only serve the functions of cultural reference and sources of identity for the members of a discipline, but also reinforce the power relations of the disciplinary hierarchy of the field and contribute to regulating contact and collaboration between (related) disciplines. They were important in the political struggle for academic autonomy that took place in the merger process. Even though the mergers gave the impression of being a radical reform aimed at changing the individualistic traditions of research practice towards more interdisciplinary collaboration, we argue that the outcomes of the process were shaped by the dominant cultural pattern (disciplinary hierarchy and identities) developed through the history of the faculty.

Two prestigious disciplines, history and philosophy, make particularly interesting cases in that respect. A few years after being merged, both managed to gain independence and became re-established as single departments.

The purpose of the reform

The proposal to merge departments at the Faculty of Arts of Oslo, was suggested as early as 1980, but was rejected then by the Faculty Senate. In 1986, the proposal was forwarded again by the Dean at that time, Professor in History, Sivert Langholm, and in 1989 it was agreed to reduce the total number of department units from 40 to 10.

Implementation of this reform was not unique for the Faculty of Arts in Oslo. During the last 10 to 15 years a number of mergers have been undertaken in the university sector. The idea of economy of scale in academic management gained hold in many (Western) countries during the late 1980s (Goedegebuure 1992). In Norway this belief was expressed in the Hernes report (NOU 1988, p.28) and in connection with the introduction of activity planning and other New Public Management reforms. Such ideas also served as important justifications for mergers in the college sector later on (Skodvin 1999). The mergers in the humanities must also be understood as a result of the lack of legitimacy of the humanities during the 1980s. The rapid decrease in the number of students and the fact that the humanities were given low priority in the national research policies had put a lid on funding of the humanities. Compared with the other faculties at the university, the Faculty of Arts was distinguished by its many and often very small departments with two to four academic staff. About 300 academic staff were spread across 40 departments. The large number of departments were partly a remnant of the former chair-faculty system, partly a result of the traditional hegemonic position of the University of Oslo. The faculty had an image of poor management and administration of its resources, and, compared with others, could be labelled a loser in the fight over scarce resources in the university at that time. It was argued that most academic staff lacked sufficient knowledge of what was going on in related disciplines and that the traditional faculty structure restricted the possibility of communication and collaboration.

Mergers were intended to accommodate a range of other goals as well, particularly administrative efficiency and management by objectives. A larger and more professional administrative staff unit in each new department would contribute to these and reduce the time spent by academic staff on administration.

Opposing arguments

Even though the majority of the academic staff represented in the council of the Faculty of Arts accepted the plans for merging departments, the specific proposals that followed were met by heavy critique from the majority of departments involved. Some feared that the status of their academic field/department would be weakened because their autonomy would be impaired by the new organisational structure. Many were apprehensive of losing disciplinary autonomy since a greater distance between the sections and centralised administration would lead to a more powerful administration. However, whether mergers actually led to a shift in the internal power structure remains an open question.

The criteria underlying the plans were considered to be rigid. It was argued that the new departments had been planned to meet administrative criteria, such as the total number employed, and on the basis of what the leadership considered to be neighbouring disciplines rather than of 'real' disciplinary affinities. Such objections were also raised by departments which one would immediately think of as closely related. Many argued against the idea that other members of the new departments should have the power to affect decisions about academic subjects of which they had little knowledge and with which they did not identify themselves. There might be bias in favour of certain disciplines due to the fact that the heads of the new departments would be elected from one of the disciplines. This, and other factors, could lead to disintegration of the respective disciplines. Some mentioned the historical responsibility for developing the disciplines. Others claimed that the particular disciplinary identities would be hard to maintain because they would no longer be institutionalised as distinctive administrative units. For example, disciplines would no longer have an independent departmental name to use in their relations with international networks. The likelihood that the administrative benefits would in the event be achieved was also questioned.

However, although no other faculty showed as much resistance as the Faculty of Arts in Oslo (Christensen 1991; Kyvik and Marheim Larsen 1993; Vabø 2000), there were different views among the academic staff. It was not simply a conflict between academics, the institutional leadership and administrators.

Identity, myths and power

Although not always identical with one particular discipline, the department is important for group formations in academia, and especially in university systems like the Norwegian. The discipline is a more crucial disintegrative force than the formal positional hierarchy since the latter, in contrast to many other countries, 'is, in practice, fairly democratic. The Norwegian university-system is characterised by a high degree of self-reproduction, and most of the faculty remains at the same department throughout their career. At the Faculty of Arts in Oslo 80 per cent of the academic staff have a master's or doctoral degree from the same faculty, usually from the department where they now work' (Vabø 2000). This phenomenon is a sustaining force of local disciplinary traditions in the formation of academic groups and their identity (see also Høstaker 1997). As a consequence, a distinctive local pattern of disciplinary 'tribes and territories', to paraphrase Becher (1989), developed.

Having said that, we do not consider the university department or the faculty culture to function as a 'scientific community' in the sense that truly distinctive norms and beliefs are incorporated and shared by the members. In the humanities especially, disciplines can be highly fragmented in terms of thematic, theoretical and method-ological approaches. In relation to this, it is important to take into consideration that most of the departments at the Faculty of Arts were established and organised on the basis of certain educational needs, especially teacher education. Traditionally, resources were dis-tributed according to the number of students and not according to research needs. It was first of all in terms of its educational tasks that the department was a joint concern and common reference point for its members.

Members' research activities were largely individualistic (see also Becher 1989). A survey undertaken at the Faculty in Oslo (in 1994) showed, for instance, that only 32 per cent collaborated with other staff and/or students (Vabø 1999). This research mode can be under-stood partly in terms of the cognitive dynamics in the humanities dis-ciplines, but also as a social strategy of the individual members to gain social recognition and scientific status in their respective fields (Bourdieu 1975). However, traditionally the department functioned as a protective body, securing the resources and autonomy necessary for the careers of its members. Since an important aim of the mergers was to separate disciplinary allegiances from administrative struc-tures, it is also reasonable to assume that academic staff thought they threatened that function.

As a consequence of the individualistic research mode and the frag-mented character of the disciplines, the departments in the human-ities are also subject to much internal disagreement and competition. For some groups, the mergers represented an opportunity to develop closer contact with peers in other departments, for instance, when a minority (of two) in the philosophy department considered the merger with the linguistics departments as a potential for strengthening research collaboration on language analysis.

How then can we explain the dominant pattern of resistance? The basic theoretical point of departure is Bourdieu's (1988) notion of the academic field as characterised by a permanent struggle for scientific hegemony, status and resources and what criteria should be legitimate in order to attain status. Relations between disciplines are regulated by the social dynamics of the disciplinary hierarchy. Regardless of position, the general pattern is that disciplinary groups will resist being influenced by others, particularly by disciplines that are closely related. The creation of myths, their content and the potential for disciplinary groups to use them in powerful ways reflects the logic of the relations in the disciplinary hierarchy of the field (Vabø 2000).

Disciplinary hierarchies are not universal, but must be analysed and understood in relation to the history of the field, such as the social, economic and intellectual status of the different disciplines in the nation over time.

As a general guideline, features such as age, size and degree of hegemony to control certain theoretical, methodological and research traditions are important. In the humanities, subjects such as ethnology and folkloristic are not, in this sense, single disciplines. They are dependent upon importing theories from other disciplines, such as anthropology, history and sociology. However, disciplinary hierarchies are expressed in many ways. In the humanities in Norway, for example, a particularly evident expression is the high degree of gender segregation between disciplines (Vabø 2000).

By treating the departments as equal, the merger process challenged the historical hierarchy of the disciplines. The concept of myth (interpreted as a simplified representation of reality) was a key dimension of the analysis. According to Christensen and Molin (1983) myths are needed to interpret the past in certain ways by putting emphasis on certain elements though neglecting others. In a political process, myths can affect decisions and contribute to legitimate plans of action and thereby contribute to reproduce the dominant cultural pattern in an organisation. In other words, studying disciplinary identity one cannot take the stories about the unique history of the disciplines at face value, a challenge for researchers on the history of disciplines (Harvey 1987). However, studying how reform policies are affecting the academic organisation, it is not the question about what is true or not that is interesting, but the organisational setting in which the myths have a function. A dominant faction in the philosophy department considered their merger with linguistics as an attempt to undermine their status as a general discipline, relevant for all disciplines, and not a selected few. Philosophy, it was said, was open to all sorts of inquiry and should not be confined to any kind of specialisation. Philosophy was 'the mother of all disciplines'.

The importance and power of myths must be understood according to their relational character. Myths about disciplines, positive or negative, are also 'reproduced' by non-members, as we observed in our interviews. One of the informants typically characterised the historians as having a 'solid research identity', in contrast to his own, the history of religions, which he dubbed an 'inferior research discipline'. Below, we exemplify how the use of myths affected the outcome of the reform policy.

The identity and myths of the historians

As a result of the merger, history was brought together with (smaller, low-status disciplines) ethnology, folkloristics, history of religion, history of ideas and social geography in a 'Department of Cultural and Social Studies'. After being merged, the group was frustrated. External consultants had been hired to evaluate and develop a better working environment between them (Eikeland and Lahn 1995). The historians claimed that the reform had failed in respect to what was promised, such as better quality of administration and secretarial services and more interdisciplinary collaboration. Furthermore, they argued that history had lost resources and not enough attention was being paid to the distinctive features of their discipline. Being part of a large and compound department was harming the historians, who were also facing a deep internal crisis within the discipline.

Even though such a definition of the situation was not unique for the historians, they succeeded in gaining independence. In order to explain why, their former position as a national centre for historical research has to be considered.

According to the evaluation report, in the 1960s the Department of History in Oslo was fairly coherent, since most of its research was concentrated upon Norwegian political history (Eikeland and Lahn 1995). Nationally and politically the department played an important role. During the 1960s and 1970s different processes contributed gradually to more academic and social fragmentation within the department. New research subjects were developed such as economic history, social history and foreign political history. In the radicalisation of the milieu in the 1970s the emergence of such subjects as women's history and non-European history contributed to fragmentation in respect to historical periods, subjects and geography, a disintegrating process which continued and became stronger. In the 1980s history departments were characterised by conflicts between different alliances. In a national context, the history department in Oslo was no longer the undisputed centre of historical research and debate. Because of decrease in student numbers and academic positions and the expansion of applied research and the college sector, younger research talents from the department were recruited elsewhere. This resulted in the development of important and vital historical research milieus at other institutions and contributed to the devaluation of the traditional academic status of the history department in Oslo.

In the 1990s, the opinions of the historians differed. Some were aware of the lack of common interests and distinct profile within the group. Others argued that due to its special traditions, history should be organised into its own independent unit. A third group was fairly optimistic about future plans for development. All in all, many argued they had a particular mandate since they belonged to a central university. In Norway the best historians were situated at the University of Oslo: it was a 'name'; 'everybody wanted to join this group' (Eikeland and Lahn 1995, p.128, our translation). It was decided to set in motion internal processes that would bring about the return of a common core and identity to the discipline and its members. In 1994 their application to the faculty senate to be re-established as their own department was accepted.

The mergers motivated an active defence of the myths about the singularities of the history department in Oslo, myths that stem from its previous position as a national centre for historical research. Despite being fragmented in the 1990s, the group became consolidated in their struggle against common enemies. The myth about the singularity of history became important to that strategy. Its success was also a result of the traditionally strong position of that department (Vabø 2000).

Established in 1811, the University of Oslo is the oldest university in Norway. In a national context, the Faculty of Arts had a long-standing hegemonic position. Therefore it is plausible to suggest that the faculty had inherited a self-understanding of being the national centre for humanistic education and research. It was true that the University of Oslo, from being the national higher education institution, had in the post-war expansion of higher education become 'just one' of several mass universities, providing educational services basically to the students of its home region. However, the resentments of the historians were indeed based on the institutional experience of belonging to a discipline with traditions closely linked to the nation-building process. It must also be remembered that compared with most others, history was a very large department.

Conservation versus subversive strategies

Mergers functioned as a catalyst for the constructions of disciplinary identities and the production of myths and disciplinary hierarchies underpinning these identities. They also shaped the outcomes of the mergers. We can therefore conclude that the mergers contributed to reproduction of the dominant cultural pattern of the faculty organisation. In other words, it is difficult to transform disciplinary identities and academic practice by imposing formal changes.

However, we do not claim that the outcome of the process should be entirely understood from a deterministic perspective. Our qualitative interviews showed that low-status disciplines, like ethnology, are more open to external influences. Consequently their identity is less dependent on distinguishing themselves from others and more open for change. A part of this picture is that they have less power to control myths about the singularity of their discipline. For instance, it is often said that ethnology is about the study and collection of material objects, and historically this is true. However, our informants described the further development of this discipline as being highly influenced by theories, subjects and methodology from sociology, history and more recently cultural theories (anthropology). While for the historians their heritage was a treasure from which they could benefit in their struggle for autonomy, for other disciplinary groups, like ethnology, their history was less of a source of strength.

The outcome of the process points to both stability and change. There were, for instance, new forms of interdisciplinary collaboration, although it must be said that they were difficult to trace back definitively to the implementation of the reforms. Our research also showed that disciplinary identities can change due to broader social processes of change, for example, decreased importance of the nation state, or that they had never been stable, in spite of the myths. (For a more detailed analysis of the merger process see Vabø 2000.)

The policy of merging departments can usefully be understood in terms of a clash between two kinds of strategy which, according to Bourdieu (1977; 1988; see also Murphy 1988), are used by academics aiming to make an impact on defined fields of knowledge or disciplines. Conservation strategies for advances are consistent with established norms, structures, conceptions of knowledge or practices. Subversive strategies are more hazardous. They are designed to challenge or undermine established structures or modes of working and to take the field in a new direction. In this instance, such strategies were employed by a combination of academic and administrative interests. They were largely, although not entirely, unsuccessful. Conservation proved the more powerful force.

The concepts of conservation and subversive strategies will emerge as useful conceptual tools in our second case study. There we note instances where academics opposing external reforms use conservation strategies that incorporate forms of subversion.

Case study 2: Quality reforms – a comparative study
Quality reforms: different countries – different meanings

We have noted that only in the 1980s and 1990s did the concept of quality find its way into national higher education policies in the three countries. Until then, as far as most of higher education was concerned, quality was a matter for the academic policy arena alone. It was implicit in the values and workings of academic institutions and disciplinary communities and could be taken for granted. Even in parts of the system, such as the UK polytechnics, which were subject to external regulation, it was largely managed by academics themselves, although there the issue was made more explicit and structures and processes were created for quality assurance.

The main difference between the quality assurance of education in the universities of the three countries was that the UK and Norway had external examiner systems, while in Sweden the assessment of undergraduate degrees was a wholly internal responsibility.

The new approaches in the three countries reflected different principles and theories of how quality was to be achieved. For all three countries quality had become a matter of national policy rather than something which only academia could control. Norwegian and Swedish policies leant towards systemic and integrated definitions and theories, while in the UK policies for quality were more specific, more centred on professional practice and its evaluation. Accountability was the key principle, while in Norway and Sweden efficiency and enhanced freedom, respectively, were primary. In the UK there had been a loss of trust between academia and government. Swedish policies were based on an increase in trust in the academic community on the part of government. In all three countries, quality policies entailed some changes in the autonomy exercised by institutions, departments and individuals and in their power to affect the autonomy of the others. In the UK disciplinary communities and their evaluative procedures were also involved in these changes.

All three countries moved from ex ante to ex post modes of control and towards an emphasis on output and performance rather than input targets and measures. All made some moves towards linking resource allocation with quality or performance measures. In the UK and Norway, the power of transparency and the public nature of evaluative judgements had a significant place in quality policies. In Norway quality was subsumed at the institutional level within a managerialist framework, through internal activity planning and evaluation against performance indicators and targets, which did have resource consequences. Departments were now rewarded, for example, for quantity of publications, the reputation of publication outlets and the production of research degree candidates.

All three countries relied to some extent on incorporating peer judgement and self-evaluation into modes of quality assurance or quality assessment. Peer judgements probably had the strongest place in the UK, but they were incorporated into state mechanisms of control in a way that had no parallel in Norway and Sweden. The UK quality assessments were also more comprehensive and intrusive into professional practice than their Scandinavian counterparts.

Academic perceptions of quality policies

Academics in English universities saw public accountability as the dominant and legitimate principle of quality policies; some explicitly distanced themselves from an exceptionalist view of higher education in this context. However, this did not mean that there was wide support for these policies, which were also thought to represent changes in political culture towards consumerism, managerialism and loss of trust in professionalism. Views about the higher education context in which they should be understood were often critical: a reduced unit of resource, explosion in student numbers and the multiplication of universities through the ending of the binary line. For some, the introduction of quality assurance was a necessary consequence of this last change: there had to be a means of determining common standards and monitoring the new universities. Others focused on the policies as a means of managing, or even masking, the decline of quality inherent in institutions being asked for more from less.

In Sweden, academics welcomed the principle of the 1993 reform, 'freedom for quality'. However, they saw the idea that higher education institutions, with their increased space for self-regulation, should develop their own systems for quality assurance not as enhancing individual academic autonomy but rather as a central directive to institutions. They felt that it encroached upon academic territory and was a denial of academic commitment to quality. 'We have always cared for quality' was a common response when the issue was raised in interviews (Bauer *et al.* 1999). Academics also observed how the huge rise in student numbers had made the university 'more like a factory', although they did not explicitly see quality assurance policies as a means of managing that phenomenon.

In Norway, as we have seen, a more explicitly managerialist approach to quality assurance was introduced into universities, in the form of activity planning and performance indicators. Here, too, academics saw this as an attack upon academic autonomy. It was represented by academics in the University of Oslo as an attempt to impose administrative control upon the universities, as if they were 'technical instruments' to be used at will by politicians (Bleiklie *et al.* 2000). In Bergen, critique focused on means rather than ends: the problem of evaluating academic quality by externally devised quantitative measures, as implied in the development of performance indicators.

Quality policies and academic identities

COLLECTIVE AND INDIVIDUAL IDENTITY

Here we highlight some particular consequences of the introduction of quality assurance policies in higher education and their implications for academic identities. We consider whether they had any impact on the dynamic between individual, discipline, department and institution in the development of academic identities and how far they constituted challenges to academic values, self-esteem and conceptions of work. Finally, we analyse how academics managed those challenges and try to determine the balance between stability and change implied in their responses.

We have already noted the strength of feeling expressed in Norway and Sweden about the value of individual academic autonomy. We have seen too, in Chapter 5, that a major implication of the introduction of quality policies was that quality was no longer perceived essentially as a matter of individual or departmental responsibility. Institutional leaders were formulating policies and setting up institution-wide structures to establish quality assurance. They also wanted to ensure that it was visible to external audiences. In all three countries they were playing a more active role in academic development.

In England and Sweden, the institutionalisation within universities of quality assurance meant that some academics found themselves taking on collective responsibilities for generic and systemic (Joss and Kogan 1995), institution-wide quality criteria or mechanisms. The assumption of institution-wide responsibilities might, however, have been a more novel experience for Swedish than for British academics used to the implications of institutional autonomy.

As such institutional activities began to take shape, they opened the way for consideration of more holistic conceptions of quality, such as the value of the whole educational environment and of coherence as a central educational value (Dill 1995). They entered the discourse at institutional and departmental levels, even if individualistic conceptions of quality were not displaced.

In Norway, the construction put upon quality policies and responses to them was strongly framed by the universities. The Universities of Oslo and Bergen interpreted the policies differently and evolved different strategic responses. However, as far as implementation was concerned, there was less evidence of any shift towards generic and institutional, as distinct from specialist and departmental, responsibilities for quality. Activity planning and quality assessments were focused on departments or disciplines. In all three countries the department was identified as the arena for working out policy changes. This implied a new focus on the idea and public image of collective effort at this level, which, as we have seen, might run counter to powerful disciplinary myths of the individual scholar.

In Sweden, departments were expected to work collectively on formulating definitions of quality and how it would be sustained within a framework established by the institution. The importance of collective self-evaluation was underlined. In England, the department was the unit of quality assessments of education and research. It was required to undertake a self-evaluation and produce an account of collective strategies and achievement. Even in research, individuals now felt that they had a responsibility to the department, as well as to themselves (or their research group in the case of scientists) and their discipline. For most this meant that because collective achievement had become more important (departments with low research grades could be vulnerable to merging or even abolition), individual achievement also took on a new urgency, as well as a new transparency.

Another consequence of the shift towards the collective was to be found in England in the nature of academic relationships. In some institutions where the myth of departmental collegialism and equality had been embedded in academics' assumptive worlds, new roles began to be identified – directors of teaching and even directors of research. They did not imply formal authority relationships with colleagues, but they did underline the idea that these academic responsibilities were not simply individual. In practice they could mean individuals not just giving support or advice to colleagues but exerting pressure on them to produce.

THE BUREAUCRATISATION OF QUALITY

A dominant theme in our empirical work in all three countries was the bureaucratisation of academic work generally and of quality in particular. In England this was most strongly associated with the assessments of the quality of education (known as teaching quality assessments, TQA), and institutions' tendencies to establish structures and procedures perceived likely to enable them to meet TQA assessment criteria. While these assessments were carried out largely by disciplinary peers, academics tended to characterise them as largely bureaucratic exercises, with a stronger emphasis on form than on substance.

In Sweden, too, the demands for explicit quality assurance programmes and measures were considered by most academics to be time consuming, costly and bureaucratic. They might have felt the contrast with previous assumptions and arrangements even more keenly than their English and Norwegian counterparts, since they had no tradition of external peer review of their undergraduate teaching and examination responsibilities. These responsibilities had been perceived as strongly individual. Systems for quality assurance emphasising the need for collective procedures and more documentation restricted individual academic autonomy.

In Sweden and England, because quality assurance was perceived by academics primarily within an administrative model of quality, it was sometimes regarded as a diversion from real academic work. Even where academics accepted the need for more systematic approaches to assuring quality, many tended to compartmentalise them as a parallel set of requirements rather than things that could be integrated into an educational model.

If in Norway academics appeared to have been more successful in resisting managerialist approaches to quality assurance and evaluation, they had nevertheless experienced a bureaucratisation of academic work.

Increasing demands for documentation and for setting up committees and meetings can be understood as a form of the 'visualisation of work' (Bleiklie *et al.* 2000; Kvalsvik 1993). Visualisation of academic work means that it 'becomes accessible to administrators and academic leaders who may evaluate academic efforts and act upon the information "from a distance" without any specialist knowledge about it' (Bleiklie *et al.* 2000). While the translation by academics of their work into a new language or form might equally be a successful strategy for sustaining their own agendas, the overall outcome could be seen as a significant shift in intra-institutional relations: a 'bureaucratisation of academic relations' (Bleiklie *et al.* 2000).

Bureaucratisation could also imply significant change in the nature and purposes of academic work. The quality principles underlying some aspects of the visualisation of work were equity, transparency, consistency and consumerism. In the context of education, clear documentation and procedures were required for students to understand expectations, rules and the rights derived from them. Such requirements could elide into orthodoxies in the presentation of lectures, teaching material or 'handouts' to students. Such developments sat uneasily with the values of individualisation, flexibility, high demands and the encouragement to take risks that constituted the ideals of elite higher education. In England, the requirements of TQA symbolised for some the coming of new bureaucratic models of education. Teaching would be more efficient, but was likely to result in 'predictable mediocrity' (senior historian, collegiate university). That might be increasingly necessary in the context of mass higher education but it signified a shift from the liberal education ideal.

MARKET MODELS OF QUALITY

Market definitions and mechanisms of quality assurance were, on the whole, more alien to academics in all three countries, despite the strong shift in political cultures towards market liberalism in the UK in the early 1980s and in Sweden in the early 1990s.

There was strong hostility in England and Sweden to the specific concept of student as customer. However, in both countries it informed a number of higher education policies and there was more ambivalence about it than at first appeared.

In England, there was some feeling that academics should pay more attention to student perspectives than had been the norm in the past, particularly in the older universities, and that students should be clearer about what they expected from higher education and more ready to complain. At the same time, some academics detected trends in expectations that they did not like, notably a shift towards regarding higher education as a credentialling as distinct from an educational process.

The idea of student as customer had most directly entered policies for quality assurance in the increasing institutionalisation of programme evaluations by students. This was reinforced not only by TQA criteria but also by the modularisation of curricula, which had encouraged more student choice of courses and more opportunities to take courses from different departments. This, in turn, affected the internal markets in universities, which were assuming growing importance.

The institutionalisation of student evaluations and its linkage with other quasi-market mechanisms had new implications for academic self-images. They raised the profile of teaching reputations. If they were incorporated into staff appraisals or departmental planning, they could constitute pressure on academics to make their courses more popular, by changing their approaches to teaching or by shifting the balance of their curricula, for example, away from 'harder' more technical material. On the other hand, academic self-images might be based more strongly on values of rigour and concern for the integrity of the discipline.

In Sweden, there were also mixed views. There, too, academics tended to be highly critical of the introduction of market values and market models of quality assurance into higher education. The academic who said that his views had changed to give more credence to 'quality as defined by external stakeholders and extrinsic values' (Bauer *et al.* 1999, p.243) was atypical: 'What has definitely changed is my view that we teachers don't have the sole right to interpret quality ... the voices of the students are important and also of others in the environment' (senior lecturer, college).

Some were appalled that resource allocations had been linked to student performance, on the grounds that this would exert pressures on academics to lower standards. However, others felt that it had led to greater effort and care for students. As we have seen in Chapter 5, it had probably also strengthened the incentives to develop innovative undergraduate programmes that would make institutions more competitive in the market for good students, by offering higher quality education.

In Norway, there is less evidence of a shift towards perceiving students as customers. The greater emphasis there on incorporating managerialism at the level of departments meant that approaches to quality based on concepts and mechanisms from the private sector might more directly influence academics. There were efforts to base resource allocation at both national and intra-institutional level on research and teaching performance but there was as yet no mechanism for seeing that these were systematically applied across institutions or disciplinary areas.

PROFESSIONAL DEFINITIONS OF QUALITY

So far we have mainly been considering how far the introduction of quality policies meant adopting definitions of quality from outside academia. We now turn to the question of whether they also represented competing conceptions or traditions of academic aims, values and beliefs that came from within the profession.

While we have seen that new and extrinsic definitions of quality had been imported into higher education, quality assurance policies in all three countries broadly reinforced the view that quality must remain in the hands of the academic profession. There was also much in them that reinforced historic beliefs about the academic profession: that academic life is rooted in research; that academic identities are primarily formed within a discipline, first in undergraduate education and then through the completion of a research degree; and that being an academic entails a combination of research, teaching and administration.

In all cases, the development of quality policies was bound to be shaped by the fact that academic reward systems were based upon achievement in research and scholarship. While there were well-developed systems for the evaluation of research, there was almost no ex post equivalent for teaching. The Council for National Academic Awards in the UK had focused primarily on quality assurance rather than on ex post quality assessment, although it had developed some work on this before it was wound up.

In all three countries, research remained dominant in the arrangements established for quality assurance, although in Norway there were the beginnings of national arrangements for integrated subject reviews. In England the separation of research and teaching assessments exacerbated the tensions being created by the increasing demands of both activities. However, the RAE was the dominant influence on academic lives. It also had some influence on conceptions of knowledge.

While the RAE was discipline-based and largely dependent on peer review, it imposed a common framework of specific output criteria to be met within a common time period. Those criteria reflected conceptions of knowledge emphasising production as distinct from reflection: beliefs that knowledge advances primarily from the cumulative effect of public articulation, exposure, criticism and exchange – 'thinking in public', as an economist in our study put it – rather than from prolonged reflection or internal dialogue with the discipline. They are criteria associated with 'normal science' (Kuhn 1970) or with the hard/pure disciplines in which the map of next problems to be solved tends to be fairly well defined (Becher 1989), even if achieving the authority to impose those definitions may be hotly contested. They are conventionally less easily accommodated within disciplines believed to progress primarily through the work of individuals engaging in recursive study or making connections between different fields of scholarship.

The RAE also had quite drastic consequences for the academic identities of some. Only those academics who could be defined in terms of the exercise as 'research active' could be entered into it. Academics who had not published enough in the prescribed period could be excluded from the category 'research active'. Once that happened, they acquired a new and undesirable semi-public status from which it was almost impossible to escape. Their teaching and administrative loads would be increased to relieve their 'active' colleagues. The development of a publication record thus became even more difficult to attain. From being a member of a community based on implicit assumptions of status, responsibilities and divisions of labour that were more complex than teaching and research (Henkel 1999; Trow 1976), a person could be consigned to an explicit category of second class and vulnerable individual. Even in the post-1992 universities, many older staff who had based their careers on the assumption that their primary identities would be as teachers were having to come to terms with the idea that their institutions were changing their missions in such a way as to call the value of those identities into question.

The approaches of the three countries to the evaluation of education differed markedly. Sweden had put its trust mainly in an institution-led approach to quality assurance and left open how the relationship between research and teaching would be dealt with. In one Swedish university the beginnings of an integrative approach had been formulated (Bowden and Marton 1998; see also Bauer and Henkel 1997). This saw the formation of knowledge within a discipline – collectively produced by research and individually attained through student learning – as having common epistemic roots, something which carries a deeper pedagogical meaning, making teaching an intellectually more challenging task. Such development implied that the role of the disciplinary expert would constitute a more integrated profession of teaching/learning and research.

The National Agency in Sweden had established some national evaluations of educational programmes that focused on content and the basic conditions for ensuring quality. However, only in England had a comprehensive system been established top-down for the evaluation of the quality of education, which did, in fact, depart from assumptions that good teaching is necessarily a product of active engagement in research.

The Funding Council intended that assessments of the quality of education would be made against self-defined aims and criteria. (To that extent, it could be said to represent the imposition of a form of activity planning on academic departments.) A self-evaluation report was required from every department or subject group. The Council was endorsing the concept of a diverse higher education system, in which 'all institutions have the potential to achieve excellence' (HEFCE 1993a, para.7). Assessments would be made on the relationship between aims and achievements and the importance of output criteria was asserted, 'the breadth and depth of student learning and student achievement'. However, the language used in the Council's guidance documentation leaned towards educational theory rather than the idea that excellence in teaching was rooted in understanding and authority in the discipline or subject area. It stressed, for example, the inseparability of teaching and learning (rather than teaching and research).

Educational assessments were predominantly in the hands of peer reviewers, but peer review in higher education was virtually unknown. Partly because of the Council's approach, peer assessors for this new form of evaluation were less likely to be acknowledged as leaders in their field. The nature of the qualifications required was contested as between academic excellence and pedagogical expertise. Making peer review key to the assessment method might not have been an effective means of commanding academic support. Rather it could be part of a process in which the exercise was externalised, stereotyped and constructed as unacceptable or irrelevant to those being assessed.

The role of pedagogical theory was one contestable element perceived as informing teaching quality assessments. A second was the concept of transferable skills and the importance to be attached to the educational aim of preparing students for the labour market. Again, in their original documentation the Council made it clear that evaluation would include 'the development of [students'] intellectual and personal skills and questions of employability and employment' (HEFCE 1993b, Annex).

In both Norway and Sweden, there was evidence of accelerating interest in different ideas about learning in higher education, although it was less clear how far these had affected academic thinking about educational practice. In 1990 a national committee in Norway proposed a range of new models for learning, teaching and the assessment of students. In a more recent public debate, it was argued that Norwegian higher education was too focused on examination and the certification of students at the expense of developing the quality of learning for its own sake (Vabø 2000).

The opposite was the case in Sweden, where there was more emphasis on the educational process than on examination and pedagogical development units had been established in the universities in the 1970s. The new demands inherent in the reforms of the 1990s contributed to a wave of interest in pedagogical development and student learning, and introduced different types of quality criteria than those used in peer review of research. However, at least in the early stages of reform, there was little central prescription or guidance in Sweden about how quality in education might be defined.

In addressing how academics in the three countries responded to these developments, it is important first to recall (see Chapter 6) the ways in which the academic profession in our three countries differed from the ideals set out above. In none of the three countries had all academics undergone doctoral research education, nor were all academics both researchers and teachers. There was substantial division between research and teaching at individual and institutional levels. Broadly, for most of our period only universities were funded for research, so that in each country there were institutions whose primary function was teaching and staff in those institutions would have to generate their own money and time for research. Certainly the Swedes, who had separated research and teaching roles in the universities in the 1960s, had made a more radical division between research and teaching than Norway or England. But there were numbers of participants in all three countries in our study who, for all or most of their careers, had regarded themselves primarily or wholly as teachers.

However, in common with academics across the world, the overwhelming majority of respondents in each country study saw their primary identity as being with their discipline (Altbach 1996). In both the English and Swedish study, specific and strong statements of discipline-based values and beliefs were made in the context of discussions about educational aims. Academics predominantly framed their aims in terms of what students could learn through studying their discipline, even if they had more generic goals in mind, such as becoming informed citizens with independent and critical minds or developing cognitive and social skills, which they could use in the labour market. A number also made it clear that they wanted students to appreciate the power, beauty or insights of their particular subject. Here the myths of these specific disciplines were evident in the language of the respondents, most noticeably, but far from only, the physicists.

Our interviews also reflected widespread commitment to the importance of maintaining research and teaching identities in academic life. There were country and discipline differences on this issue. At least in England, while many people in the social sciences and the humanities had strong views about the interdependence between research and teaching, well exemplified from their own practice, scientists were more likely to see these two activities as providing a good balance in their own working lives. A good teacher of science was not necessarily also an active researcher. However, most also thought that science teaching must take place in a research environment.

There was some evidence of trends in England and Sweden moving in opposite directions. In Sweden the separation of research and teaching roles in the 1960s had provoked sustained opposition and continuing determination that they should be integrated, although in practice the increasing pressures upon them made this extremely difficult. In England, as we saw in Chapter 6, these pressures, reinforced by quality assessments, had led institutions to find various ways of dividing teaching from research responsibilities in academic contracts, or at least reducing the tensions between them. For example, they created research-only contracts for eminent researchers or contracts in which teaching and administrative responsibilities were strictly limited. Some also employed staff on fixed-term, teaching-only contracts. Academics themselves, however, did not necessarily support this kind of solution, partly because of its divisive consequences and partly because it undermined their own intellectual dynamic. Again, natural scientists were more likely to support it, and increasingly so, because of the time spent in generating research funding and a widening range of research collaborations.

National differences and their implications

Our analysis so far has indicated that there were strong similarities between some of the developments in the three countries and academic responses to them. However, there were also marked differences. Although the patterns of these varied, the main division was between England and the two Scandinavian countries.

Some of this divide could be accounted for by the differences between the circumstances in which our empirical work was carried out. In particular, the policies for quality assurance had been established for longer in England than in either of the other two countries. Also the Norwegian study concentrated on the two universities of Oslo and Bergen, while the Swedish and English studies included a wider range of institutions, including universities and colleges in the case of Sweden and pre-1992 and post-1992 universities in the case of England.

However, there were critical differences between the English and Scandinavian policies. The English policies were more institutionalised, but were also based upon different change strategies that can be linked with the political culture of the 1980s and early 1990s. England, like Sweden, included audit of quality assurance arrangements and, like Norway, the development of national performance indicators. But as far as academics were concerned these in themselves made little impact. The assessment exercises, on the other hand, had major effects on the lives of English academics. They were comprehensive, systematically applied by a national body, mandatory and, in the case of the research assessment, had major resource consequences. They reached further into academic practices and made differential performances at the level of the basic unit transparent. While Norwegian policies also had elements of transparency built into them, they had as yet been fragmentary and allowed for some obfuscation. In England the separation between research assessment and teaching quality assessment made departments' performances clear within institutions and outside. Moreover, although individual performances were not publicly scored, they were relatively easily identified within their departments and institutions.

In the following paragraphs it is suggested that impacts discernible in England were not evident in either Sweden or Norway because of the differences in the characteristics of the policies.

There were differences in academic strategies in the face of the two forms of assessment. Research assessment was perceived as a coercive policy and aimed not only, or indeed even mainly, at quality assurance but rather at the selective allocation of resources. However, it was a joint creation of academic elites concerned about the needs of science and policy makers intent on the control of public expenditure. It was recognised as a peer review exercise, even if peer review was perceived as being used for purposes that went well beyond the operation of the academic reward system. Moreover, it could be said to be expressing and revitalising a myth of profound personal and political importance for academic professional identities, that they were grounded in research. However, it created tensions as it exposed the difference between myth and reality in the whole range of academic institutions. As we have seen, it also caused a loss of identity to many individual members of the profession. However, the importance to the dominant interests of the profession of ensuring that this gap was bridged was underlined when what had been teaching institutions were allowed to become universities at the ending of the binary line in 1992. Not only did the competition for resources become far more intense, but also conflicts about the meaning of higher education were opened up. The RAE gave strong incentives for all universities to show that they took research seriously, even those where it had not had much support before 1992.

Academics, therefore, largely accepted the research assessment exercise even if it was seen as rewarding elites, restricting some choices and, as we have seen, distorting epistemic criteria in some disciplines.

However, academic responses to the assessments of the quality of education were more mixed and ambivalent. They opened up far more uncertainties and conflicts. As already indicated, the legitimacy of these assessments was bound to be more contested, partly because they lacked precedent and partly because, although they were ostensibly also administered by peer review, the meaning of peer in this context was itself a matter of controversy. Common reactions in the academic community could be seen as an exaggerated form of those in Scandinavia. The threat of assessment that would invade not only metaphorically but physically the territory of academic encounter with students evoked from academics various forms of conservation strategy designed to undermine its legitimacy.

Fear of or resistance to external assessment resulted in stereotyping: the circulation of stories about the processes and criteria of assessment. ('Everyone must show that they use overhead projectors', 'Evaluation depends entirely on teacher performance in the classroom'.) Departments might then seek to consolidate their identity round opposition to a process based on constructions of its meaning rather than clarification of their own position. Quality assessments became a game that must be won or a matter of self-presentation that must deceive. Alternatively they could be seen as objects of ridicule so that poor performance could be construed as having no significance. Consolidation might therefore be focused around the assessment event and geared towards a short-term challenge rather than longer term confrontation of change.

In both England and Sweden, the introduction of quality assurance brought with it a strong emphasis upon self-evaluation. However, in England it was a required component of the assessment and an important component of what was judged. It could not be avoided. In Sweden it was part of the building by institutions themselves of their own systems. It was perhaps, at least in the early stages, easier to avoid or delay engaging with it.

In England, it sometimes generated another strategy: compliance. The purposes, values and language of the assessments were learnt or perhaps surmised and the department consolidated round presentation within those terms.

Probably more frequently assessment was taken seriously. Indeed, sometimes it was used for the purpose of major review. It was, in other words, accommodated within academics' own purposes and frameworks. Whole departments or subject groups, particularly in pre-1992 universities, found themselves, often for the first time, articulating their educational aims and values, examining how far they were meeting them, identifying how student needs were changing, and thinking about how they could address them. Such self-evaluation could lead to an enhanced appreciation of their subject. (A deeply sceptical professor of English had found that at the end of the exercise he had realised 'how complex is the organism that is English'.) Individuals might have a stronger identification with their department and a more collective sense of its educational responsibilities, but also a more broadly grounded sense of their discipline. The accommodation of policy requirements had made academic identities more robust in the face of new demands.

However, self-evaluation and quality assurance programmes did not necessarily result in the consolidation of identities in a particular mould. They were also the means of opening up the considerable variety of possible definitions of quality and conditions for its improvement. They could reveal divisions within the academic profession and ambivalence within individuals.

Some divisions of belief were associated with different types of institution, with individuals' length of time in the profession and with different roles. A particular line of difference was between those whose models of higher education were knowledge centred and those whose models were student centred and based on educational or learning theories. Many of the latter group also placed high value on their disciplines. However, they also tended to have more in common with consumerist thinking than their counterparts. They felt that more attention should be given to students' modes of learning, student aspirations and student perceptions of their programmes. They were more likely to be found in post-1992 universities and, within the pre-1992 universities, among young staff who had been exposed to some kind of formal induction in their teaching roles. This kind of programme tended to be run by staff development units where expertise was not discipline based but generic and strongly influenced by educational theories. Academic managers and academics who actively participated in the development or management of quality assurance were also more sympathetic to educational theories.

There were not only differences between individuals and groups. Opening up issues of quality and how it is best assured also meant the introduction of uncertainty and ambivalence. Introducing more bureaucracy was seen as part of a process in which students had become more dependent and at the same time were better informed about their courses and what was expected of them. Faculties felt that their teaching was better in that it was more focused and better organised, and at the same time that they had had to abandon liberal education ideals. The introduction of consumerist ideas in a more market-oriented system meant that students were listened to more than in the past but also that a bias had been introduced towards credentialling and student satisfaction rather than testing and stretching students.

External assessment evoked ambivalent responses. It was constructed as representing and imposing alien values but it could have the effect of consolidating departmental values. Academics resisted it, often dismissing it as irrelevant to genuine quality or core issues. It was seen as an attack on their self-esteem. However, if their department was awarded high scores, this raised their sense of self-esteem and their reputation within the institution.

Overall we have suggested that the quality reforms evoked some similar responses from academics in all three countries. They had implications for the balance between collective and individual identities and for conceptions of academic work, particularly of education. They made a stronger impression upon academics in England, but there, as elsewhere, they evoked complex patterns of resistance and change, of consolidation and ambivalence or uncertainty.

We will now look more closely at the conclusions that can be drawn from the two case studies. We consider the range of strategies employed by academics in the face of two sets of reforms and their implications for stability and change in academic identities. We note again that the relationship between specific reforms and academic identities has to be placed in a larger web of influences that will differ as between disciplines, institutional environments and countries.

Case study conclusions

We have presented two contrasting case studies. They represent different challenges to different constituencies. The first was a challenge to a prestigious discipline at the oldest university in Norway. However, the context was one where the status of the discipline had become uncertain because the contribution of humanities to higher education was under question. This was part of a wider international trend.

One purpose of the reform was to promote a more efficient mode of knowledge production, a projected outcome of which was to enable academics to give more time to their core activities of research and teaching. The reform could therefore be said to promote efficiency in the name of quality. At the same time, at least formally, it had more far-reaching implications for modes of knowledge production and knowledge development in the humanities. This was at a time when theoretical challenges to the robustness of the discipline as the organi-

sational base for the production of knowledge, at least in the humanities and the social sciences, were also making themselves felt (Geertz
1983).

The case study shows, uncertainties about the disciplines notwithstanding, the power of disciplinary myths to unite an elite discipline in
opposition and to co-opt key powerful interests in its support. It
therefore points to the continuing importance of the discipline in
academic identity; and to power as a key variable in the capacity of
academics to resist change to their academic identities. However, it
also demonstrates how strong disciplinary boundaries may be valued
differently by different disciplines with different histories.

Both studies take forward one of the main themes of Chapter 5, the
new pivotal role of institutions in higher education policy development in our period. In this chapter the stronger focus has been on
the department. Our first study shows the importance of the department to members of academic disciplines, as a source of symbolic
power but also of tangible influence and command of resources in the
institution. The second study demonstrates the critical role of the
department in the control of academic criteria. Both studies reveal
the department as a key site of academic responses to policy reforms.

The relationships between department and discipline and between
department and individual emerge as more critical to the dynamics
within which academic identities are formed and pursued. This
development also reflects the growing importance of collective insti-
tution-based identities, particularly for members of those disciplines
which tended to emphasise the less tangible and more diffuse relationship between individual and discipline.

The two studies enable us to analyse a range of largely collective
strategies used by academics in the face of challenge to their identities. We will first review them and then consider how they might be
expected to affect those identities in the longer term, as well as immediately. This implies taking into account the extent to which the
academic communities concerned were confronting the nature of the
changes facing them. It will enable us to consider again the resources
on which academic communities can draw in resisting or accommo-
dating changes that arise primarily from sources outside their own
boundaries. This set of issues is another formulation of a major theme
of the book: the relative strength of radical reform and organic or evolutionary change.

Conservation strategies were dominant and included the following:

- Using the power of *myths*: in the first study, departments
  drew on myths of a hierarchy of disciplines in academia. It
  could also be argued that, faced with a direct challenge, a

department which had not had much need to heed the fragmentation within its discipline, partly because of the power of another myth (isolation as the traditional, if not essential, condition of history scholars), drew on a third myth (historians are nevertheless a community) to unite again in the face of direct attack. In this case the strategy was successful. Why? One reason was that it meshed with the concern of the institution about its reputation, its public identity

- Consolidation of existing identities through *stereotyping* – through the successful creation of new myths about a new policy

- *Subversion*, as a form of consolidation of academic norms, not as its opposite. Quality assessments in England were in some cases treated by departments as exercises in deception or game playing

- *Compartmentalisation*: new demands, which embody values in conflict with existing values, are defined in terms that lie outside existing definitions of role and practice. So, for example, quality can be defined in terms of new bureaucratic requirements and perceived as a parallel and subordinate concern. We observed compartmentalisation strategies being adopted in both England and Sweden (see also Harvey and Knight 1996).

Some of the above strategies could be seen as relatively short term. They diverted rather than faced the implications of the changing demands on higher education. There are grounds for arguing that where academics more directly confronted these, they succeeded in reaffirming their values and beliefs, strengthening their place in a changing world.

One such longer term conservation strategy is that of *accommodation*. Academics may find ways to accommodate new demands or different priorities asserted by actors from different fields of action within their own value systems. They may be able to incorporate new evaluative criteria or procedures, such as collective self-evaluation, and use them to strengthen their own disciplinary practices. They may find ways of subsuming the knowledge priorities of external funding bodies or research customers within existing research agendas.

Transformation

All the above strategies reflect, some weakly, some with more force, the idea that policy development is inadequately conceptualised as impact or implementation. Policy consequences strongly depend upon the part played by actors in the relevant fields of action in remodelling ideas and the energy and direction they supply for their transmission: what Latour (1987) calls translation (see also Vabø 2000). We prefer to speak of transformation.

While for analytic purposes it is helpful to focus on individual reforms, in most contexts, and certainly as far as the scope of this book is concerned, they will develop as part of a wider nexus of changes. So it is possible for us to outline areas in which academics, as key actors in higher education policies, were participants in a transformation process. The following example is one in which responses to quality assurance policies were involved but as one dimension of a more complex nexus of policies and strategies.

In England a widespread response by academics to the introduction into higher education of the concepts of competence and skills within policies of economic instrumentalism and vocationalism was to interpret much of what was being advocated as what they had always done. This applied particularly to the concept of 'transferable skills' (e.g. Boys *et al.* 1988). Academics began to define such activities as developing analytic capacities or rigorous use of evidence in constructing argument or precision in the use of language as transferable skills. They could be said to be translating their own work into another externally imposed discourse and to some extent justifying it in those terms. At all events, the concept of skills became increasingly firmly embedded into higher education policies in the 1980s and 1990s, first and foremost through the government's Enterprise Initiative, but also through quality assurance. So, at one level teaching quality assessments could be regarded as providing a good example of epistemic drift (Elzinga 1985). The development of transferable skills was gradually accepted as a more or less fixed criterion in these exercises (despite the overarching definition of quality as fitness for purpose). As a result it became more firmly embedded in academic discourse about educational objectives and the curriculum.

Our interviews suggest, however, that what was occurring was not a simple shift towards instrumentalism on the part of the academics as a result of external policies. Something more complex appears to have happened of which these phenomena were a part. Several external factors, including the increase in numbers and diversity of students, vocationalist policies, modularisation and the introduction of quality assurance and performance indicators had, in combination or separately, forced departments to make quite fundamental reappraisals of their curricula in their own interests. While some academics and probably fewer departments had resolutely rejected the idea that it was a function of higher education to prepare students for the labour market, more commonly transferable skills had been incorporated into a substantially strengthened discipline-centred curriculum. It might be argued that what had occurred was a transformation of the curriculum in which internalist and externalist values had been brought together and resulted in a reaffirmation of academic identities.

Academic identities and higher education reforms

We argued at the beginning of this chapter that values, interests and beliefs, self-images and reputations are central to academic identities. They are formed and developed through interaction between individual histories and choices and the workings of key communities and structures: disciplines, departments and institutions. They reveal themselves in academic agendas, practices and conversations.

We have tried to identify stabilities and change on two main dimensions. One is the dynamic within which academic identities are shaped. The other is the substance of identities. Our analysis has throughout been suffused by the language of duality and complexity: stability and change; consolidation and weakening; collective and individual. Ambivalence and ambiguity have figured strongly in the analysis.

Some of the developments described have pointed to change in the interactions between individual, discipline, department and institution which had most significance for academic identities. We saw in Chapter 5 that institutions became pivotal for the mediation of policy developments, and as such were increasingly shaping the space of action in which academic identities were pursued. With this development, however, departments gained in significance. They were often the final arena in which the implications of policy reforms were worked out. We saw in the case studies how academics were able to unite in this arena to defend and to strengthen the discipline in the context of externally imposed reform. Disciplines continued to be the primary source of identity for the overwhelming majority of participants in our study, but departments had a stronger role in the continuing interaction between discipline and individual.

There was a shift in our period towards the importance of collective as well as individual identities, partly instrumental but partly in terms of loyalties, goals and agendas. Identification with the institution was most evidently a new development in Sweden, but in all three countries there was a growing awareness of the mutual dependency of institution, department and individual in terms of reputation, resources and autonomy.

Increased consciousness of the need for collective identity was partly a consequence of increased attention to the quality of education. However, in research too imperatives towards collective identities were strengthening. The reasons were extrinsic, efficiency and visibility to national and international markets and funding bodies, but also intrinsic, at least in science. Advances were increasingly seen by dominant scientific communities to depend on intra- and inter-disciplinary collaboration.

However, the growth in importance of collective identities did not diminish the imperatives of achieving an individual reputation and a sense of individual disciplinary identity and self-esteem. Moreover, there was no evidence in our countries of any weakening in the value attached by academic researchers to individual autonomy. While there might be some branches of science, such as high energy physics and astronomy, where teamwork was central, scientists were as insistent as social scientists and humanities scholars on their need for freedom to choose their research agendas and for acquiring an individual identity. Individual accounts of academic careers were marked by the imposition upon them of individual logic and continuity, or at least of individual control of the directions those careers had taken.

The context was undoubtedly changing. Research councils and other funding bodies were increasingly framing research agendas. As institutions, departments and individuals, too, were laying more stress on income generation and greater financial independence, private markets became more important to them. As we saw in Chapter 6, departments and individuals varied as to how far they could accommodate external agendas within their own programmes, but many did. Some, in collaboration with external partners, sought further to manage a process of transformation in which both external and internal agendas were shaped to facilitate innovation and so serve the interests of all. Intellectual, physical and social types of capital were all important in this type of endeavour. Again, individuals and departments drew on their own reputations and those of their institution. They were also variously interconnected with disciplinary hierarchies, which in turn shaped the research environment. Research councils, despite the growth of influence upon them of lay members, still relied heavily on the invisible colleges to help shape agendas and evaluate applications and outputs.

However, the emphasis on the collective dimension of research was part of a process that had significant implications for social scientists and the humanities. During the latter part of the twentieth century, the boundaries round many of the social sciences and humanities had become more permeable. There were strong currents of influence between the two and both had been influenced by similar theories from a variety of sources. If, first, some of the humanities became more scientific, soon the social sciences also became more humanistic. However, policy changes tended towards the influence of the natural sciences on the organisation and evaluation of research. Not only was there a move towards collective modes of production and an emphasis on concepts such as critical mass for determining departmental size, but there was also some shift in epistemic criteria. The emphasis on research output meant a shift towards an incremental model of knowledge in which progress is made through the public exchange of writing in papers or articles that contain relatively small-scale innovation. This contrasts with the reflective, recursive style favoured in the humanities, where strong value is placed on maturity.

Overall, however, the evidence of our study is that the values and processes within which academic identities are built and given powerful symbolic representation in disciplinary myths remain a strong source of stability. Changes in structures and institutional processes are as yet not matched by changes in values, images and ideals. Processes of change at the level of national policy are only partially co-ordinated with the rhythms of disciplines, departments and individuals.

PART IV

Conclusions

Chapter 8

Change and Continuity
Some Conclusions

Maurice Kogan, Marianne Bauer,
Ivar Bleiklie and Mary Henkel

In this chapter, we summarise the main points made in the book, discuss the main change outcomes that were discernible at T^2 and consider the sources of change and continuity. As an example of major change, we seek to interpret changes in overall structure. Finally, we note how our studies reflect on some modes of generalisation to be found in current higher education studies.

What the book said

In this book we have, through social science perspectives, compared changes in the higher education field, the change processes and their effects, in three Western European countries of different histories, polities and cultures.

In Chapter 1, we laid out the arguments for making these comparisons, which are based on the more substantive analyses of the changes contained in our national studies, and described the explicitly qualitative methods used in pursuing these lines of enquiry. We also presented an explanatory model where we assume that change is affected by bounded rational actors interacting within different institutional contexts. We noted the different stages of change since roughly the beginning of the 1970s (T^1) until the latter years of the 1990s (T^2).

In fleshing out the actor–context model and its institutionalist argument we have dealt with changes within the three tightly interwoven fields of national policy and politics (Chapters 2–4), educational institutions (Chapter 5), academic work and identity (Chapters 6–7). Our conceptualisation allows for treating change as a product of public policy and at the same time as the outcome of the actions and values of the prime actors, the academics, at the base of the system, as well as resulting from deeper structural changes affecting the university system.

Yet the countries started from different points in their modes of and assumptions about forms of government, the structures of influence and power and the very core of academic life, academic identities and preferences for different forms of knowledge.

In Chapter 2 we provided an outline of the recent higher education policy history of the three countries. A number of similar challenges that faced the systems were identified, such as sharply growing student numbers, a higher ratio of students to teachers and new forms of regulation of higher education. One set of structural changes that characterised the three systems is the movement into some sort of binary structure during the 1970s which was replaced during the 1990s by a movement towards system integration and academic drift.

We noted how all three governments urged universities to adopt explicit quality assurance practices, market behaviour, stronger vocational missions and public accountability, but the policies came out differently. In the UK and Sweden they were practically opposite. In Sweden the central regulation of study lines and courses gave way to placing the responsibility for quality on the institutions themselves. In the UK, self-regulation was overtaken by the highly prescriptive activities of first the funding agencies and later the Quality Assurance Agency. In Norway, the state was far more hesitant to insinuate nationally devised practices. The UK differed again in the assertion of selectivity in research funding which was far stronger than in Norway and Sweden. In the UK, too, policy was sharpened in the 1980s by ideology based on overt distrust of public service professionals and providers.

Thus it is possible to note parallel periods of change, largely driven by the same forces. But because they took place in different political and cultural settings and had different starting points, they produced different sets of outcomes. Common goals, different means and different contexts meant different outcomes.

Chapter 3 dealt with the policy process through a dynamic regime approach. Variations in policy can be explained in terms of policy design. Policy design has moved in all three countries from a concentration on authority tools towards the use of a wider array of policy instruments including more emphasis on incentives and learning tools. The policy field was originally characterised by participation of a few main actors within stable structural arrangements: elites in England, corporatist arrangements in Sweden and tight relations between ministry officials and academic institutions in Norway. This changed to varying degrees of wider participation within somewhat looser networks of actors. The relationship between policy regime and policy design manifested itself as different policy styles. The English policy style can be characterised as heroic, the Norwegian as incremental and the Swedish as adversarial.

Chapter 4 explored the relationship between the state and higher education. It focuses initially on how the perception of higher education has changed, as it has become larger, more complex and costly. As the system has grown and the economy has changed, the perceived importance of higher education and research to the 'knowledge' economy has put a stronger utilitarian pressure on higher education. The way in which the countries dealt with the change varied according to the point of departure when the reforms where conceived and according to national traditions. England has moved from a state–higher education relationship characterised by a devolutionary form of central planning and a comparatively high degree of autonomy. Sweden seems to have moved in the opposite direction, from a point of departure in the late 1970s characterised by extraordinarily strong state control to a more decentralised system in the 1990s. In Norway the development has been characterised by a set of seemingly contradictory moves comprising formalisation and more state influence over a wider array of higher education affairs combined with the introduction of more decentralised management procedures, particularly in the area of economic planning and budgeting.

Universities can be mapped alongside a spectrum of normative accounts of the nature of the state, from the minimalist in which it does no more than protect the natural rights of individuals, through more traditional liberal and conservative thinking, to the maximalist communitarian or absolutist views, both of which grant maximum authority to the collectivity. Alongside these are the normative accounts of the government of higher education, from the classic to the dependent model of the institution. It is possible to strip down these models by contrasting their dominant values, knowledge styles and client groups and from there educe internal and external governmental structures.

The relationship between academic institutions and national political authorities, the framing of academic authority, was the topic of Chapter 5. The increased authority of the higher education institutions, the various forms of pressure upon them to become more autonomous – although in different ways – the elements of accountability and external control of efficiency and quality seem to give the institutions quite new roles and functions in the higher education systems of today. This also raised the expectations placed on a more pronounced institutional leadership and management.

Changing assumptions about higher education systems are internalised by institutions within the framing of their space for action by government and intermediary bodies. We noted the role of institutions as key change mediators. In recent years they have taken on a more central role in transmitting political intentions to academic processes and outcomes than previously.

There are examples of efforts to find a proper balance between centralisation and decentralisation, between internal (academic) influences and external (corporate and/or market-dominated) influences, between organisational stability and flexibility, all in order to maximise the capacity for institutional development within a frame of state control.

The national contexts differed and so did the effects on institutions. In Norway, they included internal reorganisation of the departmental structure by mergers of departments, the introduction of activity planning and evaluations, and the decentralisation and strengthening of leadership at all levels of the university organisation. In Sweden, a focus on evaluation and control (of quality and efficiency) as an essential component of increased self-regulation and competition among the institutions generated demands for strong institutional leadership. In the UK, the power of the vice-chancellor was strengthened as planning and managerial practices were more firmly installed.

In Chapter 6, we noted the uncertainties surrounding the existence of the academic profession and the impact of integrating relations as well as of disintegrating forces, such as hierarchisation and divides between the disciplines. The differences between the three countries and how the position of academics has changed over the period that we cover were analysed.

The British academics living within traditional self-governing institutions contrasted with the higher civil service status of Scandinavian professors whose educational ideals were not those of producing a generally educated elite but helping the young to learn a trade. With expansion, assumptions changed in all three countries, as did those concerning the teacher–researcher divide and participation in governance of institutions by junior academic and non-teaching staff and students. With these changes, different patterns of academic leadership at the disciplinary level also emerged.

From power and authority within institutional structures our analysis in Chapter 7 turned to the ultimate criterion variables of the effects of policy changes on academic working and values. Within academia, identity is seen as a key social as well as individual concept. Identities are developed and validated within a social context, through a dynamic between individuals and significant collectives, disciplines, departments and institutions, located in national cultures and higher education histories. They provide the tangible structures and processes, and the myths and traditions that make for stability in the academic values, conceptions of knowledge and practices at the centre of academic identities.

Although the impact may vary between disciplines, institutions and countries, the analysis seems to underpin one general interpretation of the reform impact. Academics may face altered circumstances with considerable resilience, they adapt to and exploit conditions they favour, and avoid or modify reforms they resent. In a short-term perspective, counter-strategies may thus modify reforms and their impact considerably and represent an apparent conservative force in the higher education system. However, in a longer time perspective there might also be some transformation of academic values and attitudes towards knowledge. Academic staff under given circumstances act as innovators themselves.

In tracing some of the complexities of the policies and their implications for academic values and conceptions of practice, we used two case studies of contrasting policies: merging departments in Norway and quality assurance in England, Norway and Sweden. The case studies represented different challenges to different constituencies. The first shows the power of disciplinary myths to unite an elite discipline and to co-opt key powerful interests in its support. It also shows the importance of the department to members of academic disciplines. The second case study examines the patterns of similarity and difference in quality assurance policies and their implications for academics in the three countries. It notes some shifts of emphasis from individual to collective identities, the bureaucratisation of academic work and the as yet uncertainly developing influence upon academics of market values and mechanisms. It suggests that the UK policies, based on more coercive change strategies, did penetrate academic work and values more thoroughly than those in Norway and Sweden, although the implications for the longer term remain uncertain. The case studies taken together identify a range of conservation strategies used by academics, the most robust of which was probably conservation. We note some circumstances in which new demands and academic responses to them might have led to transformation of academic practices in which internalist and externalist values were brought together, and resulted in a reaffirmation of academic identities.

Change outcomes at T^2

In considering change outcomes as they emerged in our period of study, we follow two dimensions that have been our principal concerns in this book: *authority* and power relationships between higher education, the state and the market; and the *purposes* of higher education. Purposes are to be understood in terms of the forms of knowledge to be advanced in higher education and the values underlying them.

All the detailed outcomes, identified in Table 8.1 (p.206), can be categorised along these two dimensions. The model of four types of institutional autonomy, presented in Figure 4.2 (p.100), can facilitate analysis of change and continuity at all levels or in all fields of action. It makes it possible to locate the three systems at the beginning and end of our study period. It thus enables us to go beyond Clark's triangle, creative and seminal formulation though it was, which is concerned only with power or authority.

Using this diagram to illustrate various governance models, it is possible to depict the changes in the three countries from T^1 to T^2 in

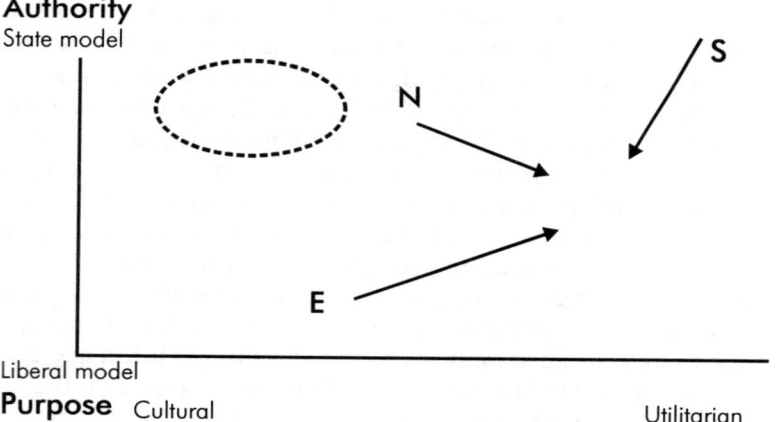

Figure 8.1 Three nations' movement towards a New Governance model

the following way (Figure 8.1). As evident from the figure, all three nations can be characterised as moving towards a market model of governance, with more emphasis on managerialism, market needs and structures, and research which is seen as 'useful'.

At T^1, the Swedish governments held a strongly utilitarian concept of higher education – the movement to T^2 partly entails a return to more cultural values. For Sweden, and arguably for Norway in certain respects, the movement reflects increased decentralisation from state authority. However, in the British case, the movement from a liberal model entails an increased degree of centralisation. It is not possible to depict such a transformation by a single point, and each nation moving towards the same point in the model does not end up with exactly the same characteristics and policies. Hence a circle is preferred to illustrate the variety between nations in their changed governance models.

We do not have enough empirical data to illustrate the corresponding movements of purposes and authority distribution in attitudes and behaviour of academic staff and leadership. However, in our interviews with academic representatives we found several expressions of adherence to the values of the Humboldtian and Newmanian models. Even if they had to adapt to new conditions, many academics continued to embrace traditional academic values.

Table 8.1 shows some of the detailed dimensions of higher education which might have changed between T^1 and T^2.

The table lists the broad categories of change that took place in the three countries between T^1 and T^2. Two reservations apply in making and using such a list, particularly one drawn up, for the sake of simplicity, in dichotomous terms. First, not all of the changes took place in the same direction. For example, in the Scandinavian countries, government became more facilitatory and less interventionist, whereas the opposite was true in the UK. All were more market driven. The UK unlike Norway and Sweden became more centralised. The system became more managerial. Professional academic control was weakened, especially in the UK, but to a lesser degree too in the other two countries.

Second, not all of the changes can be attributed to 'reform' policies. Not only, as we have shown, did contextual forces of social, economic and demographic origin help propel policies, but some, particularly those nearest academic activity, derived from changes in the configurations and developments of knowledge.

Sources of change

If it is possible to discern outcomes, it is more difficult to specify the sources of change and the processes of change. Did change evolve or was it imposed? These issues are different from but linked to the structure and actor perspectives elaborated in Chapter 3.

If we take imposition first, different concepts of change, different combinations of actors and the use of different tools did produce different outcomes in the three countries. However, it is important not to exaggerate the effects of radical policies, considerable though

Table 8.1 Outcomes at T2

Government level	
Between the facilitatory and the interventionist	Differed considerably between countries. UK more interventionist.
Between the providing and the regulative	Scandinavian countries less regulative. UK more regulative.
Between the welfare, deficiency funding and the market driven	All in direction of market.
Between the decentralised and the centralised	Norway and Sweden less, UK more centralised.
Between the professionally and the managerially led system	Moves towards managerial power.
Between control by the political and administrative laity and the academic professionals	More political and lay control, but academic control over content still strong in all countries.
Between sponsoring free enquiry and instrumental knowledge	Free enquiry strong but more deference to instrumental purposes in some areas.
Between individual development and economic and social policy values	Economic and social policy values more strongly embedded in missions.
Between peer and self-evaluation and systematic quality assurance	All stronger evaluation, but UK, though incorporating peer judgement, more external, linked to allocations.
Institutional level	
Between collegium and strong rectorate	Rectorates strengthened in all countries.
Between faculty organisation and central control and development mechanisms	Central mechanisms strengthened.
Between traditional academic and innovative styles and modes (e.g. entrepreneurial, adaptive and learning institutional models)	New models in all national rhetorics. Institutional adoption variable.
Between weak and strong accountability mechanisms	All stronger.

Table 8.1 (continued...) Outcomes at T2	
Between independent and dependent institution	More policy dependency, but more institutional earning of resources.
Between free grants and market acquired resources	More dependency on markets.
Individual academics	
Between individual to team and sponsored knowledge	Individuality strong, but more team and sponsored organisation of research and curriculum development.
Between individualistic and curiosity driven to instrumental and 'relevant' knowledge	Curiosity-driven research remained most esteemed, but more responsive, in some areas, to 'relevance'. Similar tendencies in some education.
Between individualistic and systemic and policy-driven values	Policy-driven values more salient, but individualistic remain strong.
Between scientific, progressive and humanistic, recursive models of knowledge production	Scientific model more widely imposed.
Between knowledge-led and bureaucratic or market models of quality	Knowledge-led models remained dominant but bureaucratic and market models had some impacts.
Between individual and collective identities	Collective identities became more important but not at the expense of individual identities.

they were. Academic excellence still remained the leading criterion, against all the claims of competing ideology, as represented by the allocation of funds and the award of quality assurance gradings through the RAE and the quality assurance systems. If in Norway and Sweden, expansion and the regionalisation of the universities were accompanied by equalisation of statuses, UK hierarchies of esteem, already so steep, were reinforced rather than reduced by these changes, although expansion and the implosion of the binary system certainly allowed for some readjustment, particularly in the middle of the pecking order, of statuses as between institutions. So far from enforcing single ideologies upon higher education, government, perhaps through avoidance of fundamental reappraisal, seemed content to allow several ideologies, policies and practices to run in parallel with each other.

Some changes, or at least the rhetoric surrounding them, may have come about from imitation. Thus the fashion of planning seems to have emerged strongly in the 1960s, perhaps under the advocacy of the OECD and its country reviews. The current emphases on quality review and market style arrangements almost certainly spread from country to country. But the deeper changes – massification, changing state–university relations, the stratification of systems, the new emphasis on curriculum and its delivery – might all be described as the natural evolution of systems once certain contextual factors were in place.

The three studies showed that while the countries shared many features, and particularly much of the whole vocabulary and rhetoric of reform that was common to OECD countries, the effects were varied. The changes had to operate against multiple perspectives viewed from multiple standpoints. They had to contend with different national political cultures (affecting, for example, the degree of centralisation tolerated), different institutional histories and expectations, and strong differences at the base deriving from disciplinary and other academic perspectives. Within institutions, perspectives were quite different at individual, departmental, faculty and university levels.

One generalisation that holds across the three countries is that the universities have emerged as actors with a new role and level of influence, particularly in regard to academic staff, in the policy process. However, like national systems, they were at different starting points at the beginning of our period. They reflect different national and local histories, different cultures, different mixes of expertise and multiple intellectual traditions. To try to encompass their actions or development in our period in terms of a few simple models is, we suggest, to oversimplify. For that reason we experience doubts about identifications such as 'the entrepreneurial university' (Clark 1998). That might indeed be an aspiration at the top, but is it shared by the main working parts?

Institutions' attitudes to and power to manage imposed change depend partly on various forms of capital that they inherit, but also access to assets which is entrenched in academic appointment. Universities have changed over time, but we have shown how they and the changes they have undergone are multimodal. They are multimodal because they embody many things at once. Current writing often assumes that there is an old traditional set of values and practices which is shifting under the impress of new forms of knowledge, new government university relations, new public policies. In fact, status and esteem still remain with traditional academic values and their attainment. Shifts in policy have affected practice, but we can make no presumptions about their affecting all academic working in the same ways. In particular, it was clear from the English study that the more esteemed institutions still housed academics who, if although also feeling under external pressures, remained free to go their own ways. Former largely teaching institutions would be more ready to follow new policy indications.

Whether changes evolve or are imposed by deliberate action, they evoke strategies of various kinds at the institutional, departmental and individual levels. They may be individual or collective, but in the current environments there has probably been movement from the individual to the collective level. Strategies might be broadly categorised as conservation, accommodation (perhaps the most robust form of conservation) and transformation. All of these might result in the maintenance or even reassertion of existing values. They do, however, have different potentials for generating long- as opposed to short-term change and for maintaining long-term stability or continuity. Those that take account of the changes surrounding them, rather than denying their force, are more likely to sustain the values most important to them.

There are, however, strong propensities for stability and continuity in academic communities and institutions, not least in the processes through which academic identities, collective and individual, are formed and pursued. Academic values, inherited knowledge and the agendas that drive from them are not easily disturbed and are, on the evidence of this study, slower to shift than structural changes or stronger external framing of academic work might suggest; although in the longer term these could solidify into institutions embodying new values.

The findings quoted above illustrate the interaction of structure-value driven and actor-preference driven processes of change that were conceptualised by actor–context model of change.

The historical analysis in Chapter 2 emphasised the evolutionary aspects of change and the gradual development of structures and basic values. However, when we looked more closely at the field of national policy and its development over the last 15 years (Chapter 3), we saw how policy structures and processes interacted, so that the same ideas came to be implemented within and adapted to systems which were clearly different. This shaped the preferences of the actors and the way in which they interpreted the new policies that emerged in the 1980s. Yet these conditions also seem to have provided varying degrees of leeway for actors, because actor-preference driven processes to varying degrees contributed to shaping the outcomes at T^1. This conclusion is corroborated when we look at the implications of policy changes for the state–higher education relationship in Chapters 4 and 5.

Although the relationship seemed to be affected by underlying forces that led to more convergence, they started from different points of departure and were moved by policy processes which to varying extents were driven by actor preferences and structural change. Moving our focus to the academic profession we found that it went through considerable structural changes in terms of growth, differentiation and standardisation between T^1 and T^2 in all three countries. However, the profession as such did not play the role of an actor in any of them. To the extent that we find actors within the policy processes at this level, they were representatives of academic disciplines and co-opted elites rather than of the profession as such.

In Chapter 7 we get a full impression of how broader policy and systems changes fare when faced with identities and the reactions of academics to these changes. At this level we are dealing with structures and actors that interact with national policies in particularly interesting ways since identity is closely related to academic disciplines. The disciplines constitute fields of action that to varying degrees are international and only partially sensitive to national policies or the policies of particular academic institutions.

Academic identity turned out to play an important role for the process of change in several ways. First, academic identities and modes of work constitute contextual sources of stability that seem to modify and reduce the impact of apparently radical change in policies and structural arrangements. Second, discipline is the most important source of academic identity. Third, academic identity affects attitudes towards, conceptions of and strategies of academics in relation to reforms.

Reasons for differences in national models and systems

We are left with the issue of reasons for differences in the three systems as they responded to broadly similar forces. Ultimately there is no answer to such questions as why the Norwegians opted initially for a binary system and the Swedes for a unitary pattern (they both seem likely to converge in differentiated unitary systems), or why the Scandinavian countries opted for more decentralisation while the UK has gone the other way. If we find reasons in national political cultures or patterns of regional politics, we are still left with the fact that countries have changed their policies and structures in the period of reforms. Such terms as culture may simply push the need for explanation one stage back.

However, to some extent, differences in strategies and models of state governance can be explained by the fact that the three countries started from different political cultures lending support to different overall models of government. We have noted some convergence, but underlying assumptions subsist. Thus although both the Norwegian and Swedish higher education systems developed in the continental tradition with strong governments and strong faculties, they differed in two main respects. Like England, Norway had a diversified higher education system in which the differences between institutions were not concealed but considered an important issue in regional policy. In Sweden, the national equivalence of all higher education institutions had been a core characteristic ever since the first universities were established.

Differences in outcomes between the countries in an actor–structure perspective can also be illuminated through differences in processes (not only in different points of departure and cultures), since processes of change are also dependent on direction of structural change and the resulting space for actors to utilise. For example, in England, governments distrusting the universities' quality assurance mechanisms enforced central systems for both research and education, thereby reducing the space of action for the academics leading to considerable short-term effects. In Sweden, the devolution of the responsibility for quality assurance to the institutions involved a widened space of action for institutions, faculties and departments to form their own models and activities of QA. Because the institutions were not accustomed to these tasks, however the space of action was ineffectively used.

We take as a particular example, which illustrates the difficulty of explaining national differences, the different histories of the three systems in respect to system integration. The differences cannot be interpreted in terms of the system size – Norway and Sweden differed in system arrangements as much from each other as from England.

Yet there may be a logic of institutional development that applies to systems. A first step undertaken by many has been to consolidate and enhance those parts of post-school education which, while depending for their intellectual substance on disciplined enquiry, yet look towards the world of application. For a while they remain the less 'noble' part of higher education. Increasingly, as concepts of what constitutes advanced learning and enquiry become broader, and the non-university institutions seek to emulate universities in undertaking research, a natural process of convergence sets in. Only where the most determined efforts are made to sustain a viable non-university sector, as in the Californian system, or in German *Fachhochschulen,* supported as it is by the specific requirements of professional entry to employment, is the division ultimately sustained; hence the trends in the creation of single but differentiated patterns in the USA, Australasia and Sweden. The existing binary systems such as in Finland, Norway and Greece can be predicted to go the same way within 30 years. The British system was among the strongest cases for unification since it accommodated a smaller proportion of each school-leaving age group than other countries, and assumed from the beginning that most of the higher education student body was capable of reaching degree standard. But once a system becomes unitary a hierarchy of esteem and resource is likely to assert itself. With massification, in the largest of the three systems (UK) came unification but also informal stratification, and in all systems diversification. Thus although a similar logic of system development can be traced, differences in outcome are to be expected.

Conclusions

We believe that our studies have thrown light on many areas of scholarship within political science and the theory of knowledge and its development. We have also extended such important usages as those celebrated in Clark's triangle, by adding categories from knowledge to his analysis of competing power blocks. We have linked issues concerning academic identity, already well treated by previous authors, more closely with policy processes and policy change.

Our projects have also taught us to be chary of using current depictions of universities which all contain important truths but not the whole truth. To us the traditional assumptions about universities remain secure. Research and scholarship create new truths and test old ones, and status and power within the systems rest on these primary production functions. Some writing, particularly that emanating from consultancy work undertaken for international organisations and national governments, almost assumes that the traditional qualities of higher education have or should be overtaken and replaced by such concepts as the entrepreneurial, adaptive or learning university. Indeed some universities whose primary claims to eminence are the pursuit of their traditional functions have been recruited to the lists of those defined as advancing the new styles.

In arguing that universities are multimodal we include, of course, the entrepreneurial, adaptive and learning modes in their multimodality. But that does not entail acceptance of those particular dimensions as being the fundamental characteristics of the many universities which our projects has caused us to know.

In conclusion, we bring the reader back to the assumptions for testing with which we ended our first chapter. Throughout the book we have noted that *changes in formal structures (such as higher education reform) and size (increased student enrolment) do not necessarily change behaviour or all aspects of social relationships as e.g. power and autonomy.* Our study shows that while changes at the central and institutional levels did occur, particularly as we get deeper into the system, we cannot presume that changes in social relationships and behaviour within higher education follow from structural reforms. We have shown how aspects of academic identity, values and the more important ways of working remain stable under policy pressures. These are more likely to bend under straitened resources than structural changes.

Social practices at the organisational and individual levels have changed less than formal structural changes may indicate. The formal changes have affected the space for action at the institutional and individual levels but, as our discussions of both (Chapters 5 and 7) have amply shown, they represent only one factor that affects the behaviour of individuals and organisations. Change is likely to be affected by the relationships between the types of knowledge being generated and disseminated and the higher education organisation required to sustain them.

The nature and pace of change in higher education systems are affected by national socio-political peculiarities. As we noted, some theoretical perspectives on higher education development and change, such as idealism, functionalism and rationalism, assume that the co-ordinating forces within higher education have changed fundamentally. They tend to assume, furthermore, that the autonomy of academic institutions and individual academics has been reduced, and that the influence of the market and/or public authorities has increased. But we have shown that there is a considerable variation depending on national political and educational and research traditions even though we can note commonalities across national boundaries which derive from the essential characteristics of higher education.

Events outside the realm of national politics such as changes in student preferences may affect the higher education system at least as much as national policies. Political decisions and preferences have played a key role in change, but a number of events and processes, such as educational choices made by young people, the dynamics of academic labour markets and academic prestige hierarchies, exerted equally important influences on higher education. In particular, the growth of student numbers and reduction in units of resource have affected the working styles of higher education institutions.

Processes of change at the level of national policy, within academic institutions and disciplinary groups, are only partially co-ordinated. Changes within the fields of social action are driven by different social forces. It is thus an open question how and to what extent academic institutions and practices are affected by major policy changes. This depends on the extent to which the changes are welcomed by, relevant to, moulded and absorbed by academic institutions and practices. Conversely, academic disciplines and their development may, for instance, be formed by processes such as academic drift that may go unheeded by national political actors.

We complete our joint project all the more conscious of the large agenda in both national and comparative studies that higher education presents.

References

This list contains references for the works cited in the text. More detailed bibliographies can be found in the four books on which these studies are reported.

Aarre, M. (1994) 'Akademia eller management?' Mimeo. Universitetet i Bergen: Hovedoppgave i administrasjon og organisasjonsvitenskap.

Åasen, P. (1993) 'Evaluation of Swedish Educational R&D'. In *Research Programme 1992–1995/6*. Stockholm: National Agency for Education.

Abbott, A. (1988) *The System of Professions. An Essay on the Division of Expert Labor.* Chicago and London: University of Chicago Press.

af Trolle, U. (1990) *Mot en Internationellt Konkurrenskraftig Akademisk Utbildning.* Lund: Studentlitteratur.

Alexander, J.C., Giesen, B., Münch, R. and Smelser, N.J. (1987) *The Micro-Macro Link.* Berkeley: University of California Press.

Altbach, P.G. (ed.) (1996) *The International Academic Profession. Portraits of Fourteen Countries.* San Francisco: Jossey-Bass.

Archer, M.S. (1979) *The Social Origins of Educational Systems.* London: Sage.

Archer, M.S. (1981) 'Educational politics: a model for their analysis'. In P. Broadfoot *et al.* (eds) *Politics and Educational Change.* Croom Helm.

Askling, B. (1999) *Employment and Working Conditions of Academic Staff in Higher Education. A Comparative Study of the European Community – The Case of Sweden.* Gøteborgs Universitet: Enheten för Kvalitetsutveckling och Kvalitetssäkring.

Askling, B. and Almén, E. (1997) 'From participation to competition: changes in the notion of decentralization in Swedish higher education policy.' *Tertiary Education and Management 3,* 3, 199–210.

Askling, B. and Bauer, M. (1997) 'The role, functions and impact of a national agency in the evaluation of a decentralised higher education system.' Paper presented at the CHER conference, Alicante, 19–20 September.

Askling, B. and Bauer, M. (1999) 'The role, function and impact of a national agency in the evaluation of a decentralised higher education system.' IPD report No. 1999–01. Department of Education and Didactics, Gøteborg University.

Askling, B. and Kristensen, B. (2000) 'Towards "the learning organisation": implications for institutional governance and leadership.' *Higher Education Management.*

Atkinson, M.M. and Coleman, W.D. (1992) 'Policy networks, policy communities and the problems of governance.' *Governance 5* 2, 154–180.

Aubert, V., Torgersen, U., Lindbekk, T. and Pollan, S. (1960). 'Akademikere i norsk samfunnsstruktur. 1800–1950' *Tidsskrift for samfunnsforskning 1*, 2, 185–204.

Aubert, V., Torgersen, U., Tangen, K., Lindbekk, T. and Pollan, S. (1962) *The Professions in Norwegian Social Structure, 1720–1955.* Oslo: Institutt for samfunnsforskning). 2 vols.

Audit of the Parliament (1999) *Högskoleverkets granskande och främjande roll. Rapport 1999/2000: 3. Riksdagens revisorer.* Stockholm.

Bailey, F.G. (1977) *Morality and Expediency: The Folklore of Academic Politics.* Oxford: Blackwell.

Baldridge, J.V. (1971) *Power and Conflict in the University.* New York: Wiley.

Bauer, M. and Henkel, M. (1997) 'Responses of academe to quality reforms in higher education – a comparative study of England and Sweden.' *Tertiary Education and Management 3*, 2, 211–228.

Bauer, M. and Kogan, M. (1997) 'Evaluation systems in the UK and Sweden: successes and difficulties.' *European Journal of Education 32*, 2, 129–143.

Bauer, M., Marton, Gerard, S., Askling, B. and Marton, F. (1999) *Transforming Universities. Changing Patterns of Governance, Structure and Learning in Swedish Higher Education.* Higher Education Policy Series 48. London: Jessica Kingsley Publishers.

Becher, T. (1985) 'Research policies and their impact on research.' In B. Wittrock and A. Elzinga (eds) *The University Research System.* Stockholm: Almqvist & Wiksell.

Becher, T. (1989) *Academic Tribes and Territories: Intellectual Enquiry and the Culture of Disciplines.* Buckingham: Society for Research into Higher Education and Open University Press.

Becher, T. and Kogan, M. (1980) *Process and Structure in Higher Education.* London: Heinemann.

Becher, T, and Kogan, M. (1992) *Process and Structure in Higher Education*, (2nd ed). London: Routledge.

Becher, T., Henkel, M. and Kogan, M. (1994) *Graduate Education in Britain.* London: Jessica Kingsley Publishers.

Ben-David, J. and Zloczower, A. (1991) 'Universities and academic systems in modern societies.' In J.Ben-David *Scientific Growth. Essays on the Social Organization and Ethos of Science.* Berkeley: University of California Press.

Berdahl, R. (1977) *British Universities and the State* 2nd ed. New York: Arno Press.

Berman, P. (1978) 'Macro- and micro-implementation.' *Public Policy 26*, 165–179.

Bernal, J.D. (1967) *The Social Function of Science.* Cambridge: MIT Press.

Bernstein, B. (1963) *Class, Codes and Control: Vol 3 Towards a Theory of Educational Transmission.* London: Routledge Kegan and Paul.

Birnbaum, R. (1989) *How Colleges Work. The Cybernetics of Academic Organization and Leadership.* San Francisco: Jossey-Bass.

Bleiklie, I. (1994) *The New Public Management and the Pursuit of Knowledge.* LOS-senter Notat 9411. Bergen: Norwegian Research Centre in Organisation and Management.

Bleiklie, I. (1996) 'Universitetet – fra kulturinstitutsjon til kunnskapsbedrift.' In I. Bleiklie (ed.) *Kunnskap og makt.* Oslo: Tano.

Bleiklie, I. (1997) *Service Regimes in Public Welfare Administration. Case Studies of Street-level Bureaucrats and Professionals as Decision Makers.* Oslo: Tano.

Bleiklie, I. (1998) 'Justifying the evaluative state: new public management ideals in higher education.' *European Journal of Education 33*, 3, 299–316.

Bleiklie, I. and Marton, S. (1998) *Linking Institutional Design with Policy Design – a Dynamic Network Approach.* LOS-senter Notat 9810. Bergen: Norwegian Research Centre in Organisation and Management.

Bleiklie, I. (1999) *University and Democracy.* LOS-senter Notat 9915. Bergen: Norwegian Research Centre in Organisation and Management.

Bleiklie, I., Høstaker, R. and Vabø, A. (2000) *Policy and Practice in Higher Education.* London: Jessica Kingsley Publishers.

Bleiklie, I., Marton, S. and Hanney, S. (1995) Policy Arenas, Networks and Higher Education Reform. LOS-senter Notat 9540. Bergen: Norwegian Research Centre in Organisation and Management.

Bleiklie, I., Marton, S. and Hanney, S. (1997) *Policy Regimes and Policy Design – A Dynamic Network Approach. The Cases of Higher Education in England, Sweden and Norway.* LOS-senter Notat 9718. Bergen: Norwegian Research Centre in Organisation and Management.

Blichner, L. and Sangolt, L. (1994) 'The concept of subsidiarity and the debate on European operations: pitfalls and possibilities.' *Governance 7*, 3, 284–306.

Bohlin, I. and Elzinga, A. (1998) 'Rationalistiska och relativistiska perspektiv på kvalitet och kvalitetssäkring.' In L. Berg (ed.) *Utvärdering – ett medel far att säka eller utveckla kvalitet.* Stockholm: Forskningsrå1dsnämnden, Rapport 98: 1.

Bourdieu, P. (1975) 'The specificity of the scientific field and the social conditions of progress.' *Social Sciences Information 14*, 6, 19–47.

Bourdieu, P. (1977) *Outline of a Theory of Practice.* Cambridge: Cambridge University Press.

Bourdieu, P. (1988). *Homo Academicus.* Cambridge: Polity Press.

Bowden, J. and Marton, F. (1998) *The University of Learning. Beyond Quality and Competence in Higher Education.* London: Kogan Page.

Boys, C.J., Brennan, J., Henkel, M., Kirkland, J., Kogan, M. and Youll, P. (1988) *Higher Education and the Preparation for Work.* London: Jessica Kingsley Publishers.

Brobrow, D.B. and Dryzek, J.S. (1987) *Policy Analysis by Design,* Pittsburgh: University of Pittsburgh Press.

Castles, F. (ed.) (1989) *The Comparative History of Public Policy.* Oxford: Polity Press.

Cave, M., Hanney, S., Henkel, M. and Kogan, M. (1997) *The Use of Performance Indicators in Higher Education. The Challenge of the Quality Movement,* 3rd ed. London: Jessica Kingsley Publishers.

Cawson, A. (1983) 'Functional representation and democratic politics.' In G. Duncan (ed.) *Democratic Theory and Practice*. Cambridge: Cambridge University Press, pp.178–198.

Cawson, A. (1986) *Corporatism and Political Theory*. Oxford: Blackwell.

Christensen, S. and Molin, J. (1983) *Organisationskulturer: kultur og myter, deltagestyring, ledelse og omstilling, viden og erfaring, design*. København: Akademisk forlag.

Christensen, T. (1991) *Virksomhetsplanlegging. Myteskaping eller reell problemløsning?* Oslo: Tano.

Christensen, T. and Egeberg, M. (1997) 'Noen trekk ved forholdet mellom organisasjonene og den offentlige forvaltningen.' In T. Christensen and M. Egeberg (eds) *Forvaltningskunnskap*, Oslo: Tano.

Clark B.R. (1983) *The Higher Education System: Academic Organization in Cross-National Perspective*. Berkeley: University of California Press.

Clark, B.R. (1993) *The Research Foundations of Graduate Education*. Berkeley: University of California Press.

Clark, B. R. and Youn, I.T.K. (1976) *Academic Power in the United States: Comparative Historical and Structural Perspectives*. ERIC/Higher Education Research Report No. 3. Washington: ERIC/AAHE.

Clark, B. R. (1998) *Creating Entrepreneurial Universities. Organizational Pathways of Transformation*. New York: Pergamon.

Cohen, M.D. and March, J.G. (1974) *Leadership and Ambiguity: The American College President*. New York: McGraw-Hill.

Cohen, M.D., March, J.G. and Olsen, J.P. (1972) 'A garbage can model of organisational choice.' *Administrative Science Quarterly 17*, 1, 1–25.

Daalder, H. and Shils, E. (eds) (1982) *Universities, Politicians and Bureaucrats*. Cambridge: Cambridge University Press.

Dasgupta, P. and David, P. (1994) 'Towards a new economics of science.' *Research Policy 23*, 487–521.

David, P. (1996) 'Science reorganised? Post-modern visions of research and the curse of success.' Paper presented at ESRC seminar on the regulation of science and technology, University of Warwick.

Dill, D. (1995) 'Through Deming's eyes: a cross-national analysis of quality assurance policies in higher education.' *Quality in Higher Education 1*, 2, 95–110

Dill, D (1998) 'Academic accountability and university adaptation: the architecture of an academic learning organization. Paper presented at the CHER Conference, Kassel, Germany, 3–5 September. *Architecture of an Academic Learning Organization. Higher Education 38.2 pp127–154*.

Eide, K. (1993) 'Educational research policy in the Nordic countries. Historical perspectives and a look ahead.' Unpublished paper given at Sunne OECD Conference.

Eikeland, O. and Lahn, L. C. (1995) *Organisasjon og arbeidsmiljø ved Avdeling for historie, Universitetet i Oslo*. AFIs Rapportserie nr. 2/95. Oslo.

Elmore, R.F. (1979) 'Backward mapping.' *Political Science Quarterly 94* 606–616.

Elzinga, A. (1985) 'Research, bureaucracy and the drift of epistemic criteria.' In B. Wittrock and A. Elzinga (eds) *The University Research System, the Public Policies of the Homes of Scientists*. Stockholm: Almqvist and Wicksell.

Erichsen, V. (1997) *Profesjonsmakt*. Oslo: Tano.

Etzioni-Halevy, E. (1993) *The Elite Connection. Problems and Potential of Western Democracy*. Cambridge: Polity Press.

Finer, H (1956) *Governments of the Greater European Powers*. London: Methuen.

Forland, A. (1993) 'To lover for universitetet i Bergen. Ei samanlikning av 1948-lova og 1988/89-lova med fokus på forholdet mellom universitetet og staten.' Innlegg på seminar om høyere utdanningspolitikk og organisering av kunnskaps-produksjon i samfunnsvitenskapelig og historisk perspektiv, Bergen, 3–4 mai.

Franke, S. and Frykholm, C.-U. (1998) *Vad är kvalitet i högskolan? SACO and SULF: Kunskap så det räcker?* Stockholm: SACO.

Frazer, M. (1997) 'Report on the modalities of external evaluation of higher education in Europe: 1995–1997.' *Higher Education in Europe 22, 3*.

Frederiks, M., Westerheijden, D. and Wenusthof, P. (1994) 'Stakeholders in quality.' In L. Goedegebuure and F. van Vught (eds) *Comparative Policy Studies in Higher Education*. Utrecht: Lemma.

Fridlund, M. and Sandström, U. (eds) (2000) *Universitetets värden, Bidragtill den forskningspolitiska debatten*. Stockholm: SNS.

Fulton, O. (1996) 'The academic Profession in England on the eve of structural reform.' In P.G. Altbach *The International Academic Profession*. Princeton: Carnegie Foundation for the Advancement of Teaching.

Fulton, O. (1999) 'Employment and working conditions of academic staff in higher education. The UK case.' Paper presented at the workshop Employment and Working Conditions of Academic Staff in Europe, Kassel, 15–17 April.

Geertz, C. (1964) 'Ideology as a cultural system.' In D. Apter (ed.) *Ideology and Dis-content,D. New York: Free Press.*

Geertz, C. (1983) 'The way we think now: toward an ethnography of modern thought.' In C. Geertz (ed.) *Local Knowledge: Further Essays in Interpretive Anthro-pology*. New York: Basic Books.

George, A. (1979) 'Case studies and theory development: the method of structured, focused comparison.' In P. Lauren (ed.) *Diplomacy: New Approaches in History, Theory, and Policy*. New York: Free Press.

George, A.L. and Smoke, R. (1974) *Deterrence in American Foreign Policy: Theory and Practice*. New York: Columbia University Press.

Gibbons, M., Limoges, C., Newotny, H., Schwartzman, S., Scott, P. and Trow, M. (1994) *The New Production of Knowledge. The Dynamics of Science and Research in Contemporary Societies*. London: Sage.

Giddens, A. (1991) *Modernity and Self-Identity*, Cambridge, Polity Press.

Goedegebuure, L.C.J. (1992) *Mergers in Higher Education. A Comparative Perspective*. Utrecht: Lemma.

Goedegebuure, L. and Van Vught, F. (eds) (1994) *Comparative Policy Studies in Higher Education*. Utrecht: Lemma.

Goedegebuure, L., Kaiser, F., Maassen, P., Meek, L., van Vught, F., and de Weert, E, (1994) 'Higher education policy: international perspectives on trends and issues in higher education.' In L. Goedegebuure, F. Kaiser, P. Maassen, L. Meek, F. van Vught and E. de Weert (eds) *Higher Education Policy: An International Comparative Perspective*. Oxford: Pergamon.

Government Bill 1990/91 (Swedish).

Government Bill 1992/93 (Swedish).

Government Bill 1994/95 (Swedish).

Grant, W. (ed.) (1985) *The Political Economy of Corporatism*. New York: St Martin's.

Halsey, A.H. (1992) *Decline of Donnish Domination: The British Academic Professions in the Twentieth Century*. Oxford: Clarendon Press.

Halsey, A.H. and Trow, M. (1971) *The British Academics*. London: Faber.

Harvey, L. (1987) *Myths of the Chicago School of Sociology*. Aldershot: Avebury.

Harvey, L. and Knight, P. (1996) *Transforming Higher Education*. Buckingham: Open University Press.

Heady, F. (1990) 'Introduction.' In O.P. Dwivedi and K.M. Henderson (eds) *Public Administration in World Perspective*. Iowa: Iowa State University Press.

Heclo, H. (1972) 'Review article: policy analysis.' *British Journal of Political Science 2*, 83–108.

Heclo, H. and Wildavsky, A. (1974) *The Private Government of Public Money: Community and Policy inside British Politics*. London: Macmillan.

Heidenheimer, A.J., Heclo, H. and Adams, C.T. (1983) *Comparative Public Policy. The Politics of Social Choice in Europe and America*. New York: St Martin's Press.

Henkel, M. (1999) 'The modernisation of research evaluation: the case of the UK.' *Higher Education 38*, 1, 105–122.

Henkel, M. (2000) *Academic Identities and Policy Change in Higher Education*. London: Jessica Kingsley Publishers.

Henkel, M., Hanney, S., Vaux, J. and Von Walden Laing, D. (2000) *Academic Responses to the UK Foresight Initiative. Research Report*. Uxbridge: CEPPP, Brunel University.

Hernes Commission (1988) Report NOU 1988: 28 Med viten og vilje (the Hernes Report), Innstilling fra Universitets- og høyskoleutvalet oppnevnt ved kongelig resolusjon av 22. juli 1987. Avgitt til Kultur- og vitenskapsdepartementet 9. september 1988.

Higher Education Funding Council for England (HEFCE) (1993a) 'Assessment of the quality of higher education.' Circular 3/93. Bristol: HEFCE.

Higher Education Funding Council for England (HEFCE) (1993b) *Quality Assessment Division. Assessors' Handbook*. Bristol: HEFCE.

Hölttä, S. (1995) *Towards the Self-Regulative University*. University of Joensuu: University of Joensuu Publications in Social Science.

Høstaker, R. (1997) *University life. A Study of the Relations between Political Processes and Institutional Conditions in two University Faculties*. Bergen: LOS-Senteret, Rapport 9707.

Hunter, F. (1953) *Community Power Structure*. Chapel Hill: University of North Carolina Press.

Ingram, H. and Schneider, A. (1990) 'Behavioral assumptions of policy tools.' *Journal of Politics 52*, 2, 510–529.

Ingram, H. and Schneider, A. (1993) 'Constructing citizenship: the subtle messages of policy design.' In H. Ingram and S.R. Smith (eds) *Public Policy for Democracy*. Washington DC: Brookings Institution.

Jarratt Report (1985) Committee of Vice Chancellors and Principals' Report of the Steering Committee for Efficiency Studies in Universities. London: CVCP.

Jerdal, E. (1996) 'Distriktshøgskolen –alternativ utdanning?' In I. Bleiklie (ed.) *Kunnskap og makt. Norsk høyere utdanning i endring*. Oslo, Tano.

Johansson, J. (1989) *Den geografiska rörligheten hos svenska universitetslärare*. Arbetsrapport från utredningssektionen nr. 21. UHÄ.

John, P. and Cole, A. (1997) 'Networks or networking? The importance of power, position and values in local economic policy networks in Britain and France.' Paper presented at the Annual Meeting of the American Political Science Association, Washington, 28–31 August.

Johnson, T. (1982) 'The state and professions: peculiarities of the British.' In A. Giddens and G. McKenzie (eds) *Social Class and the Division of Labour*. Cambridge: Cambridge University Press.

Jordan, G. and Schubert, K. (1992) 'A preliminary ordering of policy network labels.' *European Journal of Political Research 21*, 7–27.

Joss, R. and Kogan, M. (1995) *Advancing Quality. Total Quality Management in the National Health Service*. Buckingham: Open University Press.

Kells, H. (1992) *Self-regulation in Higher Education: A Multi-national Perspective on Collaborative Systems of Quality Assurance and Control*. London: Jessica Kingsley Publishers.

Kells, H. and van Vught, F. (eds) (1988) *Self-regulation, Self-study and Program Review in Higher Education*. Culemborg: Lemma.

Kleppe Commission (1961) Report concerning the further expansion of universities and colleges. The University and College Commission 1960. Submitted to the Royal Ministry of Ecclesiastical and Educational Affairs, 28 March 1961.

Knoke, D., Pappi, F.U., Broadbent, J., and Tsujinaka, Y. (1996) *Comparing Policy Networks. Labor Politics in the U.S., Germany and Japan*. Cambridge: Cambridge University Press.

Kogan, M. (1969) 'Audit, control and freedom.' *Higher Education Review 1*, 2, 16–27.

Kogan, M. (1975) *Educational Policy-making. A Study of Interest Groups and Parliament*. London: Allen and Unwin.

Kogan, M. (1984) 'The political view.' In B.R. Clark *Perspectives on Higher Education. Eight Disciplinary and Comparative Views*. Berkeley: University of California Press.

Kogan, M. (1992) 'Political Science.' In B.R. Clark and G. Neave (eds) *The International Encyclopedia of Higher Education*. Oxford: Pergamon.

Kogan, M. (1996) 'Comparing higher education systems.' *Higher Education 21*, 4, 395–402.

Kogan, M. (1999) 'The academic–administrative interface.' In M. Henkel and B. Little (eds) *Changing Relationships Between Higher Education and the State.* London: Jessica Kingsley Publishers.

Kogan, M. and Hanney, S. (1999) *Reforming Higher Education.* Higher Education Policy Series 50. London: Jessica Kingsley Publishers.

Kogan, M. and Kogan, D. (1983) *The Attack on Higher Education.* London: Kogan Page.

Kuhn, T.S. (1970) *The Structure of Scientific Revolutions.* Chicago: University of Chicago Press.

Kvalsvik, B. N. (1993) 'Skiljemerka mellom folk. Introdusere Pierre Bourdieu?' In *LITINORs skriftserie* nr. 2, NAVF, Program for kultur- og tradisjonsformidlande forsking (KULT).

Kyvik, S. (1991) *Productivity in Academia. Scientific Publishing at Norwegian Universities.* Oslo: Norwegian University Press.

Kyvik, S. and Marheim Larsen, I. (1993) *Nye styringsformer på instituttnivå. Rapport 8/93.* Oslo: NFRs utredningsinstitutt.

Laegreid, P. and Pedersen. O.K. (eds) (1999) *Fra opbygning til ombygning I staten. Organisationsforandringer I tre nordiske lande.* Copenhagen: Jurist- og Økonomforbundets Forlag.

Lane, J.-E. (1990) *Institutional Reform. A Public Policy Perspective.* Aldershot: Dartmouth.

Lane, J.-E. (1992) 'Sweden.' In B. Clark and G. Neave (eds) *The Encyclopedia of Higher Education.* Oxford: Pergamon.

Latour, B. (1987) *Science in Action, How to Follow Scientists and Engineers through Society.* Cambridge MA: Harvard University Press.

Lester, J.P. and Goggin, M. (1999) 'Back to the future: the rediscovery of implementation studies.' *Policy Currents 8*, 1–9.

Maassen, P.A.M. (1996) *Governmental Steering and the Academic Culture. The Intangibility of the Human Factor in Dutch and German Universities.* Utrecht: De Tijdstroom.

Maassen, P. and van Vught, F. (1994) 'Alternative models of governmental steering in higher education.' In L. Goedegebuure and F. van Vught (eds) *Comparative Policy Studies in Higher Education.* Utrecht: Lemma.

MacIntyre, A. (1981) *After Virtue: A Study in Moral Theory.* London: Duckworth.

March, J.M. and Olsen, J.P. (1986) *Ambiguity and Choice in Organizations.* Oslo: Universitetsforlaget.

March, J.M. and Olsen, J.P. (1989) *Discovering Institutions.* New York: Free Press.

March, J.M. and Olsen, J.P. (1994) 'Institutional perspectives on governance.' In *Systemrationalität und Partialinteresse: Festschrift für Renate Mayntz/Hans Ulrich Derlien.* Baden-Baden: Nomos.

March, J.M. and Olsen, J.P. (1995) *Democratic Governance.* New York: Free Press.

Marton, S. (1994) 'Issues in comparative methodology.' Annex to M. Bauer, M. Henkel, M. Kogan and S. Marton, 'The impacts of reform on higher education: an Anglo-Swedish comparative study.' Paper presented at Conference of Consortium of Higher Education Researchers, Enschede, 5–7 October.

Marton, S. (forthcoming) *The Mind of the State: The Politics of University Autonomy in Sweden, 1968–1998*. Göteborg: Göteborg Studies in Politics.

Marton, S., Hanney, S. and Kogan, M. (1995) 'Interest groups and elites in higher education policy making: the cases of England and Sweden.' Paper presented at the European Consortium of Political Research, Bordeaux, 27 April to 2 May.

Merton, R.K. (1973) *The Sociology of Science*. Chicago: Chicago University Press.

Mill, J.S. (1962) 'On liberty.' In M. Warnock (ed.) *Utilitarianism*. London: Collins.

Mulhall, S. and Swift, A. (1992) *Liberals and Communitarians*. Oxford: Blackwell.

Mulkay, M.J. (1977) 'Sociology of the scientific research community.' In I. Spiegel-Rosing and D. de Solla Price *Science, Technology and Society*. London: Sage.

Murphy, R. (1988) *Social Closure. The Theory of Monopolization and Exclusion*. Oxford: Clarendon Press.

NAVF (1991) Evaluation of English Studies in Norway. Report from the Evaluation Committee.

Neave, G. (1986) 'On shifting sands.' *European Journal of Education 20*, 2–3.

Neave, G. and Rhoades, G. (1987) 'The academic estate in Western Europe.' In B.R.Clark (ed.) *The Academic Profession: National, Disciplinary and Institutional Settings*. Berkeley: University of California Press.

Neave, G. and Van vught, F.A. (1991) *Prometheus Bound. The Changing Relationship Between Government and Higher Education in Western Europe*. Oxford: Pergamon.

Neave, G. and van Vught, F.A. (1994) *Government and Higher Education Relationships Across Three Continents*. Oxford: Pergamon.

NOU (1988): 28 Med viten og vilje (the Hernes Report), Innstilling fra Universitets- og høyskoleutvalet oppnevnt ved kongelig resolusjon av 22. juli 1987. Avgitt til Kultur- og vitenskapsdepartementet 9. september 1988.

Nozick, R. (1974) *Anarchy, State and Utopia*. New York: Basic Books.

Olsen, J.P. (1978) "Folkestyre, byråkrati og korporativisme.' In J.P. Olsen (ed.) *Politisk organisering*. Oslo: Universitetsforlaget.

Olsen, J.P. (1983) *Organized Democracy*. Bergen: Universitetsforlaget.

Olsen, J.P. and Peters, B.G. (1996) (eds) *Lessons from Experience*. Oslo: Scandinavian University Press.

Olsen, T.B. (1988) *Doktorgrader i Norge. En kvantitativ oversikt*. Oslo, NAVF's utredningsinstitutt, Notat 9/88.

Ostrom, E. (1990) *Governing the Commons. The Evolution of Institutions for Collective Action*. Cambridge: Cambridge University Press.

Ottosen Commission (1965) Report No.1 on Further education for secondary school graduates. Royal Ministry of Ecclesiastical Affairs, Oslo.

Øverland, O. (1988) 'Kan de norske universitetene bli bedre?' *Nytt norsk tidsskrift 5, 4*, 63–70.

Page, E.C. (1995) 'Comparative public administration in Britain.' *Public Administration 73*, 1, 123–141.

Parsons, T. (1939) 'The professions and social structure.' *Social Forces 17*, 457–467.

Peters, B.G. (1999) *Institutional Theory in Political Science. The 'New Institutionalism'*. London: Pinter.

Petersson, O. (ed.) (1990) *Demokrati och Makt i Sverige*. SOU, 1990: 44 Huvudrapport. Stockholm: Allmänna Förlaget.

Petersson, O. (1993) *Svensk Politik*. Stockholm: Publica.

Polanyi, M. (1962) 'The republic of science: its political and economic theory.' *Minerva 1*, 1, 54–73.

Pollitt, C. (1990) *Managerialism and the Public Services: The Anglo-American Experience*. Oxford: Blackwell.

Pollitt, C. (1993) *Managerialism and the Public Services. The Anglo-American Experience*. Oxford: Blackwell.

Pollitt, C. (1995) 'Justification by works or by faith? Evaluation of new public management.' EVANPM for EGPA workshop 'Administrative Reforms and Modernization'. Rotterdam, September.

Powell, W.W. and P.J. Dimaggio (eds) (1991) *The New Institutionalism in Organizational Analysis*. Chicago: University of Chicago Press.

Premfors, R. (1980) *The Politics of Higher Education in a Comparative Perspective: France, Sweden, United Kingdom*. Studies in Politics 15. Stockholm: University of Stockholm.

Premfors, R. (1983) Oral contribution to seminar at London Business School.

Premfors, R. and and Östergren, B (1978) *Systems of Higher Education: Sweden*. New Haven: ICED.

Prop. 1992/93 (Swedish).

Prop. 1993/94 (Swedish).

Raab, C. (1994) 'Theorising the governance of education.' *British Journal of Educational Studies 42*, 1, 6–22.

Ragin, C. (1987) *The Comparative Method, Moving Beyond Qualitative and Quantitative Strategies*. Berkeley: University of California Press.

Ramsden, P. (1998) *Learning to Lead in Higher Education*. London: Routledge.

Rein, M. (1983) *From Policy to Practice*. London: Macmillan.

Rhodes, R.A.W. and Marsh, D. (1992) 'New directions in the study of policy networks.' *European Journal of Political Research 21*, 181–205.

Richardson, J. (1997) 'Interest groups, multi-arena politics and policy change.' Paper presented at Annual Meeting of the American Political Science Association, Washington, 28–31 August.

Richardson, G. and Fielden, J. (1997) *Measuring the Grip of the State: The Relationship Between Governments and Universities in Selected Commonwealth Countries*. London: Commonwealth Higher Education Management Service.

Robbins Report (1963) *Higher Education. Report of the Committee appointed by the Prime Minister under the Chairmanship of Lord Robbins, 1961–63*. Cmnd 2154. London: HMSO.

Rokkan, S. (1966) 'Norway: numerical democracy and corporate pluralism.' In R.A. Dahl (ed.) *Political Oppositions in Western Democracies*. New Haven: Yale University Press.

Rommetveit, K. (1995) *Personellressurser, aktivitetsnivå og innflytelsemugligheter I et Storting I vekst.* LOS-senter Notat 9501. Bergen: Norwegian Research Centre in Organisation and Manaegement.

Rothblatt, S. and Wittrock, B. (eds) (1993) *The European and American University since 1900. Historical and Sociological Essays.* Cambridge: Cambridge University Press.

Rothstein, B. (2000) Universitetets värden, Bidragtill den forskningspolitiska debatten. Stockholm: SNS.

Sabatier, P.A. (1986) 'Top-down and bottom-up approaches to implementation research: a critical analysis and suggested synthesis.' *Journal of Public Policy 6,* 21–48.

Sabatier, P.A. and Jenkins-Smith, H. (eds) (1993) *Policy Change and Learning: An Advocacy Coalition Framework.* Boulder CO: Westview Press.

Salter, B. and Tapper, T. (1994) *The State and Higher Education.* London: Woburn Press.

Sartori, G. (1970) 'Concept misinformation in comparative politics.' *American Political Science Review 64,* 1033–1053.

Saward, M. (1992) *Co-optive Politics and State Legitimacy.* Aldershot: Dartmouth.

Schmitter, P. (1974) 'Still the century of corporatism.' In F. Pike and Th. Strich (eds) *The New Corporatism.* Paris: University of Notre Dame.

Scharpf, F.W. (1997) Games Real Actors Play: Actor-Centred Institutionalism in Policy Research. Boulder, CO: Westview Press.

Schmitter, P. and Lehmbruch, G. (eds) (1979) *Trends Toward Corporatist Intermediation.* Sage: Beverly Hills.

Schneider, A.L. and Ingram, H. (1997) *Policy Design for Democracy.* Lawrence KA: University of Kansas Press.

Scott, P. (1994) 'Recent developments in quality assurance in Great Britain.' In D. Westerheiden, J. Brennan and P. Maassen (eds) *Changing Contexts of Quality Assurance: Recent Trends in West European Higher Education.* Utrecht: LEMMA.

Scott, P. (1995) *The Meanings of Mass Higher Education.* Buckingham and Philadelphia: Society for Research into Higher Education and Open University Press.

Scruton, R. (1980) *The Meaning of Conservatism.* London: Macmillan.

Selznick, P. (1966) *TVA and the Grass Roots.* New York: Harper and Row.

Senge, P. (1990) *The Fifth Discipline.* London: Century.

Skocpol, T. (1980) Emerging agendas and recurrent strategies in historical sociology.' In T. Skocpol (ed.) *Vision and Method in Historical Sociology.* Cambridge: Cambridge University Press.

Skocpol, T. (1992) *Protecting Soldiers and Mothers. The Political Origins of Social Policy in the United States.* Cambridge MA: Belknap Press.

Skodvin, O.-J. (1999) 'Mergers in higher education – success or failure?' *Tertiary Education and Management 5,* 65–80.

Smith, D., Scott, P., Bocock, J. and Bargh, C. (1999) 'Vice chancellors and executive leadership in UK universities: new roles and relationships?' In M. Henkel and B.

Little (eds) *Changing Relationships between Higher Education and the State*. London: Jessica Kingsley Publishers.

Sporn, B. (1999) 'Towards more adaptive universities: trends of institutional reform in Europe.' *Higher Education in Europe 24*, 1, 23–33.

Ståhle, B. (1996) *Universiteten og forskarane –från stagnation til fornyelse. Universitetsforskare, forskarutbildning och forskarrekruttering i Norden*. Nord 1996: 39, Copenhagen: Nordiska forskningspolitiske rådet.

Statens Offentliga Utredningar (SOU) (1992) *Frihet, Ansvar, Kompetens: Grundutbildningens villkor i högskolan*. Stockholm: Allmänna Förlaget.

Svensson, L. (1987) *State Control and Academic Autonomy*. Stockholm: UHÄ.

Tapper, T. and Salter, B. (1978) *Education and the Political Order*. London: Macmillan.

Tapper, T. and Salter, B. (1995) 'The changing idea of university autonomy.' *Studies in Higher Education 20*, 1, 59–71.

Tasker, M.E. and Packham, D.E. (1990) 'Freedom, funding and the future of the universities.' *Studies in Higher Education 15*, 2, 181–195.

Taylor, C. (1989) *Sources of the Self: the Making of the Modern Identity*. Cambridge: Cambridge University Press.

Teichler, U. (1993) 'Research on higher education in Europe: some aspects of recent developments.' In E, Frackmann and P. Maassen (eds) *Towards Excellence in European Higher Education in the 90s Proceedings of 11th European AIR Forum*. University of Trier, 27–30 August 1989, EAIR.

Thelen, K. and Steinmo, S. (1995) 'Historical institutionalism in comparative politics.' In S. Steinmo, K. Thelen and F. Lonstreth (eds) *Structuring Politics*. Cambridge: Cambridge University Press.

Torgersen, U. (1994) *Profesjoner og offentlig sector*. Oslo: Tano.

Trow, M. (1970) 'Reflections on the transition from mass to universal higher education.' *Daedalus 99*, 1–42.

Trow, M. (1974) 'Problems in the transition from elite to mass higher education.' *In Policies for Higher Education. General Report to the Conference on Future Structure and Post-Secondary Education*. Paris: OECD.

Trow, M. (1976) 'The American university department as a context for learning.' *Studies in Higher Education 1*, 1, 11–22.

Tvede, O. (1992) *Forskerrekruttering og forskerutdanning: fortsatt vekst?* Rapport 6/92. Oslo: NAVF's utredningsinstitutt.

Universit af Trolle, U. (1990) *Mot en internationellt konkurrenskraftig akademisk utbildning*. Lund: Studentlitteratur.

Vabø, A. (1999) 'Universitet og endring. Belyst gjennom instituttsammenslåingsprosessen ved Det historisk-filosofiske fakultet.' Bergen: Universitetet i Oslo, Draft polit. thesis.

Vabø, A. (2000) *Eksamens- og evalueringsformer i høyere utdanning: en sammenlignende studie*. Oslo: Norsk institutt for studier av forskning og utdanning.

Välimaa, J. (1995) *Higher Education Cultural Approach*. Jyväskylä Studies in Education, Psychology and Social Research 113. University of Jyväskylä

Van den daele, W., Krahn, W. and Weingart, P. (1977) 'The political direction of scientific development.' In E. Mendelsohn, P. Weingart and R. Whitley (eds) *The Social Production of Scientific Knowledge*, vol. 1. Dordrecht and Boston: Reidel and Boston Publishing.

Van Vught, F. (1988) 'A new autonomy in European higher education? An exploration and analysis of the strategy of self-regulation in higher education governance.' *International Journal of Institutional Management in Higher Education 12*, 1, 16–26.

Van Vught, F. (ed) (1989) *Governmental Strategies and Innovation in Higher Education*. London: Jessica Kingsley Publishers.

Van Waarden, F. (1992) 'Dimensions and types of policy networks.' *European Jourrnal of Political Research 21*, 29–52.

Weber, M. (1978) *Economy and Society*. Berkeley: University of California Press.

Wennerås, C. and Wold, A. (1997) 'Nepotism and sexism in peer-review.' *Nature 387*.

Wilensky, H.L. (1964) 'The professionalization of everyone?' *American Journal of Sociology 70* 2, 137–158.

Wirt, F. (1981) 'Professionalism and political conflict: a developmental model.' *Journal of Public Policy 1*, 1

Woodward, J. (1965) *Industrial Theory and Practice*. Oxford: Oxford University Press.

The Contributors

Berit Askling is Professor in the Department of Education and Educational Research at Göteborg University.

Marianne Bauer is Emerita Professor at Göteborg University.

Ivar Bleiklie is Professor in Administration and Organisation Theory and Director of the Norwegian Research Center in Organisation and Management at the University of Bergen.

Mary Henkel is Reader in Goverment at Brunel University.

Roar Høstaker is an Associate Professor at Lillehammer College.

Maurice Kogan is Professor Emeritus of Government and Director of the Centre for the Evaluation of Public Policy and Practice at Brunel University.

Susan Gerard Marton is a Researcher at the Department of Political Science, Göteborg University specialising in comparative public policy.

Agnete Vabø is a Researcher at the Norwegian Institute for Studies in Higher Education and Research in Oslo.

Subject Index

Author Index